Teen Health Series

Cancer Information For Teens, Fourth Edition

Teen Health Series

Cancer Information For Teens, Fourth Edition

Health Tips About Cancer Prevention, Risks, Diagnosis, And Treatment

Including Facts About Cancers Of Most Concern To Teens And Young Adults, Coping Strategies, Survivorship, And Dealing With Cancer In Loved Ones

OMNIGRAPHICS
615 Griswold, Ste. 901
Detroit, MI 48226

Bibliographic Note
Because this page cannot legibly accommodate all the copyright notices, the Bibliographic Note portion of the Preface constitutes an extension of the copyright notice.

* * *

OMNIGRAPHICS
Greg Mullin, *Managing Editor*

* * *

Copyright © 2018 Omnigraphics

ISBN 978-0-7808-1615-2
E-ISBN 978-0-7808-1616-9

Library of Congress Cataloging-in-Publication Data

Names: Omnigraphics, Inc., issuing body.

Title: Cancer information for teens: health tips about cancer prevention, risks, diagnosis, and treatment including facts about cancers of most concern to teens and young adults, coping strategies, survivorship, and dealing with cancer in loved ones.

Description: Fourth edition. | Detroit, MI: Omnigraphics, Inc., [2018] | Series: Teen health series | Audience: Age 11+ | Audience: Grade 9 to 12. | Includes bibliographical references and index.

Identifiers: LCCN 2017052247 (print) | LCCN 2017053490 (ebook) | ISBN 9780780816169 (eBook) | ISBN 9780780816152 (hardcover: alk. paper)

Subjects: LCSH: Cancer--Juvenile literature.

Classification: LCC RC264 (ebook) | LCC RC264.C36 2018 (print) | DDC 616.99/4--dc23

LC record available at https://lccn.loc.gov/2017052247

Table Of Contents

Part Three: Cancer Awareness, Diagnosis, Treatment, And Prevention

Part Four: Cancer Survivorship

Part Five: When A Loved One Has Cancer

Part Six: If You Need More Information

Preface

About This Book

In 2017, it was estimated that more than 5,000 teens would be diagnosed with cancer and more than 600 would die from the disease. Though there is a decline in the number due to the advancements made in cancer diagnosis, treatment, and prognosis, cancer still remains the leading cause of death among teens.

Cancer affects teens differently than older adults or young children. Additionally, teens face environmental factors and make lifestyle choices that may influence their disease risk.

Cancer Information For Teens, Fourth Edition presents updated facts about cancer causes, prevention, diagnosis, and treatment. It explains how cancer occurs in the body and describes some warning signs. A chapter focused on cancer myths helps teens sort fact from fiction. For teens who do have cancer, the book gives practical advice about important topics, such as which questions to ask healthcare providers and how to cope with treatment side effects and changes in body image. Social worries at school and among friends are addressed, and cancer survivorship issues, including fertility concerns, are discussed frankly. A separate section focuses on teens with friends or family members who have cancer. Finally, a resource section provides suggestions for additional reading, a directory of web-based support sources and mobile apps, and list of websites for finding cancer trials.

How To Use This Book

This book is divided into parts and chapters. Parts focus on broad areas of interest; chapters are devoted to single topics within a part.

Part One: Cancer Facts And Risk Factors explains that cancer is a variety of diseases that begin the same way: cells divide in an uncontrolled manner with the ability to attack the body's tissues. This part also discusses risk factors for cancer. These include familial or genetic predisposition, outdoor and indoor tanning, tobacco use, obesity, chemicals in the environment, and human papillomavirus infection. Ways to reduce modifiable risks are suggested.

Part Two: Cancers Of Most Concern To Teens And Young Adults gives facts on the cancer types most often diagnosed in adolescents and young adults. Among these are bone cancer, brain and spinal cord tumors, leukemia, lymphoma, oral, and testicular cancer.

Part Three: Cancer Awareness, Diagnosis, Treatment, And Prevention provides prevention strategies, and describes how doctors diagnose the disease and determine how advanced it is. Chapters in this part discuss commonly used cancer treatments, including surgery, chemotherapy, hormone therapy, immunotherapy, precision medicine, radiation, and bone marrow and stem cell transplantation. The part also offers information on supportive care and cancer clinical research.

Part Four: Cancer Survivorship acknowledges the wide-ranging and sometimes long-term impact that cancer can have on teens' lives. It describes temporary effects of treatment during recovery. The part includes a summary of chronic health problems that can result after cancer, including fertility issues.

Part Five: When A Loved One Has Cancer gives guidance for teens with a parent, sibling, or friend who has cancer. It explains how to cope with the sometimes-confusing emotions that can arise and how teens can plan in advance for helping others while still taking of themselves.

Part Six: If You Need More Information includes suggestions for additional reading about cancers, a directory of web-based resources including teen-focused support groups, and guidance for people who want to learn more about specific clinical trials.

Bibliographic Note

This volume contains documents and excerpts from publications issued by the following government agencies: Centers for Disease Control and Prevention (CDC); National Cancer Institute (NCI); National Institute of Environmental Health Sciences (NIEHS); National Institutes of Health (NIH); Office on Women's Health (OWH); U.S. Department of Health and Human Services (HHS); and U.S. Food and Drug Administration (FDA).

It may also contain original material produced by Omnigraphics and reviewed by medical consultants.

The photograph on the front cover is © Sasa Prudkov.

Medical Review

Omnigraphics contracts with a team of qualified, senior medical professionals who serve as medical consultants for the *Teen Health Series*. As necessary, medical consultants review reprinted and originally written material for currency and accuracy. Citations including the phrase, "Reviewed (month, year)" indicate material reviewed by this team. Medical consultation services are provided to the *Teen Health Series* editors by:

Dr. Vijayalakshmi, MBBS, DGO, MD
Dr. Senthil Selvan, MBBS, DCH, MD
Dr. K. Sivanandham, MBBS, DCH, MS (Research), PhD

About The *Teen Health Series*

At the request of librarians serving today's young adults, the *Teen Health Series* was developed as a specially focused set of volumes within Omnigraphics' *Health Reference Series*. Each volume deals comprehensively with a topic selected according to the needs and interests of people in middle school and high school. Teens seeking preventive guidance, information about disease warning signs, medical statistics, and risk factors for health problems will find answers to their questions in the *Teen Health Series*. The *Series*, however, is not intended to serve as a tool for diagnosing illness, in prescribing treatments, or as a substitute for the physician/patient relationship. All people concerned about medical symptoms or the possibility of disease are encouraged to seek professional care from an appropriate healthcare provider.

If there is a topic you would like to see addressed in a future volume of the *Teen Health Series*, please write to:

Editor
Teen Health Series
Omnigraphics
615 Griswold, Ste. 901
Detroit, MI 48226

A Note About Spelling And Style

Teen Health Series editors use *Stedman's Medical Dictionary* as an authority for questions related to the spelling of medical terms and the *Chicago Manual of Style* for questions related to grammatical structures, punctuation, and other editorial concerns. Consistent adherence is not always possible, however, because the individual volumes within the *Series* include many documents from a wide variety of different producers and copyright holders, and the editor's primary goal is to present material from each source as accurately as is possible following the terms specified by each document's producer. This sometimes means that information in different chapters may follow other guidelines and alternate spelling authorities. For example, occasionally a copyright holder may require that eponymous terms be shown in possessive forms (Crohn's disease vs. Crohn disease) or that British spelling norms be retained (leukaemia vs. leukemia).

Part One
Cancer Facts And Risk Factors

What Is Cancer?

Cancer is the name given to a collection of related diseases. In all types of cancer, some of the body's cells begin to divide without stopping and spread into surrounding tissues. Cancer can start almost anywhere in the human body, which is made up of trillions of cells. Normally, human cells grow and divide to form new cells as the body needs them. When cells grow old or become damaged, they die, and new cells take their place.

When cancer develops, however, this orderly process breaks down. As cells become more and more abnormal, old or damaged cells survive when they should die, and new cells form when they are not needed. These extra cells can divide without stopping and may form growths called tumors. Many cancers form solid tumors, which are masses of tissue. Cancers of the blood, such as leukemias, generally do not form solid tumors.

Cancerous tumors are malignant, which means they can spread into, or invade, nearby tissues. In addition, as these tumors grow, some cancer cells can break off and travel to distant places in the body through the blood or the lymph system and form new tumors far from the original tumor.

Unlike malignant tumors, benign tumors do not spread into, or invade, nearby tissues. Benign tumors can sometimes be quite large, however. When removed, they usually don't grow back, whereas malignant tumors sometimes do. Unlike most benign tumors elsewhere in the body, benign brain tumors can be life threatening.

About This Chapter: Text in this chapter begins with excerpts from "What Is Cancer?" National Cancer Institute (NCI), February 9, 2015; Text under the heading "Statistics At A Glance: The Burden Of Cancer In The United States" is excerpted from "Cancer Statistics," National Cancer Institute (NCI), March 22, 2017.

Differences Between Cancer Cells And Normal Cells

Cancer cells differ from normal cells in many ways that allow them to grow out of control and become invasive. One important difference is that cancer cells are less specialized than normal cells. That is, whereas normal cells mature into very distinct cell types with specific functions, cancer cells do not. This is one reason that, unlike normal cells, cancer cells continue to divide without stopping.

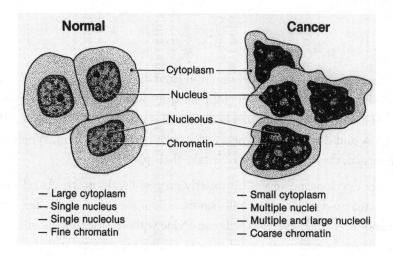

Figure 1.1. Normal Cell Versus Cancer Cell

(Source: "Normal And Cancer Cells Structure," National Cancer Institute (NCI).)

In addition, cancer cells are able to ignore signals that normally tell cells to stop dividing or that begin a process known as programmed cell death, or apoptosis, which the body uses to get rid of unneeded cells. Cancer cells may be able to influence the normal cells, molecules, and blood vessels that surround and feed a tumor—an area known as the microenvironment. For instance, cancer cells can induce nearby normal cells to form blood vessels that supply tumors with oxygen and nutrients, which they need to grow. These blood vessels also remove waste products from tumors.

Cancer cells are also often able to evade the immune system, a network of organs, tissues, and specialized cells that protects the body from infections and other conditions. Although the immune system normally removes damaged or abnormal cells from the body, some cancer cells are able to "hide" from the immune system.

Tumors can also use the immune system to stay alive and grow. For example, with the help of certain immune system cells that normally prevent a runaway immune response, cancer cells can actually keep the immune system from killing cancer cells.

How Cancer Arises

Cancer is a genetic disease—that is, it is caused by changes to genes that control the way our cells function, especially how they grow and divide.

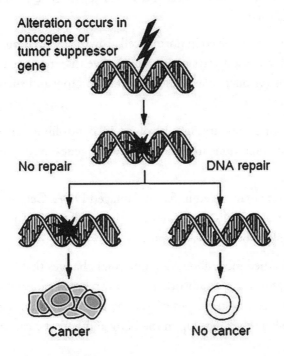

Figure 1.2. How Cancer Arises

(Source: "Cancer And The Environment," National Institute of Environmental Health Sciences (NIEHS).)

Genetic changes that cause cancer can be inherited from our parents. They can also arise during a person's lifetime as a result of errors that occur as cells divide or because of damage to deoxyribonucleic acid (DNA) caused by certain environmental exposures. Cancer causing environmental exposures include substances, such as the chemicals in tobacco smoke, and radiation, such as ultraviolet (UV) rays from the sun. Each person's cancer has a unique combination of genetic changes. As the cancer continues to grow, additional changes will occur.

Even within the same tumor, different cells may have different genetic changes. In general, cancer cells have more genetic changes, such as mutations in DNA, than normal cells. Some of these changes may have nothing to do with the cancer; they may be the result of the cancer, rather than its cause.

"Drivers" Of Cancer

The genetic changes that contribute to cancer tend to affect three main types of genes—proto-oncogenes, tumor suppressor genes, and DNA repair genes. These changes are sometimes called "drivers" of cancer.

- **Proto-oncogenes** are involved in normal cell growth and division. However, when these genes are altered in certain ways or are more active than normal, they may become cancer-causing genes (or oncogenes), allowing cells to grow and survive when they should not.

- **Tumor suppressor genes** are also involved in controlling cell growth and division. Cells with certain alterations in tumor suppressor genes may divide in an uncontrolled manner.

- **DNA repair genes** are involved in fixing damaged DNA. Cells with mutations in these genes tend to develop additional mutations in other genes. Together, these mutations may cause the cells to become cancerous.

As scientists have learned more about the molecular changes that lead to cancer, they have found that certain mutations commonly occur in many types of cancer. Because of this, cancers are sometimes characterized by the types of genetic alterations that are believed to be driving them, not just by where they develop in the body and how the cancer cells look under the microscope.

When Cancer Spreads

A cancer that has spread from the place where it first started to another place in the body is called metastatic cancer. The process by which cancer cells spread to other parts of the body is called **metastasis.** Metastatic cancer has the same name and the same type of cancer cells as the original, or primary, cancer. For example, breast cancer that spreads to and forms a metastatic tumor in the lung is metastatic breast cancer, not lung cancer.

Under a microscope, metastatic cancer cells generally look the same as cells of the original cancer. Moreover, metastatic cancer cells and cells of the original cancer usually have some molecular features in common, such as the presence of specific chromosome changes. Treatment may help prolong the lives of some people with metastatic cancer. In general, though, the primary goal of treatments for metastatic cancer is to control the growth of the cancer or to relieve symptoms caused by it. Metastatic tumors can cause severe damage to how the body functions, and most people who die of cancer die of metastatic disease.

Tissue Changes That Are Not Cancer

Not every change in the body's tissues is cancer. Some tissue changes may develop into cancer if they are not treated, however. Here are some examples of tissue changes that are not cancer but, in some cases, are monitored:

- **Hyperplasia** occurs when cells within a tissue divide faster than normal and extra cells buildup, or proliferate. However, the cells and the way the tissue is organized look normal under a microscope. Hyperplasia can be caused by several factors or conditions, including chronic irritation.

- **Dysplasia** is a more serious condition than hyperplasia. In dysplasia, there is also a buildup of extra cells. But the cells look abnormal and there are changes in how the tissue is organized. In general, the more abnormal the cells and tissue look, the greater the chance that cancer will form. Some types of dysplasia may need to be monitored or treated. An example of dysplasia is an abnormal mole (called a dysplastic nevus) that forms on the skin. A dysplastic nevus can turn into melanoma, although most do not.

- An even more serious condition is **carcinoma in situ.** Although it is sometimes called cancer, carcinoma in situ is not cancer because the abnormal cells do not spread beyond the original tissue. That is, they do not invade nearby tissue the way that cancer cells do. But, because some carcinomas in situ may become cancer, they are usually treated.

Types Of Cancer

There are more than 100 types of cancer. Types of cancer are usually named for the organs or tissues where the cancers form. For example, lung cancer starts in cells of the lung, and brain cancer starts in cells of the brain. Cancers also may be described by the type of cell that formed them, such as an epithelial cell or a squamous cell. Here are some categories of cancers that begin in specific types of cells:

Carcinoma

Carcinomas are the most common type of cancer. They are formed by epithelial cells, which are the cells that cover the inside and outside surfaces of the body. There are many types of epithelial cells, which often have a column-like shape when viewed under a microscope.

Carcinomas that begin in different epithelial cell types have specific names:

- **Adenocarcinoma** is a cancer that forms in epithelial cells that produce fluids or mucus. Tissues with this type of epithelial cell are sometimes called glandular tissues. Most cancers of the breast, colon, and prostate are adenocarcinomas.

- **Basal cell carcinoma** is a cancer that begins in the lower or basal (base) layer of the epidermis, which is a person's outer layer of skin.

- **Squamous cell carcinoma** is a cancer that forms in squamous cells, which are epithelial cells that lie just beneath the outer surface of the skin. Squamous cells also line many other organs, including the stomach, intestines, lungs, bladder, and kidneys. Squamous cells look flat, like fish scales, when viewed under a microscope. Squamous cell carcinomas are sometimes called epidermoid carcinomas.

- **Transitional cell carcinoma** is a cancer that forms in a type of epithelial tissue called transitional epithelium, or urothelium. This tissue, which is made up of many layers of epithelial cells that can get bigger and smaller, is found in the linings of the bladder, ureters, and part of the kidneys (renal pelvis), and a few other organs. Some cancers of the bladder, ureters, and kidneys are transitional cell carcinomas.

Sarcoma

Sarcomas are cancers that form in bone and soft tissues, including muscle, fat, blood vessels, lymph vessels, and fibrous tissue (such as tendons and ligaments).

Osteosarcoma is the most common cancer of bone. The most common types of soft tissue sarcoma are leiomyosarcoma, Kaposi sarcoma, malignant fibrous histiocytoma, liposarcoma, and dermatofibrosarcoma protuberans.

Leukemia

Cancers that begin in the blood-forming tissue of the bone marrow are called leukemias. These cancers do not form solid tumors. Instead, large numbers of abnormal white blood cells (leukemia cells and leukemic blast cells) buildup in the blood and bone marrow, crowding out normal blood cells. The low level of normal blood cells can make it harder for the body to get oxygen to its tissues, control bleeding, or fight infections.

There are four common types of leukemia, which are grouped based on how quickly the disease gets worse (acute or chronic) and on the type of blood cell the cancer starts in (lymphoblastic or myeloid).

Lymphoma

Lymphoma is cancer that begins in lymphocytes (T cells or B cells). These are disease-fighting white blood cells that are part of the immune system. In lymphoma, abnormal lymphocytes buildup in lymph nodes and lymph vessels, as well as in other organs of the body.

There are two main types of lymphoma:

- **Hodgkin lymphoma.** People with this disease have abnormal lymphocytes that are called Reed-Sternberg cells. These cells usually form from B cells.

- **Non-Hodgkin lymphoma.** This is a large group of cancers that start in lymphocytes. The cancers can grow quickly or slowly and can form from B cells or T cells.

Multiple Myeloma

Multiple myeloma is cancer that begins in plasma cells, another type of immune cell. The abnormal plasma cells, called myeloma cells, buildup in the bone marrow and form tumors in bones all through the body. Multiple myeloma is also called plasma cell myeloma and Kahler disease.

Melanoma

Melanoma is cancer that begins in cells that become melanocytes, which are specialized cells that make melanin (the pigment that gives skin its color). Most melanomas form on the skin, but melanomas can also form in other pigmented tissues, such as the eye.

Brain And Spinal Cord Tumors

There are different types of brain and spinal cord tumors. These tumors are named based on the type of cell in which they formed and where the tumor first formed in the central nervous system. For example, an astrocytic tumor begins in star-shaped brain cells called astrocytes, which help keep nerve cells healthy. Brain tumors can be benign (not cancer) or malignant (cancer).

Other Types Of Tumors

Germ Cell Tumors

Germ cell tumors are a type of tumor that begins in the cells that give rise to sperm or eggs. These tumors can occur almost anywhere in the body and can be either benign or malignant.

Neuroendocrine Tumors

Neuroendocrine tumors form from cells that release hormones into the blood in response to a signal from the nervous system. These tumors, which may make higher-than-normal amounts of hormones, can cause many different symptoms. Neuroendocrine tumors may be benign or malignant.

Carcinoid Tumors

Carcinoid tumors are a type of neuroendocrine tumor. They are slow growing tumors that are usually found in the gastrointestinal system (most often in the rectum and small intestine). Carcinoid tumors may spread to the liver or other sites in the body, and they may secrete substances such as serotonin or prostaglandins, causing carcinoid syndrome.

Statistics At A Glance: The Burden Of Cancer In The United States

- In 2016, an estimated 1,685,210 new cases of cancer will be diagnosed in the United States and 595,690 people will die from the disease.

- The most common cancers in 2016 are projected to be breast cancer, lung and bronchus cancer, prostate cancer, colon and rectum cancer, bladder cancer, melanoma of the skin, non-Hodgkin lymphoma, thyroid cancer, kidney and renal pelvis cancer, leukemia, endometrial cancer, and pancreatic cancer.

- The number of new cases of cancer (cancer incidence) is 454.8 per 100,000 men and women per year (based on 2008–2012 cases).

- The number of cancer deaths (cancer mortality) is 171.2 per 100,000 men and women per year (based on 2008–2012 deaths).

- Cancer mortality is higher among men than women (207.9 per 100,000 men and 145.4 per 100,000 women). It is highest in African American men (261.5 per 100,000) and lowest in Asian/Pacific Islander women (91.2 per 100,000). (Based on 2008–2012 deaths.)

- The number of people living beyond a cancer diagnosis reached nearly 14.5 million in 2014 and is expected to rise to almost 19 million by 2024.

- Approximately 39.6 percent of men and women will be diagnosed with cancer at some point during their lifetimes (based on 2010–2012 data).

- In 2014, an estimated 15,780 children and adolescents ages 0 to 19 were diagnosed with cancer and 1,960 died of the disease.

- National expenditures for cancer care in the United States totaled nearly $125 billion in 2010 and could reach $156 billion in 2020.

Chapter 2

Cancer In Young People: An Overview

How Common Is Cancer In Children?

Although cancer in children is rare, it is the leading cause of death by disease past infancy among children in the United States. In 2017, it is estimated that 15,270 children and adolescents ages 0–19 years will be diagnosed with cancer and 1,790 will die of the disease in the United States. Among children ages 0–14 years, it is estimated that 10,270 will be diagnosed with cancer and 1,190 will die of the disease in 2017.

The most common types of cancer diagnosed in children ages 0–14 years in the United States are leukemias, followed by brain and other central nervous system tumors, lymphomas, soft tissue sarcomas (of which half are rhabdomyosarcoma), neuroblastoma, and kidney tumors. The most common types of cancer diagnosed in 15–19-year-olds are lymphomas, followed by brain and other central nervous system tumors, leukemias, gonadal (testicular and ovarian) germ cell tumors, thyroid cancer, and melanoma. As of January 1, 2014, approximately 419,000 survivors of childhood and adolescent cancer (diagnosed at ages 0–19 years) were alive in the United States. The number of survivors will continue to increase, given that the incidence of childhood cancer has been rising slightly in recent decades and that survival rates overall are improving.

About This Chapter: This chapter includes text excerpted from "Cancer In Children And Adolescents," National Cancer Institute (NCI), August 24, 2017.

Leading Causes Of Cancer Death In Children Aged 0–19

In 2014, the most commonly diagnosed cancers and leading causes of cancer death in children aged 0–19 years were:

- Leukemias
  - Highest incidence rate (8.4) found among children aged 1–4 years.
  - Highest death rate (0.8) found among children aged 15–19 years.
- Brain and central nervous system cancer
  - Highest incidence rate (4.3) found among children aged 1–4 years.
  - Highest death rate (0.9) found among children aged 5–9 years.

(Source: "Cancer Facts For Demographic Groups—Cancer Among Children," Centers for Disease Control and Prevention (CDC).)

What Are The Possible Causes Of Cancer In Children?

Inherited Genetic Mutation

The causes of most childhood cancers are not known. About 5 percent of all cancers in children are caused by an inherited genetic mutation (a mutation that can be passed from parents to their children). For example, 25–30 percent of cases of retinoblastoma, a cancer of the eye that develops mainly in children, are caused by an inherited mutation in a gene called *RB1*. However, retinoblastoma accounts for only about 4 percent of all cancers in children ages 0–14 years. Inherited mutations associated with certain familial syndromes, such as Li-Fraumeni syndrome, Beckwith-Wiedemann syndrome, Fanconi anemia syndrome, Noonan syndrome, and von Hippel-Lindau syndrome, also increase the risk of childhood cancer.

Genetic mutations that initiate cancer development can also arise during the development of a fetus in the womb. Evidence for this comes from studies of monozygotic (identical) twins in which both twins developed leukemia with an identical leukemia-initiating gene mutation.

Children who have Down syndrome (DS), a genetic condition caused by the presence of an extra copy of chromosome 21, are 10–20 times more likely to develop leukemia than children without Down syndrome. However, only a very small proportion of childhood leukemia is linked to Down syndrome.

Mutations In Genes

Most cancers in children, like those in adults, are thought to develop as a result of mutations in genes that lead to uncontrolled cell growth and eventually cancer. In adults, these gene mutations are often the result of exposure to environmental factors, such as cigarette smoke, asbestos, and ultraviolet radiation from the sun. However, environmental causes of childhood cancer have been difficult to identify, partly because cancer in children is rare, and partly because it is difficult to determine what children might have been exposed to early in their development.

Exposure To Radiation

Many studies have shown that exposure to ionizing radiation can damage deoxyribonucleic acid (DNA), which can lead to the development of childhood leukemia and possibly other cancers. For example, children and adolescents who were exposed to radiation from the World War II atomic bomb blasts had an elevated risk of leukemia, and children and adults who were exposed to radiation from accidents at nuclear power plants had an elevated risk for thyroid cancer. Children whose mothers had X-rays during pregnancy (that is, children who were exposed before birth) and children who were exposed after birth to diagnostic medical radiation from computed tomography scans also have an increased risk of some cancers.

Other Potential Risks

Studies of other possible environmental risk factors, including parental exposure to cancer-causing chemicals, prenatal exposure to pesticides, childhood exposure to common infectious agents, and living near a nuclear power plant, have produced mixed results. Whereas some studies have found associations between these factors and risk of some cancers in children, other studies have found no such associations. Higher risks of cancer have not been seen in children who have a parent who was diagnosed with and treated for a childhood cancer that was not caused by an inherited mutation.

How Do Cancers In Adolescents And Young Adults Differ From Those In Younger Children?

Cancer occurs more frequently in adolescents and young adults ages 15–39 years than in younger children, although incidence in this group is still much lower than in older adults.

- 2 cancer diagnoses per 100,000 children ages 0–14 years

15

- 71 cancer diagnoses per 100,000 adolescents and young adults ages 15–39 years

- 1 cancer diagnoses per 100,000 people aged 40 years or older

About 102,130 adolescents and young adults ages 15–39 years were diagnosed with cancer in the United States each year in 2010–2014.

Adolescents and young adults are often diagnosed with different types of cancer than either younger children or older adults. For example, adolescents and young adults are more likely than either younger children or older adults to be diagnosed with Hodgkin lymphoma and testicular cancer. However, the incidence of specific cancer types varies widely across the adolescent and young adult age continuum.

The 5-year overall survival rate among adolescents ages 15–19 years with cancer exceeded 80 percent in 2007–2013, similar to that among younger children (84% versus 83%). However, for specific diagnoses, survival is lower for 15–19-year-olds than for younger children. For example, the 5-year survival rate for acute lymphoblastic leukemia in 2007–2013 was 91 percent for children younger than 15 years, compared with 74 percent for adolescents ages 15–19 years.

Some evidence suggests that adolescents and young adults with acute lymphoblastic leukemia may have better outcomes if they are treated with pediatric treatment regimens than if they receive adult treatment regimens. The improvement in 5-year survival rates for 15–19-year-olds with acute lymphoblastic leukemia—from approximately 50 percent in the early 1990s to 74 percent in 2007–2013—may reflect greater use of these pediatric treatment regimens. Between 1999 and 2014, the cancer death rate dropped the most for 1–4-year-olds (26%), followed by that for 15–19-year-olds (22%), 10–14-year-olds (19%), and 5–9-year-olds (14%).

What Is The Outlook For Children With Cancer?

The overall outlook for children with cancer has improved greatly over the last half-century. In 1975, just over 50 percent of children diagnosed with cancer before age 20 years survived at least 5 years. In 2007–2013, 83 percent of children diagnosed with cancer before age 20 years survived at least 5 years. Although survival rates for most childhood cancers have improved in recent decades, the improvement has been especially dramatic for a few cancers, particularly acute lymphoblastic leukemia, which is the most common childhood cancer. Improved treatments introduced beginning in the 1960s and 1970s raised the 5-year survival rate for children diagnosed with acute lymphoblastic leukemia before age 20 years from less than 10 percent in the 1960s to about 88 percent in 2007–2013. The 5-year survival rate for children diagnosed with non-Hodgkin lymphoma before age 20 years has also increased dramatically, from less than 50 percent in the late 1970s to about 89 percent in 2007–2013.

A notable example of how treatment advances have improved the outlook for children with leukemia is reflected in recent data showing that during 1999–2014, brain cancer replaced leukemia as the leading cause of cancer death among 1–19-year-olds. By contrast, survival rates remain very low for some cancer types, for some age groups, and for some cancers within a site. For example, median survival for children with diffuse intrinsic pontine glioma (a type of brain tumor) is less than 1 year from diagnosis. Among children with Wilms tumor (a type of kidney cancer), older children (those diagnosed between ages 10 and 16 years) have worse 5-year survival rates than younger children. For soft tissue sarcomas, 5-year survival rates in 2007–2013 among children and adolescents ages 0–19 years ranged from 65 percent (rhabdomyosarcoma) to 95 percent (chondrosarcoma), but children with sarcomas who present with metastatic disease have much lower 5-year survival rates.

The cancer mortality rate—the number of deaths due to cancer per 100,000 people per year—among children ages 0–19 years declined by more than 50 percent from 1975–1977 to 2010–2014. Specifically, the mortality rate was slightly more than 5 per 100,000 children in 1975 and about 2.1 per 100,000 children in 2010–2014. However, despite the overall decrease in mortality, approximately 1,800 children die of cancer each year in the United States, indicating that new advances and continued research to identify effective treatments are required to further reduce childhood cancer mortality.

Chapter 3

Cancer Facts, Myths, And Misconceptions

Certain popular ideas about how cancer starts and spreads—though scientifically wrong—can seem to make sense, especially when those ideas are rooted in old theories. But wrong ideas about cancer can lead to needless worry and even hinder good prevention and treatment decisions.

Is Cancer A Death Sentence?

In the United States, the likelihood of dying from cancer has dropped steadily since the 1990s. Five-year survival rates for some cancers, such as breast, prostate, and thyroid cancers, now exceed 90 percent. The 5-year survival rate for all cancers combined is currently about 66 percent. It is important to note, however, that these rates are based on data from large numbers of people. How long an individual cancer patient will live and whether he or she will die from the disease depend on many factors, including whether the cancer is slow or fast growing, how much the cancer has spread in the body, whether effective treatments are available, the person's overall health, and more.

Will Eating Sugar Make My Cancer Worse?

No. Although research has shown that cancer cells consume more sugar (glucose) than normal cells, no studies have shown that eating sugar will make your cancer worse or that, if you stop eating sugar, your cancer will shrink or disappear. However, a high-sugar diet may contribute to excess weight gain, and obesity is associated with an increased risk of developing several types of cancer.

About This Chapter: This chapter includes text excerpted from "Common Cancer Myths And Misconceptions," National Cancer Institute (NCI), February 3, 2014. Reviewed December 2017.

Do Artificial Sweeteners Cause Cancer?

No. Researchers have conducted studies on the safety of the artificial sweeteners (sugar substitutes) saccharin (Sweet 'N Low®, Sweet Twin®, NectaSweet®); cyclamate; aspartame (Equal®, NutraSweet®); acesulfame potassium (Sunett®, Sweet One®); sucralose (Splenda®); and neotame and found no evidence that they cause cancer in humans. All of these artificial sweeteners except for cyclamate have been approved by the U.S. Food and Drug Administration (FDA) for sale in the United States.

What Are Artificial Sweeteners?

Artificial sweeteners, also called sugar substitutes, are substances that are used instead of sucrose (table sugar) to sweeten foods and beverages. Saccharin, aspartame, sucralose, acesulfame potassium, neotame, advantame, and cyclamate are a few of the popular artificial sweeteners.

(Source: "Artificial Sweeteners And Cancer," National Cancer Institute (NCI).)

Is Cancer Contagious?

In general, no. Cancer is not a contagious disease that easily spreads from person to person. The only situation in which cancer can spread from one person to another is in the case of organ or tissue transplantation. A person who receives an organ or tissue from a donor who had cancer in the past may be at increased risk of developing a transplant-related cancer in the future. However, that risk is extremely low—about 2 cases of cancer per 10,000 organ transplants. Doctors avoid the use of organs or tissue from donors who have a history of cancer. In some people, cancers may be caused by certain viruses (some types of human papillomavirus, or HPV, for example) and bacteria (such as *Helicobacter pylori*). While a virus or bacterium can spread from person to person, the cancers they sometimes cause cannot spread from person to person.

Does My Attitude—Positive Or Negative—Determine My Risk Of, Or Likely Recovery From, Cancer?

To date, there is no convincing scientific evidence that links a person's "attitude" to his or her risk of developing or dying from cancer. If you have cancer, it's normal to feel sad, angry, or discouraged sometimes and positive or upbeat at other times. People with a positive attitude may be more likely to maintain social connections and stay active, and physical activity and emotional support may help you cope with your cancer.

Can Cancer Surgery Or A Tumor Biopsy Cause Cancer To Spread In The Body?

The chance that surgery will cause cancer to spread to other parts of the body is extremely low. Following standard procedures, surgeons use special methods and take many steps to prevent cancer cells from spreading during biopsies or surgery to remove tumors. For example, if they must remove tissue from more than one area of the body, they use different surgical tools for each area.

Will Cancer Get Worse If Exposed To Air?

No. Exposure to air will not make tumors grow faster or cause cancer to spread to other parts of the body.

Do Cell Phones Cause Cancer?

No, not according to the best studies completed so far. Cancer is caused by genetic mutations, and cell phones emit a type of low-frequency energy that does not damage genes.

Do Power Lines Cause Cancer?

No, not according to the best studies completed so far. Power lines emit both electric and magnetic energy. The electric energy emitted by power lines is easily shielded or weakened by walls and other objects. The magnetic energy emitted by power lines is a low-frequency form of radiation that does not damage genes.

Are There Herbal Products That Can Cure Cancer?

No. Although some studies suggest that alternative or complementary therapies, including some herbs, may help patients cope with the side effects of cancer treatment, no herbal products have been shown to be effective for treating cancer. In fact, some herbal products may be harmful when taken during chemotherapy or radiation therapy because they may interfere with how these treatments work. Cancer patients should talk with their doctor about any complementary and alternative medicine products—including vitamins and herbal supplements—they may be using.

Whenever starting a new routine, whether an exercise program or use of a multivitamin, you should always consult your doctor first. It is important to clearly communicate all medications you take, including dietary supplements, vitamins, and herbals to prevent potential drug interactions. Some supplements may interfere with the effectiveness of chemotherapy, radiation, or prescription medications.

(Source: "Talking About Complementary And Alternative Medicine With Healthcare Providers: A Workbook And Tips," National Cancer Institute (NCI).)

If Someone In My Family Has Cancer, Am I Likely To Get Cancer, Too?

Not necessarily. Cancer is caused by harmful changes (mutations) in genes. Only about 5–10 percent of cancers are caused by harmful mutations that are inherited from a person's parents. In families with an inherited cancer-causing mutation, multiple family members will often develop the same type of cancer. These cancers are called "familial" or "hereditary" cancers. The remaining 90–95 percent of cancers are caused by mutations that happen during a person's lifetime as a natural result of aging and exposure to environmental factors, such as tobacco smoke and radiation. These cancers are called "nonhereditary" or "spontaneous" cancers.

If No One In My Family Has Had Cancer, Does That Mean I'm Risk-Free?

No. Based on the most recent data, about 40 percent of men and women will be diagnosed with cancer at some point during their lives. Most cancers are caused by genetic changes that occur throughout a person's lifetime as a natural result of aging and exposure to environmental factors, such as tobacco smoke and radiation. Other factors, such as what kind of food you eat, how much you eat, and whether you exercise, may also influence your risk of developing cancer.

Do Antiperspirants Or Deodorants Cause Breast Cancer?

No. The best studies so far have found no evidence linking the chemicals typically found in antiperspirants and deodorants with changes in breast tissue.

Does Hair Dye Use Increase The Risk Of Cancer?

There is no convincing scientific evidence that personal hair dye use increases the risk of cancer. Some studies suggest, however, that hairdressers and barbers who are regularly exposed to large quantities of hair dye and other chemical products may have an increased risk of bladder cancer.

Many people in the United States and Europe use hair dyes. It is estimated that more than one-third of women over age 18 and about 10 percent of men over age 40 use some type of hair dye. Over 5,000 different chemicals are used in hair dye products, some of which are reported to be carcinogenic (cancer-causing) in animals.

(Source: "Hair Dyes And Cancer Risk," National Cancer Institute (NCI).)

Chapter 4

Genes, Genetic Disorders, And Cancer

Genetic Changes And Cancer

Cancer is a genetic disease—that is, cancer is caused by certain changes to genes that control the way our cells function, especially how they grow and divide.

Genes carry the instructions to make proteins, which do much of the work in our cells. Certain gene changes can cause cells to evade normal growth controls and become cancer. For example, some cancer-causing gene changes increase production of a protein that makes cells grow. Others result in the production of a misshapen, and therefore nonfunctional, form of a protein that normally repairs cellular damage.

Genetic changes that promote cancer can be inherited from our parents if the changes are present in germ cells, which are the reproductive cells of the body (eggs and sperm). Such changes, called germline changes, are found in every cell of the offspring.

Cancer-causing genetic changes can also be acquired during one's lifetime, as the result of errors that occur as cells divide or from exposure to carcinogenic substances that damage deoxyribonucleic acid (DNA), such as certain chemicals in tobacco smoke, and radiation, such as ultraviolet rays from the sun. Genetic changes that occur after conception are called somatic (or acquired) changes.

There are many different kinds of DNA changes. Some changes affect just one unit of DNA, called a nucleotide. One nucleotide may be replaced by another, or it may be missing entirely. Other changes involve larger stretches of DNA and may include rearrangements, deletions, or duplications of long stretches of DNA.

About This Chapter: This chapter includes text excerpted from "The Genetics Of Cancer," National Cancer Institute (NCI), October 12, 2017.

Sometimes the changes are not in the actual sequence of DNA. For example, the addition or removal of chemical marks, called epigenetic modifications, on DNA can influence whether the gene is "expressed"—that is, whether and how much messenger ribonucleic acid (RNA) is produced. (Messenger RNA in turn is translated to produce the proteins encoded by the DNA.)

In general, cancer cells have more genetic changes than normal cells. But each person's cancer has a unique combination of genetic alterations. Some of these changes may be the result of cancer, rather than the cause. As the cancer continues to grow, additional changes will occur. Even within the same tumor, cancer cells may have different genetic changes.

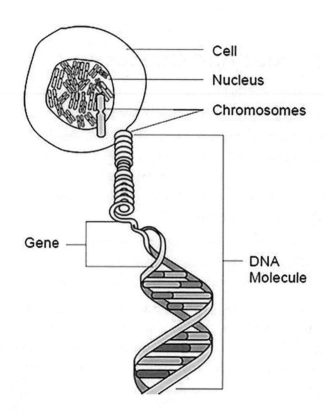

Figure 4.1. DNA (Deoxyribonucleic Acid)

Tightly coiled strands of DNA, which carry the instructions that allow cells to make proteins, are packaged in units called chromosomes. Subunits of DNA are known as genes.

(Source: "Cancer And The Environment," National Institute of Environmental Health Sciences (NIEHS).)

Hereditary Cancer Syndromes

Inherited genetic mutations play a major role in about 5–10 percent of all cancers. Researchers have associated mutations in specific genes with more than 50 hereditary cancer syndromes, which are disorders that may predispose individuals to developing certain cancers.

Genetic tests for hereditary cancer syndromes can tell whether a person from a family that shows signs of such a syndrome has one of these mutations. These tests can also show whether family members without obvious disease have inherited the same mutation as a family member who carries a cancer-associated mutation.

Many experts recommend that genetic testing for cancer risk be considered when someone has a personal or family history that suggests an inherited cancer risk condition, as long as the test results can be adequately interpreted (that is, they can clearly tell whether a specific genetic change is present or absent) and when the results provide information that will help guide a person's future medical care.

Cancers that are not caused by inherited genetic mutations can sometimes appear to "run in families." For example, a shared environment or lifestyle, such as tobacco use, can cause similar cancers to develop among family members. However, certain patterns in a family—such as the types of cancer that develop, other noncancer conditions that are seen, and the ages at which cancer develops—may suggest the presence of a hereditary cancer syndrome.

Even if a cancer-predisposing mutation is present in a family, not everyone who inherits the mutation will necessarily develop cancer. Several factors influence the outcome in a given person with the mutation, including the pattern of inheritance of the cancer syndrome.

Here are examples of genes that can play a role in hereditary cancer syndromes.

- The most commonly mutated gene in all cancers is *TP53*, which produces a protein that suppresses the growth of tumors. In addition, germline mutations in this gene can cause Li-Fraumeni syndrome, a rare, inherited disorder that leads to a higher risk of developing certain cancers.

- Inherited mutations in the *BRCA1* and *BRCA2* genes are associated with hereditary breast and ovarian cancer syndrome, which is a disorder marked by an increased lifetime risk of breast and ovarian cancers in women. Several other cancers have been associated with this syndrome, including pancreatic and prostate cancers, as well as male breast cancer.

- Another gene that produces a protein that suppresses the growth of tumors is *PTEN*. Mutations in this gene are associated with Cowden syndrome, an inherited disorder that increases the risk of breast, thyroid, endometrial, and other types of cancer.

Genetic Tests For Hereditary Cancer Syndromes

Genetic tests for mutations that cause hereditary cancer syndromes are usually requested by a person's doctor or other healthcare provider. Genetic counseling can help people consider the risks, benefits, and limitations of genetic testing in their particular situations.

A genetic counselor, doctor, or other healthcare professional trained in genetics can help an individual or family understand their test results and explain the possible implications of test results for other family members.

People considering genetic testing should understand that their results may become known to other people or organizations that have legitimate, legal access to their medical records, such as their insurance company or employer, if their employer provides the patient's health insurance as a benefit. Legal protections are in place to prevent genetic discrimination, including the Genetic Information Nondiscrimination Act (GINA) of 2008 and the Privacy Rule of the Health Information Portability and Accountability Act (HIPAA) of 1996.

The Genetic Information Nondiscrimination Act (GINA)

In 2008, President George W. Bush signed the Genetic Information Nondiscrimination Act (GINA) into law. Under GINA, employers and health insurers can no longer discriminate against individuals based upon their genetic information. GINA protects Americans from genetic discrimination while encouraging each patient to seek out medical care that is specifically tailored to his or her genetic makeup.

(Source: "The Genetic Information Nondiscrimination Act (GINA)," National Institutes of Health (NIH).)

Identifying Genetic Changes In Cancer

Lab tests called DNA sequencing tests can "read" DNA. By comparing the sequence of DNA in cancer cells with that in normal cells, such as blood or saliva, scientists can identify genetic changes in cancer cells that may be driving the growth of an individual's cancer. This information may help doctors sort out which therapies might work best against a particular tumor. Tumor DNA sequencing can also reveal the presence of inherited mutations. Indeed, in some cases, the genetic testing of tumors has shown that a patient's cancer could be associated with a hereditary cancer syndrome that the family was not aware of. As with testing for specific mutations in hereditary cancer syndromes, clinical DNA sequencing has implications that patients need to consider. For example, they may learn incidentally about the presence of inherited mutations that may cause other diseases, in them or in their family members.

Tumor DNA Sequencing

Each person's cancer has a unique combination of genetic changes, and tumor DNA sequencing—sometimes called genetic profiling or genetic testing—is a test to identify these unique DNA changes. Tumor DNA sequencing is at the crux of precision medicine: care tailored to the molecular characteristics of each patient's disease.

(Source: "Tumor DNA Sequencing In Cancer Treatment," National Cancer Institute (NCI).)

Chapter 5

Cancer And The Environment

Cancer arises when cells are unable to repair deoxyribonucleic acid (DNA) damage and experience abnormal cell growth and division. The process known as metastasis occurs when cancer cells travel to other parts of the body via the bloodstream and replace normal tissue. According to the American Cancer Society (ACS), this chronic disease is the second leading cause of death in the United States with half of all men and one-third of all women developing some form of cancer during their lifetimes. Although cancer is responsible for 23 percent of all deaths in the United States, millions of Americans have recovered from the disease. People may reduce their chances of getting cancer by employing prevention methods such as having regular screenings and living a healthy lifestyle.

Factors Outside The Body

Exposure to a wide variety of natural and man-made substances in the environment accounts for at least two-thirds of all the cases of cancer in the United States. These environmental factors include lifestyle choices like cigarette smoking, excessive alcohol consumption, poor diet, lack of exercise, excessive sunlight exposure, and sexual behavior that increases exposure to certain viruses. Other factors include exposure to certain medical drugs, hormones, radiation, viruses, bacteria, and environmental chemicals that may be present in the air, water, food, and workplace. The cancer risks associated with many environmental chemicals have been identified through studies of occupational groups that have higher exposures to these chemicals than the general population.

About This Chapter: This chapter includes text excerpted from "Cancer," National Institute of Environmental Health Sciences (NIEHS), June 7, 2017.

The importance of the environment can be seen in the differences in cancer rates throughout the world and the change in cancer rates when groups of people move from one country to another. For example, when Asians, who have low rates of prostate and breast cancer and high rates of stomach cancer in their native countries, immigrate to the United States, their prostate and breast cancer rates rise over time until they are nearly equal to or greater than the higher levels of these cancers in the United States. Likewise, their rates of stomach cancer fall, becoming nearly equal to the lower U.S. rates. Lifestyle factors such as diet, exercise, and being overweight are thought to play a major role in the trends for breast and prostate cancers, and infection with the *Helicobacter pylori* bacterium is an important risk factor for stomach cancer. Recently, the rapid rise in the rates of colorectal cancer in Japan and China suggests an environmental cause such as lifestyle factors.

Different environmental exposures are linked to specific kinds of cancer. For example, exposure to asbestos is linked primarily to lung cancer, whereas exposure to benzidine, a chemical found in certain dyes, is associated with bladder cancer. In contrast, smoking is linked to cancers of the lung, bladder, mouth, colon, kidney, throat, voice box, esophagus, lip, stomach, cervix, liver, and pancreas.

Factors Inside The Body

Certain factors inside the body make some people more likely to develop cancer than others. For instance, some people either inherit or acquire the following conditions: altered genes in the body's cells, abnormal hormone levels in the bloodstream, or a weakened immune system. Each of these factors may make an individual more susceptible to cancer.

One of the ways scientists know that genes play an important role in the development of cancer is from studying certain rare families where family members over several generations develop similar cancers. It appears that these families are passing on an altered gene that carries with it a high chance of getting cancer. Several genes that greatly increase a person's chance of developing certain cancers (e.g., colon, breast, and ovary) have been identified. Only a very small percentage of people in the general population have abnormal copies of these genes. Cancers caused by these genes, known as familial cancers, account for only two to five percent of all cancers.

Gene alterations may also contribute to individual differences in susceptibility to environmental carcinogens (cancer-causing substances). For instance, people differ in their ability to eliminate cancer-causing agents from their body to which they have been exposed, or to repair deoxyribonucleic acid (DNA) damage that was caused by such agents. These gene alterations may also be passed on in families and account for higher rates of cancer in these families. Higher rates of cancer in families may also be related to shared environmental exposures like diet or exposure to carcinogens at work. One of the main objectives of a growing field in cancer research called molecular epidemiology is to identify gene alterations that increase or decrease a person's chance of developing cancer after an environmental exposure.

Interaction Of Environmental Factors And Genes

Environmental factors such as viruses, sunlight, and chemicals interact with cells throughout our lives. Mechanisms to repair damage to our genes and healthy lifestyle choices (wearing protective clothing for sun exposure or not smoking) help to protect us from harmful exposures. However, over time, substances in the environment may cause gene alterations, which accumulate inside our cells. While many alterations have no effect on a person's health, permanent changes in certain genes can lead to cancer.

The chance that an individual will develop cancer in response to a particular environmental agent depends on several interacting factors—how long and how often a person is exposed to a particular substance, his/her exposure to other agents, genetic factors, diet, lifestyle, health, age, and gender. For example, diet, alcohol consumption, and certain medications can affect the levels of chemicals in the body that break down cancer-causing substances.

Because of the complex interplay of many factors, it is not possible to predict whether a specific environmental exposure will cause a particular person to develop cancer. We know that certain genetic and environmental factors increase the risk of developing cancer, but we rarely know exactly which combination of factors is responsible for a person's specific cancer. This also means that we usually don't know why one person gets cancer and another does not.

Chapter 6

Indoor Tanning And Cancer Risk

What Is Indoor Tanning?

Using a tanning bed, booth, or sunlamp to get tan is called indoor tanning. Exposure to ultraviolet (UV) rays while indoor tanning can cause skin cancers including melanoma (the deadliest type of skin cancer), basal cell carcinoma, and squamous cell carcinoma. UV exposure also can cause cataracts and cancers of the eye (ocular melanoma). UV exposure from the sun and from indoor tanning is classified as a human carcinogen (causes cancer in humans) by the International Agency for Research on Cancer (IARC) (part of the World Health Organization (WHO)) and by the U.S. Department of Health and Human Services (HHS).

Facts About Indoor Tanning

Tanning Indoors Is Not Safer Than Tanning In The Sun

Indoor tanning and tanning outside are both dangerous. Although indoor tanning devices operate on a timer, the exposure to UV rays can vary based on the age and type of light bulbs. Indoor tanning is designed to give you high levels of UV radiation in a short time. You can get a burn from tanning indoors, and even a tan indicates damage to your skin.

About This Chapter: Text beginning with the heading "What Is Indoor Tanning?" is excerpted from "Skin Cancer—Indoor Tanning Is Not Safe," Centers for Disease Control and Prevention (CDC), April 26, 2017; Text beginning with the heading "Preventing From Ultraviolet (UV) Rays" is excerpted from "Skin Cancer—Are There Benefits To Spending Time Outdoors?" Centers for Disease Control and Prevention (CDC), April 25, 2017.

> ## What Are UV Rays, And How Do They Affect The Skin?
>
> Sunlight travels to earth as a mixture of both visible and invisible rays. Some of the rays are harmless to people. But one kind, ultraviolet (UV) rays, can cause problems. They are a form of radiation. UV rays do help your body make vitamin D, but too much exposure damages your skin. Most people can get the vitamin D that they need with only about 5–15 minutes of sun exposure two to three times a week. There are three types of UV rays. Two of them, UVA and UVB, can reach the earth's surface and affect your skin. Using a tanning bed also exposes you to UVA and UVB.
>
> *(Source: "Tanning," MedlinePlus, National Institutes of Health (NIH).)*

A Base Tan Is Not A Safe Tan

A tan is the body's response to injury from UV rays. A base tan does little to protect you from future damage to your skin caused by UV exposure. In fact, people who indoor tan are more likely to report getting sunburned.

The best way to protect your skin from the sun is by using these tips for skin cancer prevention.

Indoor Tanning Is Not A Safe Way To Get Vitamin D

Although it is important to get enough vitamin D, the safest way to do so is through what you eat. Tanning harms your skin, and the amount of UV exposure you need to get enough vitamin D is hard to measure because it is different for every person and also varies with the weather, latitude, altitude, and more.

Dangers Of Indoor Tanning

Indoor tanning exposes users to two types of UV rays, UVA and UVB, which damage the skin and can lead to cancer. Indoor tanning is particularly dangerous for younger users; people who begin indoor tanning during adolescence or early adulthood have a higher risk of getting melanoma. This may be due to greater use of indoor tanning among those who begin tanning at earlier ages.

Every time you tan you increase your risk of getting skin cancer, including melanoma. Indoor tanning also:

- Causes premature skin aging, like wrinkles and age spots.

- Changes your skin texture.

- Increases the risk of potentially blinding eye diseases, if eye protection is not used.

Is Base Tan Risk Free?

Some people think that getting a "base tan" in a tanning salon can protect you when you go in the sun. But a "base tan" causes damage to your skin and will not prevent you from getting sunburn when you go outside.

Indoor tanning is particularly dangerous for younger people. You have a higher risk of melanoma if you started doing indoor tanning while you were a teen or young adult. Some research shows that frequent tanning may even be addictive. This can be dangerous because the more often you tan, the more damage you do to your skin.

(Source: "Tanning," MedlinePlus, National Institutes of Health (NIH).)

Preventing Overexposure To Ultraviolet (UV) Rays

Spending time outdoors can improve overall health and wellness. The outdoors offers many opportunities to be physically active. Time outdoors may also promote mental health and stress reduction. While enjoying the benefits of being outdoors, people can decrease skin cancer risk from too much UV exposure by using sun protection. Protect yourself by staying in the shade, wearing protective clothing, and applying and re-applying a broad spectrum sunscreen with a sun protection factor (SPF) of 15 or higher.

Ultraviolet (UV) rays from the sun can stimulate production of vitamin D in the skin. Having little or no sun exposure may put a person at risk for low levels of vitamin D, but too much UV exposure from the sun or artificial sources can increase risk of skin cancers and eye disease. The amount of vitamin D a person's skin makes when they are in the sun depends on many factors, including skin tone, geographic location, weather conditions, time of year, and time of day. The skin can produce only a limited amount of vitamin D at one time. Once the body has reached this limit, spending more time in the sun will not continue to increase vitamin D levels. However, continued time in the sun will increase your skin cancer risk. There is no known level of UV exposure that would increase vitamin D levels without also increasing skin cancer risk. Vitamin D can be obtained safely through food and dietary supplements without the risks associated with overexposure to UV.

Sun Safety

The sun's ultraviolet (UV) rays can damage your skin in as little as 15 minutes.

Follow these recommendations to help protect yourself and your family.

Shade

You can reduce your risk of skin damage and skin cancer by seeking shade under an umbrella, tree, or other shelter before you need relief from the sun. Your best bet to protect your skin is to use sunscreen or wear protective clothing when you're outside—even when you're in the shade.

Clothing

When possible, long-sleeved shirts and long pants and skirts can provide protection from UV rays. Clothes made from tightly woven fabric offer the best protection. A wet T-shirt offers much less UV protection than a dry one, and darker colors may offer more protection than lighter colors. Some clothing certified under international standards comes with information on its ultraviolet protection factor.

If wearing this type of clothing isn't practical, at least try to wear a T-shirt or a beach cover-up. Keep in mind that a typical T-shirt has an SPF rating lower than 15, so use other types of protection as well.

Hat

For the most protection, wear a hat with a brim all the way around that shades your face, ears, and the back of your neck. A tightly woven fabric, such as canvas, works best to protect your skin from UV rays. Avoid straw hats with holes that let sunlight through. A darker hat may offer more UV protection.

If you wear a baseball cap, you should also protect your ears and the back of your neck by wearing clothing that covers those areas, using a broad spectrum sunscreen with at least SPF 15, or by staying in the shade.

Sunglasses

Sunglasses protect your eyes from UV rays and reduce the risk of cataracts. They also protect the tender skin around your eyes from sun exposure.

Sunglasses that block both UVA and UVB rays offer the best protection. Most sunglasses sold in the United States, regardless of cost, meet this standard. Wrap-around sunglasses work best because they block UV rays from sneaking in from the side.

Sunscreen

Put on broad spectrum sunscreen with at least SPF 15 before you go outside, even on slightly cloudy or cool days. Don't forget to put a thick layer on all parts of exposed skin. Get help for hard-to-reach places like your back. And remember, sunscreen works best when combined with other options to prevent UV damage.

How sunscreen works. Most sunscreen products work by absorbing, reflecting, or scattering sunlight. They contain chemicals that interact with the skin to protect it from UV rays. All products do not have the same ingredients; if your skin reacts badly to one product, try another one or call a doctor.

Sun protection factor (SPF). Sunscreens are assigned a sun protection factor (SPF) number that rates their effectiveness in blocking UV rays. Higher numbers indicate more protection. You should use a broad spectrum sunscreen with at least SPF 15.

Reapplication. Sunscreen wears off. Put it on again if you stay out in the sun for more than two hours and after swimming, sweating, or toweling off.

Expiration date. Check the sunscreens' expiration date. Sunscreen without an expiration date has a shelf life of no more than three years, but its shelf life is shorter if it has been exposed to high temperatures.

Cosmetics. Some makeup and lip balms contain some of the same chemicals used in sunscreens. If they do not have at least SPF 15, don't use them by themselves.

Watch the UV Index. The UV Index provides important information that can help you plan your outdoor activities to avoid getting too much of the sun's rays. You can learn more about the UV Index in the Sun section of girlshealth.gov. Also, you can check the UV Index on most weather websites or at the Environmental Protection Agency (EPA).

(Source: "How To Protect Yourself From The Sun," girlshealth.gov, Office on Women's Health (OWH).)

Chapter 7

Vitamin D And Cancer Prevention

What Is Vitamin D?

Vitamin D is the name given to a group of fat-soluble prohormones (substances that usually have little hormonal activity by themselves but that the body can turn into hormones). Vitamin D helps the body use calcium and phosphorus to make strong bones and teeth. Skin exposed to sunshine can make vitamin D, and vitamin D can also be obtained from certain foods. Vitamin D deficiency can cause a weakening of the bones that is called rickets in children and osteomalacia in adults.

Two major forms of vitamin D that are important to humans are vitamin D_2, or ergocalciferol, and vitamin D_3, or cholecalciferol. Vitamin D_2 is made naturally by plants, and vitamin D_3 is made naturally by the body when skin is exposed to ultraviolet radiation in sunlight. Both forms are converted to 25-hydroxyvitamin D in the liver. 25-Hydroxyvitamin D then travels through the blood to the kidneys, where it is further modified to 1, 25-dihydroxyvitamin D, or calcitriol, the active form of vitamin D in the body. The most accurate method of evaluating a person's vitamin D status is to measure the level of 25-hydroxyvitamin D in the blood.

Most people get at least some of the vitamin D they need through sunlight exposure. Dietary sources include a few foods that naturally contain vitamin D, such as fatty fish, fish liver oil, and eggs. However, most dietary vitamin D comes from foods fortified with vitamin D, such as milk, juices, and breakfast cereals. Vitamin D can also be obtained through dietary supplements.

About This Chapter: This chapter includes text excerpted from "Vitamin D And Cancer Prevention," National Cancer Institute (NCI), October 21, 2013. Reviewed December 2017.

The Institute of Medicine (IOM) of the National Academies has developed the following recommended daily intakes of vitamin D, assuming minimal sun exposure:

- For those between 1 and 70 years of age, including women who are pregnant or lactating, the recommended dietary allowance (RDA) is 15 micrograms (μg) per day. Because 1 μg is equal to 40 International Units (IU), this RDA can also be expressed as 600 IU per day.

- For infants, the IOM could not determine an RDA due to a lack of data. However, the IOM set an Adequate Intake level of 10 μg per day (400 IU per day), which should provide sufficient vitamin D.

Although the average dietary intakes of vitamin D in the United States are below guideline levels, data from the National Health and Nutrition Examination Survey (NHANES) revealed that more than 80 percent of Americans had adequate vitamin D levels in their blood.

Even though most people are unlikely to have high vitamin D intakes, it is important to remember that excessive intake of any nutrient, including vitamin D, can cause toxic effects. Too much vitamin D can be harmful because it increases calcium levels, which can lead to calcinosis (the deposit of calcium salts in soft tissues, such as the kidneys, heart, or lungs) and hypercalcemia (high blood levels of calcium). The safe upper intake level of vitamin D for adults and children older than 8 years of age is 100 μg per day (4000 IU per day). Toxicity from too much vitamin D is more likely to occur from high intakes of dietary supplements than from high intakes of foods that contain vitamin D. Excessive sun exposure does not cause vitamin D toxicity. However, the IOM states that people should not try to increase vitamin D production by increasing their exposure to sunlight because this will also increase their risk of skin cancer.

Why Are Cancer Researchers Studying A Possible Connection Between Vitamin D And Cancer Risk?

Early epidemiologic research showed that incidence and death rates for certain cancers were lower among individuals living in southern latitudes, where levels of sunlight exposure are relatively high, than among those living at northern latitudes. Because exposure to ultraviolet light from sunlight leads to the production of vitamin D, researchers hypothesized that variation in vitamin D levels might account for this association. However, additional research based on stronger study designs is required to determine whether higher vitamin D levels are related to lower cancer incidence or death rates.

Experimental evidence has also suggested a possible association between vitamin D and cancer risk. In studies of cancer cells and of tumors in mice, vitamin D has been found to have several activities that might slow or prevent the development of cancer, including promoting cellular differentiation, decreasing cancer cell growth, stimulating cell death (apoptosis), and reducing tumor blood vessel formation (angiogenesis).

What Is The Evidence That Vitamin D Can Help Reduce The Risk Of Cancer In People?

A number of epidemiologic studies have investigated whether people with higher vitamin D intakes or higher blood levels of vitamin D have lower risks of specific cancers. The results of these studies have been inconsistent, possibly because of the challenges in carrying out such studies. For example, dietary studies do not account for vitamin D made in the skin from sunlight exposure, and the level of vitamin D measured in the blood at a single point in time (as in most studies) may not reflect a person's true vitamin D status. Also, it is possible that people with higher vitamin D intakes or blood levels are more likely to have other healthy behaviors. It may be one of these other behaviors, rather than vitamin D intake, that influences cancer risk.

Several randomized trials of vitamin D intake have been carried out, but these were designed to assess bone health or other noncancer outcomes. Although some of these trials have yielded information on cancer incidence and mortality, the results need to be confirmed by additional research because the trials were not designed to study cancer specifically.

The cancers for which the most human data are available are colorectal, breast, prostate, and pancreatic cancer. Numerous epidemiologic studies have shown that higher intake or blood levels of vitamin D are associated with a reduced risk of colorectal cancer. In contrast, the Women's Health Initiative randomized trial found that healthy women who took vitamin D and calcium supplements for an average of 7 years did not have a reduced incidence of colorectal cancer. Some scientists have pointed out that the relatively low level of vitamin D supplementation (10 µg, or 400 IU, once a day), the ability of participants to take additional vitamin D on their own, and the short duration of participant follow-up in this trial might explain why no reduction in colorectal cancer risk was found. Evidence on the association between vitamin D and the risks of all other malignancies studied is inconclusive.

How Is Vitamin D Being Studied Now In Clinical Cancer Research?

Taken together, the available data are not comprehensive enough to establish whether taking vitamin D can prevent cancer. To fully understand the effects of vitamin D on cancer and other health outcomes, new randomized trials need to be conducted. However, the appropriate dose of vitamin D to use in such trials is still not clear. Other remaining questions include when to start taking vitamin D, and for how long, to potentially see a benefit.

To begin addressing these issues, researchers are conducting two phase I trials to determine what dose of vitamin D may be useful for chemoprevention of prostate, colorectal, and lung cancers (trial descriptions here and here). In addition, larger randomized trials have been initiated to examine the potential role of vitamin D in the prevention of cancer. The Vitamin D/ Calcium Polyp Prevention Study, which has finished recruiting approximately 2,200 participants, is testing whether vitamin D supplements, given alone or with calcium, can prevent the development of colorectal adenomas (precancerous growths) in patients who previously had an adenoma removed. The study's estimated completion date is December 2017. The Vitamin D and Omega-3 Trial (VITAL) will examine whether vitamin D supplements can prevent the development of a variety of cancer types in healthy older men and women.

Researchers are also beginning to study vitamin D analogs—chemicals with structures similar to that of vitamin D—which may have the anticancer activity of vitamin D but not its ability to increase calcium levels.

Chapter 8

Cancer Risks Associated With Smoking And Other Tobacco Use

Tobacco Use And Youth

Youth use of tobacco in any form is unsafe.

If smoking continues at the current rate among youth in this country, 5.6 million of today's Americans younger than 18 will die early from a smoking-related illness. That's about 1 of every 13 Americans aged 17 years or younger alive today.

Preventing tobacco use among youth is critical to ending the tobacco epidemic in the United States.

- Tobacco use is started and established primarily during adolescence.

    - Nearly 9 out of 10 cigarette smokers first tried smoking by age 18, and 99 percent first tried smoking by age 26.

    - Each day in the United States, more than 3,200 youth aged 18 years or younger smoke their first cigarette, and an additional 2,100 youth and young adults become daily cigarette smokers.

- Flavorings in tobacco products can make them more appealing to youth.

    - In 2014, 73 percent of high school students and 56 percent of middle school students who used tobacco products in the past 30 days reported using a flavored tobacco product during that time.

About This Chapter: Text under the heading "Youth And Tobacco Use" is excerpted from "Tobacco Use And Youth," Centers for Disease Control and Prevention (CDC), September 20, 2017; Text under the heading "Tobacco Use And Cancer" is excerpted from "Risk Factors: Tobacco," National Cancer Institute (NCI), January 23, 2017; Text beginning with the heading "How Is Smoking Related To Cancer?" is excerpted from "Diseases/Conditions Featured In The Campaign—Smoking And Cancer," Centers for Disease Control and Prevention (CDC), January 23, 2017.

Estimates Of Current Tobacco Use Among Youth

Cigarettes

- From 2011 to 2016, current cigarette smoking declined among middle and high school students.

    - About 2 of every 100 middle school students (2.2%) reported in 2016 that they smoked cigarettes in the past 30 days—a decrease from 4.3 percent in 2011.

    - 8 of every 100 high school students (8.0%) reported in 2016 that they smoked cigarettes in the past 30 days—a decrease from 15.8 percent in 2011.

Electronic Cigarettes

- Current use of electronic cigarettes increased among middle and high school students from 2011 to 2016.

    - About 4 of every 100 middle school students (4.3%) reported in 2016 that they used electronic cigarettes in the past 30 days—an increase from 0.6 percent in 2011.

    - About 11 of every 100 high school students (11.3%) reported in 2016 that they used electronic cigarettes in the past 30 days—an increase from 1.5 percent in 2011.

Hookahs

- From 2011 to 2016, current use of hookahs increased among middle and high school students.

    - 2 of every 100 middle school students (2.0%) reported in 2016 that they had used hookah in the past 30 days—an increase from 1.0 percent in 2011.

    - Nearly 5 of every 100 high school students (4.8%) reported in 2016 that they had used hookah in the past 30 days—an increase from 4.1 percent in 2011.

Smokeless Tobacco

- In 2016:

    - About 2 of every 100 middle school students (2.2%) reported current use of smokeless tobacco.

    - Nearly 6 of every 100 high school students (5.8%) reported current use of smokeless tobacco.

All Tobacco Product Use

- In 2016, about 7 of every 100 middle school students (7.2%) and about 20 of every 100 high school students (20.2%) used some type of tobacco product.

- In 2013, nearly 18 of every 100 middle school students (17.7%) and nearly half (46.0%) of high school students said they had ever tried a tobacco product.

Use of multiple tobacco products is prevalent among youth.

- In 2016, about 3 of every 100 middle school students (3.1%) and nearly 10 of every 100 high school students (9.6%) reported use of two or more tobacco products in the past 30 days.

- In 2013, more than 31 of every 100 high school students (31.4%) said they had ever tried two or more tobacco products.

Tobacco Use: Leading Cause Of Cancer Deaths

Tobacco use is the leading preventable cause of cancer and cancer deaths. It can cause not only lung cancer—but also cancers of the mouth and throat, voice box, esophagus, stomach, kidney, pancreas, liver, bladder, cervix, colon and rectum, and a type of leukemia. Each year, 660,000 people in the United States are diagnosed with and 343,000 people die from a cancer related to tobacco use.

(Source: "Cancer And Tobacco Use," Centers for Disease Control and Prevention (CDC).)

Tobacco Use And Cancer

Tobacco use is a leading cause of cancer and of death from cancer. People who use tobacco products or who are regularly around environmental tobacco smoke (also called secondhand smoke) have an increased risk of cancer because tobacco products and secondhand smoke have many chemicals that damage deoxyribonucleic acid (DNA). Tobacco use causes many types of cancer, including cancer of the lung, larynx (voice box), mouth, esophagus, throat, bladder, kidney, liver, stomach, pancreas, colon and rectum, and cervix, as well as acute myeloid leukemia. People who use smokeless tobacco (snuff or chewing tobacco) have increased risks of cancers of the mouth, esophagus, and pancreas. There is no safe level of tobacco use. People who use any type of tobacco product are strongly urged to quit. People who quit smoking, regardless of their age, have substantial gains in life expectancy compared with those who continue to smoke. Also, quitting smoking at the time of a cancer diagnosis reduces the risk of death.

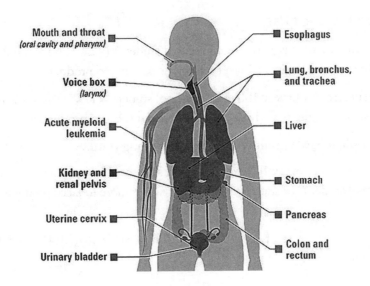

Figure 8.1. Tobacco Use Causes Cancer Throughout The Body

Tobacco use includes smoked (cigarettes and cigars) and smokeless (snuff and chewing tobacco) tobacco products that, to date, have been shown to cause cancer.

(Source: "Cancer And Tobacco Use," Centers for Disease Control and Prevention (CDC).)

How Is Smoking Related To Cancer?

Smoking can cause cancer and then block your body from fighting it:

- Poisons in cigarette smoke can weaken the body's immune system, making it harder to kill cancer cells. When this happens, cancer cells keep growing without being stopped.

- Poisons in tobacco smoke can damage or change a cell's DNA. DNA is the cell's "instruction manual" that controls a cell's normal growth and function. When DNA is damaged, a cell can begin growing out of control and create a cancer tumor.

Doctors have known for years that smoking causes most lung cancers. It's still true today, when nearly 9 out of 10 lung cancers are caused by smoking cigarettes. In fact, smokers have a greater risk for lung cancer today than they did in 1964, even though they smoke fewer cigarettes. One reason may be changes in how cigarettes are made and what chemicals they contain.

Treatments are getting better for lung cancer, but it still kills more men and women than any other type of cancer. In the United States, more than 7,300 nonsmokers die each year from lung cancer caused by secondhand smoke. Secondhand smoke is the combination of smoke from the burning end of a cigarette and the smoke breathed out by smokers.

Smokeless Tobacco

Smokeless tobacco is tobacco that is not burned. It is also known as chewing tobacco, oral tobacco, spit or spitting tobacco, dip, chew, and snuff. Most people chew or suck (dip) the tobacco in their mouth and spit out the tobacco juices that build up, although "spitless" smokeless tobacco has also been developed.

There are two main types of smokeless tobacco: chewing tobacco and snuff. At least 28 chemicals in smokeless tobacco have been found to cause cancer. Smokeless tobacco causes oral cancer, esophageal cancer, and pancreatic cancer.

(Source: "Smokeless Tobacco And Cancer," National Cancer Institute (NCI).)

Smoking can cause cancer almost anywhere in your body, including the:

- Blood (acute myeloid leukemia)

- Bladder

- Cervix

- Colon and rectum

- Esophagus

- Kidney and renal pelvis

- Larynx

- Liver

- Lungs

- Mouth and throat

- Pancreas

- Stomach

- Trachea, lung, and bronchus

Men with prostate cancer who smoke may be more likely to die from these diseases than nonsmokers.

Smokeless tobacco, such as chewing tobacco, also causes cancer, including cancers of the:

- Esophagus

- Mouth and throat

- Pancreas

How Can Smoking-Related Cancers Be Prevented?

Quitting smoking lowers the risks for cancers of the lung, mouth, throat, esophagus, and larynx.

- Within five years of quitting, your chance of getting cancer of the mouth, throat, esophagus, and bladder is cut in half.

- Ten years after you quit smoking, your risk of dying from lung cancer drops by half.

If nobody smoked, one of every three cancer deaths in the United States would not happen.

Secondhand Smoke Affects Children

Secondhand smoke is smoke from burning tobacco products, such as cigarettes, cigars, or pipes. Secondhand smoke also is smoke that has been exhaled, or breathed out, by the person smoking.

In children, secondhand smoke causes the following:

- Ear infections
- More frequent and severe asthma attacks
- Respiratory symptoms (for example, coughing, sneezing, and shortness of breath)
- Respiratory infections (bronchitis and pneumonia)
- A greater risk for sudden infant death syndrome (SIDS)

(Source: "Smoking And Tobacco Use—Secondhand Smoke (SHS) Facts," Centers for Disease Control and Prevention (CDC).)

Chapter 9

Chemicals In Meat Cooked At High Temperatures And Cancer Risk

What Are Heterocyclic Amines (HCAs) And Polycyclic Aromatic Hydrocarbons (PAHs), And How Are They Formed In Cooked Meats?

Heterocyclic amines (HCAs) and polycyclic aromatic hydrocarbons (PAHs) are chemicals formed when muscle meat, including beef, pork, fish, or poultry, is cooked using high-temperature methods, such as pan frying or grilling directly over an open flame. In laboratory experiments, HCAs and PAHs have been found to be mutagenic—that is, they cause changes in deoxyribonucleic acid (DNA) that may increase the risk of cancer.

HCAs are formed when amino acids (the building blocks of proteins), sugars, and creatine (a substance found in muscle) react at high temperatures. PAHs are formed when fat and juices from meat grilled directly over an open fire drip onto the fire, causing flames. These flames contain PAHs that then adhere to the surface of the meat. PAHs can also be formed during other food preparation processes, such as smoking of meats. HCAs are not found in significant amounts in foods other than meat cooked at high temperatures. PAHs can be found in other charred foods, as well as in cigarette smoke and car exhaust fumes.

About This Chapter: This chapter includes text excerpted from "Chemicals In Meat Cooked At High Temperatures And Cancer Risk," National Cancer Institute (NCI), October 19, 2015.

What Factors Influence The Formation Of HCA And PAH In Cooked Meats?

The formation of HCAs and PAHs varies by meat type, cooking method, and "doneness" level (rare, medium, or well done). Whatever the type of meat, however, meats cooked at high temperatures, especially above 300°F (as in grilling or pan frying), or that are cooked for a long time tend to form more HCAs. For example, well done, grilled, or barbecued chicken and steak all have high concentrations of HCAs. Cooking methods that expose meat to smoke or charring contribute to PAH formation.

HCAs and PAHs become capable of damaging DNA only after they are metabolized by specific enzymes in the body, a process called "bioactivation." Studies have found that the activity of these enzymes, which can differ among people, may be relevant to cancer risks associated with exposure to these compounds.

What Evidence Is There That HCAs And PAHs In Cooked Meats May Increase Cancer Risk?

Studies have shown that exposure to HCAs and PAHs can cause cancer in animal models. In many experiments, rodents fed a diet supplemented with HCAs developed tumors of the breast, colon, liver, skin, lung, prostate, and other organs. Rodents fed PAHs also developed cancers, including leukemia and tumors of the gastrointestinal tract and lungs. However, the doses of HCAs and PAHs used in these studies were very high—equivalent to thousands of times the doses that a person would consume in a normal diet.

Population studies have not established a definitive link between HCA and PAH exposure from cooked meats and cancer in humans. One difficulty with conducting such studies is that it can be difficult to determine the exact level of HCA and/or PAH exposure a person gets from cooked meats. Although dietary questionnaires can provide good estimates, they may not capture all the detail about cooking techniques that is necessary to determine HCA and PAH exposure levels. In addition, individual variation in the activity of enzymes that metabolize HCAs and PAHs may result in exposure differences, even among people who ingest (take in) the same amount of these compounds. Also, people may have been exposed to PAHs from other environmental sources, such as pollution and tobacco smoke. Nevertheless, numerous epidemiologic studies have used detailed questionnaires to examine participants' meat consumption and meat cooking methods to estimate HCA and PAH exposures. Researchers found that high consumption of well-done, fried, or barbecued meats was associated with increased risks of colorectal, pancreatic, and prostate cancer.

Do Guidelines Exist For The Consumption Of Food Containing HCAs And PAHs?

Currently, no Federal guidelines address the consumption of foods containing HCAs and PAHs. The World Cancer Research Fund (WCRF) / American Institute for Cancer Research (AICR) issued a report with dietary guidelines that recommended limiting the consumption of red and processed (including smoked) meats; however, no recommendations were provided for HCA and PAH levels in meat.

Are There Ways To Reduce HCA And PAH Formation In Cooked Meats?

Even though no specific guidelines for HCA/PAH consumption exist, concerned individuals can reduce their exposure by using several cooking methods:

- Avoiding direct exposure of meat to an open flame or a hot metal surface and avoiding prolonged cooking times (especially at high temperatures) can help reduce HCA and PAH formation.

- Using a microwave oven to cook meat prior to exposure to high temperatures can also substantially reduce HCA formation by reducing the time that meat must be in contact with high heat to finish cooking.

- Continuously turning meat over on a high heat source can substantially reduce HCA formation compared with just leaving the meat on the heat source without flipping it often.

- Removing charred portions of meat and refraining from using gravy made from meat drippings can also reduce HCA and PAH exposure.

What Research Is Being Conducted On The Relationship Between The Consumption Of HCAs And PAHs And Cancer Risk In Humans?

Researchers in the United States are investigating the association between meat intake, meat cooking methods, and cancer risk. Ongoing studies include the National Institutes of Health (NIH)-AARP Diet and Health Study, the American Cancer Society's (ACS) Cancer Prevention Study II, the Multiethnic Cohort, and studies from Harvard University. Similar research in a European population is being conducted in the European Prospective Investigation into Cancer and Nutrition (EPIC) study.

Chapter 10

Obesity And Cancer Risk

What Is Obesity?

Obesity is a condition in which a person has an unhealthy amount and/or distribution of body fat. To measure obesity, researchers commonly use a scale known as the body mass index (BMI). BMI is calculated by dividing a person's weight (in kilograms) by their height (in meters) squared (commonly expressed as kg/m^2). BMI provides a more accurate measure of obesity than weight alone, and for most people it is a fairly good (although indirect) indicator of body fatness. Other measurements that reflect the distribution of body fat—that is, whether more fat is carried around the hips or the abdomen—are increasingly being used along with BMI as indicators of obesity and disease risks. These measurements include waist circumference and the waist-to-hip ratio (the waist circumference divided by the hip circumference).

For children and adolescents (younger than 20 years of age), overweight and obesity are based on the Centers for Disease Control and Prevention's (CDC) BMI-for-age growth charts.

The CDC has a BMI percentile calculator for children and teens at nccd.cdc.gov/dnpabmi/calculator.aspx

Compared with people of normal weight, those who are overweight or obese are at greater risk for many diseases, including diabetes, high blood pressure, cardiovascular disease, stroke, and many cancers. Extreme or severe obesity is also associated with an increased death rate; heart disease, cancer, and diabetes are responsible for most of the excess deaths.

About This Chapter: This chapter includes text excerpted from "Obesity And Cancer," National Cancer Institute (NCI), January 17, 2017.

Table 10.1. BMI For Children And Adolescents (Younger Than 20 Years Of Age)

BMI	Weight Category
BMI-for-age at or above sex-specific 85th percentile, but less than 95th percentile	Overweight
BMI-for-age at or above sex-specific 95th percentile	Obese

How Common Is Overweight Or Obesity?

Results from the National Health and Nutrition Examination Survey (NHANES) showed that the percentage of children and adolescents who are overweight or obese has also increased. In 2011–2014, an estimated 9 percent of 2–5-year-olds, 17 percent of 6–11-year-olds, and 20 percent of 12–19-year-olds were overweight or obese. In 1988–1994, those figures were only 7 percent, 11 percent, and 10 percent, respectively. In 2011–2014, about 17 percent of U.S. youth ages 2–19 years old were obese. In 1988–1994, by contrast, only about 10 percent of 2–19-year old were obese. According to the CDC, the prevalence of obesity in the United States differs among racial/ethnic groups. For example, among children and adolescents ages 2–19 years, the prevalence of obesity in 2011–2012 was 21.9 percent among Hispanics, 19.5 percent among non-Hispanic blacks, 14.7 percent among non-Hispanic whites, and 8.6 percent among non-Hispanic Asians.

What Is Known About The Relationship Between Obesity And Cancer?

Nearly all of the evidence linking obesity to cancer risk comes from large cohort studies, a type of observational study. However, data from observational studies can be difficult to interpret and cannot definitively establish that obesity causes cancer. That is because obese or overweight people may differ from lean people in ways other than their body fat, and it is possible that these other differences—rather than their body fat—are what explains their different cancer risk.

Despite the limitations of the study designs, there is consistent evidence that higher amounts of body fat are associated with increased risks of a number of cancers, including:

- **Endometrial cancer.** Obese and overweight women are two to about four times as likely as normal-weight women to develop endometrial cancer (cancer of the lining of the uterus), and extremely obese women are about seven times as likely to develop the more common of the two main types of this cancer. The risk of endometrial cancer increases with increasing weight gain in adulthood, particularly among women who have never used menopausal hormone therapy.

- **Esophageal adenocarcinoma.** People who are overweight or obese are about twice as likely as normal-weight people to develop a type of esophageal cancer called esophageal adenocarcinoma, and people who are extremely obese are more than four times as likely.

- **Gastric cardia cancer.** People who are obese are nearly twice as likely as normal-weight people to develop cancer in the upper part of the stomach, that is, the part that is closest to the esophagus.

- **Liver cancer.** People who are overweight or obese are up to twice as likely as normal-weight people to develop liver cancer. The association between overweight/obesity and liver cancer is stronger in men than women.

- **Kidney cancer.** People who are overweight or obese are nearly twice as likely as normal-weight people to develop renal cell cancer, the most common form of kidney cancer. The association of renal cell cancer with obesity is independent of its association with high blood pressure, a known risk factor for kidney cancer.

- **Multiple myeloma.** Compared with normal-weight individuals, overweight and obese individuals have a slight (10%–20%) increase in the risk of developing multiple myeloma.

- **Meningioma.** The risk of this slow-growing brain tumor that arises in the membranes surrounding the brain and the spinal cord is increased by about 50 percent in people who are obese and about 20 percent in people who are overweight.

- **Pancreatic cancer.** People who are overweight or obese are about 1.5 times as likely to develop pancreatic cancer as normal-weight people.

- **Colorectal cancer.** People who are obese are slightly (about 30%) more likely to develop colorectal cancer than normal-weight people.

A higher BMI is associated with increased risks of colon and rectal cancers in both men and in women, but the increases are higher in men than in women.

- **Gallbladder cancer.** Compared with normal-weight people, people who are overweight have a slight (about 20%) increase in risk of gallbladder cancer, and people who are obese have a 60 percent increase in risk of gallbladder cancer. The risk increase is greater in women than men.

- **Breast cancer.** Many studies have shown that, in postmenopausal women, a higher BMI is associated with a modest increase in risk of breast cancer. For example, a 5-unit increase in BMI is associated with a 12 percent increase in risk. Among postmenopausal women, those who are obese have a 20–40 percent increase in risk of developing breast cancer compared with normal-weight women. The higher risks are seen mainly in women who have never used menopausal hormone therapy and for tumors that express hormone receptors. Obesity is also a risk factor for breast cancer in men.

In premenopausal women, by contrast, overweight and obesity have been found to be associated with a 20 percent decreased risk of breast tumors that express hormone receptors.

- **Ovarian cancer.** Higher BMI is associated with a slight increase in the risk of ovarian cancer, particularly in women who have never used menopausal hormone therapy. For example, a 5-unit increase in BMI is associated with a 10 percent increase in risk among women who have never used menopausal hormone therapy.

- **Thyroid cancer.** Higher BMI (specifically, a 5-unit increase in BMI) is associated with a slight (10%) increase in the risk of thyroid cancer.

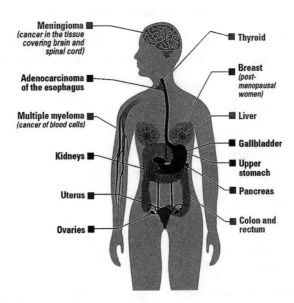

Figure 10.1. Cancers Associated With Obesity And Overweight

(Source: "Cancer And Obesity," Centers for Disease Control and Prevention (CDC).)

How Might Obesity Increase The Risk Of Cancer?

Several possible mechanisms have been suggested to explain how obesity might increase the risks of some cancers.

- Obese people often have chronic low-level inflammation, which can, over time, cause deoxyribonucleic acid (DNA) damage that leads to cancer. Overweight and obese individuals are more likely than normal-weight individuals to have conditions or disorders that are linked to or that cause chronic local inflammation and that are risk factors for certain cancers. For example, chronic local inflammation induced by gastroesophageal reflux disease or Barrett esophagus is a likely cause of esophageal adenocarcinoma. Obesity is a risk factor for gallstones, a condition characterized by chronic gallbladder inflammation, and a history of gallstones is a strong risk factor for gallbladder cancer. Chronic ulcerative colitis (a chronic inflammatory condition) and hepatitis (a disease of the liver causing inflammation) are risk factors for different types of liver cancer.

- Fat tissue (also called adipose tissue) produces excess amounts of estrogen, high levels of which have been associated with increased risks of breast, endometrial, ovarian, and some other cancers.

- Obese people often have increased blood levels of insulin and insulin-like growth factor-1 (IGF-1). (This condition, known as hyperinsulinemia or insulin resistance, precedes the development of type 2 diabetes.) High levels of insulin and IGF-1 may promote the development of colon, kidney, prostate, and endometrial cancers.

- Fat cells produce adipokines, hormones that may stimulate or inhibit cell growth. For example, the level of an adipokine called leptin, which seems to promote cell proliferation, in the blood increases with increasing body fat. And another adipokine, adiponectin—which is less abundant in obese people than in those of normal weight—may have antiproliferative effects.

- Fat cells may also have direct and indirect effects on other cell growth regulators, including mammalian target of rapamycin (mTOR) and AMP-activated protein kinase.

Other possible mechanisms by which obesity could affect cancer risk include changes in the mechanical properties of the scaffolding that surrounds breast cells and altered immune responses, effects on the nuclear factor kappa beta system, and oxidative stress.

How Many Cancer Cases May Be Due To Obesity?

A population-based study using BMI and cancer incidence data from the GLOBOCAN project estimated that, in 2012 in the United States, about 28,000 new cases of cancer in men (3.5%) and 72,000 in women (9.5%) were due to overweight or obesity. The percentage of cases attributed to overweight or obesity varied widely for different cancer types but was as high as 54 percent for gallbladder cancer in women and 44 percent for esophageal adenocarcinoma in men. A study summarizing worldwide estimates of the fractions of different cancers attributable to overweight/obesity reported that, compared with other countries, the United States had the highest fractions attributable to overweight/obesity for colorectal cancer, pancreatic cancer, and postmenopausal breast cancer.

Does Avoiding Weight Gain Or Losing Weight Decrease The Risk Of Cancer?

Most of the data about whether avoiding weight gain or losing weight reduces cancer risk comes from cohort and case-control studies. As with observational studies of obesity and cancer risk, these studies can be difficult to interpret because people who lose weight or avoid weight gain may differ in other ways from people who do not.

Nevertheless, when the evidence from multiple observational studies is consistent, the association is more likely to be real. Many observational studies have provided consistent evidence that people who have lower weight gain during adulthood have lower risks of colon cancer, kidney cancer, and—for postmenopausal women—breast, endometrial, and ovarian cancers.

Fewer studies have examined possible associations between weight loss and cancer risk. Some of these have found decreased risks of breast, endometrial, colon, and prostate cancers among people who have lost weight. However, most of these studies were not able to evaluate whether the weight loss was intentional or unintentional (and possibly related to underlying health problems).

Stronger evidence for a relationship between weight loss and cancer risk comes from studies of people who have undergone bariatric surgery (surgery performed on the stomach or intestines to induce weight loss). Obese people who have bariatric surgery appear to have lower risks of obesity-related cancers than obese people who do not have bariatric surgery.

Nevertheless, the follow-up study of weight and breast cancer in the Women's Health Initiative (WHI) found that for women who were already overweight or obese at baseline, weight change (either gain or loss) was not associated with breast cancer risk during follow-up.

However, for women who were of normal weight at baseline, gaining more than 5 percent of body weight was associated with increased breast cancer risk.

How Does Obesity Affect Cancer Survivorship?

Most of the evidence about obesity in cancer survivors comes from people who were diagnosed with breast, prostate, or colorectal cancer. Research indicates that obesity may worsen several aspects of cancer survivorship, including quality of life, cancer recurrence, cancer progression, and prognosis (survival).

For example, obesity is associated with increased risks of treatment-related lymphedema in breast cancer survivors and incontinence in prostate cancer survivors treated with radical prostatectomy. In a large clinical trial of patients with stage II and stage III rectal cancer, those with a higher baseline BMI (particularly men) had an increased risk of local recurrence. Death from multiple myeloma is 50 percent more likely for people at the highest levels of obesity compared with people at normal weight.

Several randomized clinical trials in breast cancer survivors have reported weight loss interventions that resulted in both weight loss and beneficial changes in biomarkers that have been linked to the association between obesity and prognosis. However, there is little evidence about whether weight loss improves cancer recurrence or prognosis. The National Cancer Institute (NCI)-sponsored Breast Cancer WEight Loss (BWEL) Study, a randomized phase III trial that is currently recruiting participants, will compare recurrence rate in overweight and obese women who take part in a weight loss program after breast cancer diagnosis with that in women who do not take part in the weight loss program.

Chapter 11

Human Papillomavirus (HPV) And Cancer Risk

What Are Human Papillomaviruses (HPV)?

Human papillomaviruses (HPVs) are a group of more than 200 related viruses. More than 40 HPV types can be easily spread through direct sexual contact, from the skin and mucous membranes of infected people to the skin and mucous membranes of their partners. They can be spread by vaginal, anal, and oral sex. Other HPV types are responsible for nongenital warts, which are not sexually transmitted.

Sexually transmitted HPV types fall into two categories:

- **Low-risk HPVs,** which do not cause cancer but can cause skin warts (technically known as condylomata acuminata) on or around the genitals and anus. For example, HPV types 6 and 11 cause 90 percent of all genital warts. HPV types 6 and 11 also cause recurrent respiratory papillomatosis, a less common disease in which benign tumors grow in the air passages leading from the nose and mouth into the lungs.

- **High-risk HPVs,** which can cause cancer. About a dozen high-risk HPV types have been identified. Two of these, HPV types 16 and 18, are responsible for most HPV-caused cancers.

HPV infections are the most common sexually transmitted infections in the United States. About 14 million new genital HPV infections occur each year. In fact, the Centers for Disease Control and Prevention (CDC) estimates that more than 90 percent and 80 percent,

About This Chapter: This chapter includes text excerpted from "HPV And Cancer," National Cancer Institute (NCI), February 19, 2015.

respectively, of sexually active men and women will be infected with at least one type of HPV at some point in their lives. Around one-half of these infections are with a high-risk HPV type.

Most high-risk HPV infections occur without any symptoms, go away within 1–2 years, and do not cause cancer. Some HPV infections, however, can persist for many years. Persistent infections with high-risk HPV types can lead to cell changes that, if untreated, may progress to cancer.

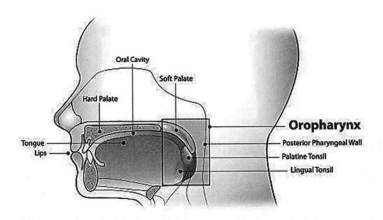

Figure 11.1. *Cancers Associated With Human Papillomavirus (HPV)*

(Source: "Cancers Associated With Human Papillomavirus (HPV)," Centers for Disease Control and Prevention (CDC).)

Which Cancers Are Caused By HPV?

High-risk HPVs cause several types of cancer.

- **Cervical cancer.** Virtually all cases of cervical cancer are caused by HPV, and just two HPV types, 16 and 18, are responsible for about 70 percent of all cases.

- **Anal cancer.** About 95 percent of anal cancers are caused by HPV. Most of these are caused by HPV type 16.

- **Oropharyngeal cancers (cancers of the middle part of the throat, including the soft palate, the base of the tongue, and the tonsils).** About 70 percent of oropharyngeal cancers are caused by HPV. In the United States, more than half of cancers diagnosed in the oropharynx are linked to HPV type 16.

- **Rarer cancers.** HPV causes about 65 percent of vaginal cancers, 50 percent of vulvar cancers, and 35 percent of penile cancers. Most of these are caused by HPV type 16.

High-risk HPV types cause approximately 5 percent of all cancers worldwide. In the United States, high-risk HPV types cause approximately 3 percent of all cancer cases among women and 2 percent of all cancer cases among men.

Who Gets HPV Infections?

Anyone who has ever been sexually active (that is, engaged in skin-to-skin sexual conduct, including vaginal, anal, or oral sex) can get HPV. HPV is easily passed between partners through sexual contact. HPV infections are more likely in those who have many sex partners or have sex with someone who has had many partners. Because the infection is so common, most people get HPV infections shortly after becoming sexually active for the first time. A person who has had only one partner can get HPV. Someone can have an HPV infection even if they have no symptoms and their only sexual contact with an HPV-infected person happened many years ago.

Can HPV Infections Be Prevented?

People who are not sexually active almost never develop genital HPV infections. In addition, HPV vaccination before sexual activity can reduce the risk of infection by the HPV types targeted by the vaccine. The U.S. Food and Drug Administration (FDA) has approved three vaccines to prevent HPV infection: Gardasil®, Gardasil® 9, and Cervarix®. These vaccines provide strong protection against new HPV infections, but they are not effective at treating established HPV infections or disease caused by HPV. Correct and consistent condom use is associated with reduced HPV transmission between sexual partners, but less frequent condom use is not. However, because areas not covered by a condom can be infected by the virus, condoms are unlikely to provide complete protection against the infection.

Can HPV Infections Be Detected?

HPV infections can be detected by testing a sample of cells to see if they contain viral deoxyribonucleic acid (DNA) or ribonucleic acid (RNA). Several HPV tests are currently approved by the FDA for three cervical screening indications: for follow-up testing of women who seem to have abnormal Pap test results, for cervical cancer screening in combination with a Pap test among women over age 30, and for use alone as a first-line primary cervical cancer screening test for women ages 25 and older.

The most common HPV test detects DNA from several high-risk HPV types in a group, but it cannot identify the specific type(s) that are present. Other tests do tell in addition whether there is DNA or RNA from HPV types 16 and 18, the two types that cause most HPV-associated cancers. These tests can detect HPV infections before abnormal cell changes are evident, and before any treatment for cell changes is needed. There are no FDA-approved tests to detect HPV infections in men. There are also no currently recommended screening methods similar to a Pap test for detecting cell changes caused by HPV infection in anal, vulvar, vaginal, penile, or oropharyngeal tissues. However, this is an area of ongoing research.

What Are Treatment Options For HPV-Infected Individuals?

There is currently no medical treatment for persistent HPV infections that are not associated with abnormal cell changes. However, the genital warts, benign respiratory tract tumors, precancerous changes at the cervix, and cancers resulting from HPV infections can be treated. Methods commonly used to treat precancerous cervical changes include cryosurgery (freezing that destroys tissue), LEEP (loop electrosurgical excision procedure, or the removal of cervical tissue using a hot wire loop), surgical conization (surgery with a scalpel, a laser, or both to remove a cone-shaped piece of tissue from the cervix and cervical canal), and laser vaporization conization (use of a laser to destroy cervical tissue). Treatments for other types of benign respiratory tract tumors and precancerous changes caused by HPV (vaginal, vulvar, penile, and anal lesions) and genital warts include topical chemicals or drugs, excisional surgery, cryosurgery, electrosurgery, and laser surgery. Treatment approaches are being tested in clinical trials, including a randomized controlled trial that will determine whether treating anal precancerous lesions will reduce the risk of anal cancer in people who are infected with human immunodeficiency virus (HIV).

HPV-infected individuals who develop cancer generally receive the same treatment as patients whose tumors do not harbor HPV infections, according to the type and stage of their tumors. However, people who are diagnosed with HPV-positive oropharyngeal cancer may be treated differently than people with oropharyngeal cancers that are HPV-negative. Research has shown that patients with HPV-positive oropharyngeal tumors have a better prognosis and may do just as well on less intense treatment. Ongoing clinical trials are investigating this question.

How Does High-Risk HPV Cause Cancer?

HPV infects epithelial cells. These cells, which are organized in layers, cover the inside and outside surfaces of the body, including the skin, the throat, the genital tract, and the anus. Once

HPV enters an epithelial cell, the virus begins to make the proteins it encodes. Two of the proteins made by high-risk HPVs (E6 and E7) interfere with cell functions that normally prevent excessive growth, helping the cell to grow in an uncontrolled manner and to avoid cell death.

Many times these infected cells are recognized by the immune system and eliminated. Sometimes, however, these infected cells are not destroyed, and a persistent infection results. As the persistently infected cells continue to grow, they may develop mutations in cellular genes that promote even more abnormal cell growth, leading to the formation of an area of precancerous cells and, ultimately, a cancerous tumor.

Other factors may increase the risk that an infection with a high-risk HPV type will persist and possibly develop into cancer. These include:

- Smoking or chewing tobacco (for increased risk of oropharyngeal cancer)
- Having a weakened immune system
- Having many children (for increased risk of cervical cancer)
- Long-term oral contraceptive use (for increased risk of cervical cancer)
- Poor oral hygiene (for increased risk of oropharyngeal cancer)
- Chronic inflammation

Researchers believe that it can take between 10 and 30 years from the time of an initial HPV infection until a tumor forms. However, even when severely abnormal cells are seen on the cervix (a condition called cervical intraepithelial neoplasia 3, or CIN3), these do not always lead to cancer. The percentage of CIN3 lesions that progress to invasive cervical cancer has been estimated to be 50 percent or less.

Chapter 12

Oral Contraceptives And Cancer Risk

What Is The Birth Control Pill?

The birth control pill, also known as oral contraceptive or "the pill," is a medication taken daily to prevent pregnancy. Some women take the pill for reasons other than preventing pregnancy. There are two main kinds of birth control pills:

- **Combined pills.** Contain two hormones, estrogen and progestin. Hormones are chemicals that control how different parts of your body work. These pills are taken every day and prevent pregnancy by keeping the ovaries from releasing eggs. The pills also cause cervical mucus to thicken and the lining of the uterus to thin. This keeps sperm from meeting with and fertilizing an egg.

- **Progestin-only pills** (or "mini-pills"). Contain only one hormone, progestin, which causes cervical mucus to thicken and the lining of the uterus to thin. This keeps sperm from reaching the egg. Less often, mini-pills prevent pregnancy by keeping the ovaries from releasing eggs.

How Do I Use It?

Combined pills are typically packaged as 21 "active" pills that contain hormones. One pill is taken daily for three weeks, followed by one week of not taking pills. Others are packaged as

About This Chapter: Text beginning with the heading "What Is The Birth Control Pill?" is excerpted from "Birth Control Pill," U.S. Department of Health and Human Services (HHS), June 8, 2017; Text beginning with the heading "What Types Of Oral Contraceptives Are Available In The United States Today?" is excerpted from "Oral Contraceptives And Cancer Risk," National Cancer Institute (NCI), March 21, 2012. Reviewed December 2017.

28 pills that include 21 "active" pills taken daily, followed by one week of "inactive" reminder pills that do not contain hormones. Some newer formulations have increased the number of active pills to 24 and reduced the inactive pills to four. With all combined pill formulations, protection against pregnancy continues during the week that no active pills are taken.

Mini-pills come only in packages of 28-day "active" pills. Like combined pills, it is important to take mini-pills every day and to take them at the same time each day. If you are late taking a mini-pill by more than three hours, you will need to not have sex or use an additional type of birth control (such as a condom or sponge) for two consecutive days to prevent pregnancy, but continue also to take the mini-pill every day. All types of birth control pills should be taken exactly as directed by your healthcare provider, even on days when you do not have sex.

Advantages Of The Birth Control Pills

Combination pills may offer other benefits such as fewer menstrual cramps, decreased menstrual blood loss, and less acne. These pills also may reduce the risk of some cancers that affect reproductive organs.

What Types Of Oral Contraceptives Are Available In The United States Today?

Two types of oral contraceptives (birth control pills) are currently available in the United States. The most commonly prescribed type of oral contraceptive contains man-made versions of the natural female hormones estrogen and progesterone. This type of birth control pill is often called a "combined oral contraceptive." The second type is called the minipill. It contains only progestin, which is the man-made version of progesterone that is used in oral contraceptives.

How Could Oral Contraceptives Influence Cancer Risk?

Naturally occurring estrogen and progesterone have been found to influence the development and growth of some cancers. Because birth control pills contain female hormones, researchers have been interested in determining whether there is any link between these widely used contraceptives and cancer risk. The results of population studies to examine associations between oral contraceptive use and cancer risk have not always been consistent. Overall, however, the risks of endometrial and ovarian cancer appear to be reduced with the use of oral contraceptives, whereas the risks of breast, cervical, and liver cancer appear to be increased.

How Do Oral Contraceptives Affect Breast Cancer Risk?

A woman's risk of developing breast cancer depends on several factors, some of which are related to her natural hormones. Hormonal and reproductive history factors that increase the risk of breast cancer include factors that may allow breast tissue to be exposed to high levels of hormones for longer periods of time, such as the following:

- Beginning menstruation at an early age
- Experiencing menopause at a late age
- Later age at first pregnancy
- Not having children at all

A analysis of epidemiologic data from more than 50 studies worldwide by the Collaborative Group on Hormonal Factors in Breast Cancer found that women who were current or recent users of birth control pills had a slightly higher risk of developing breast cancer than women who had never used the pill. The risk was highest for women who started using oral contraceptives as teenagers. However, 10 or more years after women stopped using oral contraceptives, their risk of developing breast cancer had returned to the same level as if they had never used birth control pills, regardless of family history of breast cancer, reproductive history, geographic area of residence, ethnic background, differences in study design, dose and type of hormone(s) used, or duration of use. In addition, breast cancers diagnosed in women who had stopped using oral contraceptives for 10 or more years were less advanced than breast cancers diagnosed in women who had never used oral contraceptives.

What Are *BRCA1* And *BRCA2*?

BRCA1 and *BRCA2* are human genes that produce tumor suppressor proteins. These proteins help repair damaged deoxyribonucleic acid (DNA) and, therefore, play a role in ensuring the stability of the cell's genetic material. When either of these genes is mutated, or altered, such that its protein product either is not made or does not function correctly, DNA damage may not be repaired properly. As a result, cells are more likely to develop additional genetic alterations that can lead to cancer.

(Source: "BRCA1 And BRCA2: Cancer Risk And Genetic Testing," National Cancer Institute (NCI).)

A analysis of data from the Nurses' Health Study, which has been following more than 116,000 female nurses who were 24–43 years old when they enrolled in the study, found that the participants who used oral contraceptives had a slight increase in breast cancer risk. However, nearly all of the increased risk was seen among women who took a specific type of oral contraceptive, a "triphasic" pill, in which the dose of hormones is changed in three stages over the course of a woman's monthly cycle. Because the association with the triphasic formulation was unexpected, more research will be needed to confirm the findings from the Nurses' Health Study.

How Do Oral Contraceptives Affect Ovarian Cancer Risk?

Oral contraceptive use has consistently been found to be associated with a reduced risk of ovarian cancer. In a analysis of 20 studies, researchers found that the longer a woman used oral contraceptives the more her risk of ovarian cancer decreased. The risk decreased by 10–12 percent after 1 year of use and by approximately 50 percent after 5 years of use.

Researchers have studied how the amount or type of hormones in oral contraceptives affects ovarian cancer risk. The Cancer and Steroid Hormone (CASH) study, found that the reduction in ovarian cancer risk was the same regardless of the type or amount of estrogen or progestin in the pill. A analysis of data from the CASH study, however, indicated that oral contraceptive formulations with high levels of progestin were associated with a lower risk of ovarian cancer than formulations with low progestin levels. In another study, the Steroid Hormones and Reproductions (SHARE) Study, researchers investigated new, lower-dose progestins that have varying androgenic (testosterone-like) effects. They found no difference in ovarian cancer risk between androgenic and nonandrogenic pills.

Oral contraceptive use by women at increased risk of ovarian cancer due to a genetic mutation in the *BRCA1* or *BRCA2* gene has been studied. One study showed a reduction in risk among *BRCA1*- or *BRCA2*-mutation carriers who took oral contraceptives, whereas another study showed no effect. A third study found that women with *BRCA1* mutations who took oral contraceptives had about half the risk of ovarian cancer as those who did not.

How Do Oral Contraceptives Affect Endometrial Cancer Risk?

Women who use oral contraceptives have been shown to have a reduced risk of endometrial cancer. This protective effect increases with the length of time oral contraceptives are used and continues for many years after a woman stops using oral contraceptives.

How Do Oral Contraceptives Affect Cervical Cancer Risk?

Long-term use of oral contraceptives (5 or more years) is associated with an increased risk of cervical cancer. An analysis of 24 epidemiologic studies found that the longer a woman used oral contraceptives, the higher her risk of cervical cancer. However, among women who stopped taking oral contraceptives, the risk tended to decline over time, regardless of how long they had used oral contraceptives before stopping.

In a report by the International Agency for Research on Cancer (IARC), which is part of the World Health Organization (WHO), data from eight studies were combined to assess the association between oral contraceptive use and cervical cancer risk among women infected with the human papillomavirus (HPV). Researchers found a nearly threefold increase in risk among women who had used oral contraceptives for 5–9 years compared with women who had never used oral contraceptives. Among women who had used oral contraceptives for 10 years or longer, the risk of cervical cancer was four times higher.

Virtually all cervical cancers are caused by persistent infection with high-risk, or oncogenic, types of HPV, and the association of cervical cancer with oral contraceptive use is likely to be indirect. The hormones in oral contraceptives may change the susceptibility of cervical cells to HPV infection, affect their ability to clear the infection, or make it easier for HPV infection to cause changes that progress to cervical cancer. Questions about how oral contraceptives may increase the risk of cervical cancer will be addressed through ongoing research.

How Do Oral Contraceptives Affect Liver Cancer Risk?

Oral contraceptive use is associated with an increase in the risk of benign liver tumors, such as hepatocellular adenomas. Benign tumors can form as lumps in different areas of the liver, and they have a high risk of bleeding or rupturing. However, these tumors rarely become malignant. Whether oral contraceptive use increases the risk of malignant liver tumors, also known as hepatocellular carcinomas, is less clear. Some studies have found that women who take oral contraceptives for more than 5 years have an increased risk of hepatocellular carcinoma, but others have not.

Chapter 13

Cell Phones And Cancer Risk

Why Is There Concern That Cell Phones May Cause Cancer Or Other Health Problems?

There are three main reasons why people are concerned that cell phones (also known as "mobile" or "wireless" telephones) might have the potential to cause certain types of cancer or other health problems:

- Cell phones emit radiofrequency energy (radio waves), a form of nonionizing radiation, from their antennas. Tissues nearest to the antenna can absorb this energy.

- The number of cell phone users has increased rapidly. There were more than 327.5 million cell phone subscribers in the United States, according to the Cellular Telecommunications and Internet Association (CTIA). This is a nearly threefold increase from the 110 million users in 2000. Globally, the number of subscriptions is estimated by the International Telecommunication Union (ITU) to be 5 billion.

- Over time, the number of cell phone calls per day, the length of each call, and the amount of time people use cell phones have increased. However, improvements in cell phone technology have resulted in devices that have lower power outputs than earlier models.

About This Chapter: This chapter includes text excerpted from "Cell Phones And Cancer Risk," National Cancer Institute (NCI), May 27, 2016.

Can Using A Cell Phone Cause Cancer?

There is no scientific evidence that provides a definite answer to that question. Some organizations recommend caution in cell phone use. More research is needed before we know if using cell phones causes health effects.

(Source: "Radiation In Everyday Objects—Frequently Asked Questions About Cell Phones And Your Health," Centers for Disease Control and Prevention (CDC).)

What Is Radiofrequency Energy And How Does It Affect The Body?

Radiofrequency energy is a form of electromagnetic radiation. Electromagnetic radiation can be categorized into two types: ionizing (e.g., X-rays, radon, and cosmic rays) and nonionizing (e.g., radiofrequency and extremely low frequency, or power frequency). Electromagnetic radiation is defined according to its wavelength and frequency, which is the number of cycles of a wave that pass a reference point per second. Electromagnetic frequencies are described in units called hertz (Hz).

The energy of electromagnetic radiation is determined by its frequency; ionizing radiation is high frequency, and therefore high energy, whereas nonionizing radiation is low frequency, and therefore low energy.

The frequency of radiofrequency electromagnetic radiation ranges from 30 kilohertz (30 kHz, or 30,000 Hz) to 300 gigahertz (300 GHz, or 300 billion Hz). Electromagnetic fields in the radiofrequency range are used for telecommunications applications, including cell phones, televisions, and radio transmissions. The human body absorbs energy from devices that emit radiofrequency electromagnetic radiation. The dose of the absorbed energy is estimated using a measure called the specific absorption rate (SAR), which is expressed in watts per kilogram of body weight.

Exposure to ionizing radiation, such as from X-rays, is known to increase the risk of cancer. Nonionizing. However, although many studies have examined the potential health effects of nonionizing radiation from radar, microwave ovens, cell phones, and other sources, there is currently no consistent evidence that nonionizing radiation increases cancer risk.

The only consistently recognized biological effect of radiofrequency energy is heating. The ability of microwave ovens to heat food is one example of this effect of radiofrequency energy.

Radiofrequency exposure from cell phone use does cause heating to the area of the body where a cell phone or other device is held (ear, head, etc.). However, it is not sufficient to measurably increase body temperature, and there are no other clearly established effects on the body from radiofrequency energy.

It has been suggested that radiofrequency energy might affect glucose metabolism, but two small studies that examined brain glucose metabolism after use of a cell phone showed inconsistent results. Whereas one study showed increased glucose metabolism in the region of the brain close to the antenna compared with tissues on the opposite side of the brain, the other study found reduced glucose metabolism on the side of the brain where the phone was used.

Another study investigated whether exposure to the radiofrequency energy from cell phones affects the flow of blood in the brain and found no evidence of such an effect. The authors of these studies noted that the results are preliminary and that possible health outcomes from changes in glucose metabolism are still unknown. Such inconsistent findings are not uncommon in experimental studies of the biological effects of radiofrequency electromagnetic radiation. Some contributing factors include assumptions used to estimate doses, failure to consider temperature effects, and lack of blinding of investigators to exposure status.

How Is Radiofrequency Energy Exposure Measured In Epidemiologic Studies?

Epidemiologic studies use information from several sources, including questionnaires and data from cell phone service providers. Direct measurements are not yet possible outside of a laboratory setting. Estimates take into account the following:

- How "regularly" study participants use cell phones (the number of calls per week or month)

- The age and the year when study participants first used a cell phone and the age and the year of last use (allows calculation of the duration of use and time since the start of use)

- The average number of cell phone calls per day, week, or month (frequency)

- The average length of a typical cell phone call

- The total hours of lifetime use, calculated from the length of typical call times, the frequency of use, and the duration of use

What Has Research Shown About The Possible Cancer Causing Effects Of Radiofrequency Energy?

Radiofrequency energy, unlike ionizing radiation, does not cause deoxyribonucleic acid (DNA) damage that can lead to cancer. It's only consistently observed biological effect in humans is tissue heating. In animal studies, it has not been found to cause cancer or to enhance the cancer causing effects of known chemical carcinogens. The National Institute of Environmental Health Sciences (NIEHS), which is part of the National Institutes of Health (NIH), is carrying out a large scale study in rodents of exposure to radiofrequency energy (the type used in cell phones). This investigation is being conducted in highly specialized labs that can specify and control sources of radiation and measure their effects.

Researchers have carried out several types of epidemiologic studies to investigate the possibility of a relationship between cell phone use and the risk of malignant (cancerous) brain tumors, such as gliomas, as well as benign (noncancerous) tumors, such as acoustic neuromas (tumors in the cells of the nerve responsible for hearing), most meningiomas (tumors in the meninges, membranes that cover and protect the brain and spinal cord), and parotid gland tumors (tumors in the salivary glands).

In one type of study, called a case-control study, cell phone use is compared between people with these types of tumors and people without them. In another type of study, called a cohort study, a large group of people who do not have cancer at study entry is followed over time and the rate of these tumors in people who did and didn't use cell phones is compared. Cancer incidence data can also be analyzed over time to see if the rates of cancer changed in large populations during the time that cell phone use increased dramatically. These studies have not shown clear evidence of a relationship between cell phone use and cancer. However, researchers have reported some statistically significant associations for certain subgroups of people. Three large epidemiologic studies have examined the possible association between cell phone use and cancer: Interphone, a case-control study; the Danish Study, a cohort study; and the Million Women Study, another cohort study.

- **Interphone**

  How the study was done: This is the largest health-related case-control study of cell phone use and the risk of head and neck tumors. It was conducted by a consortium of researchers from 13 countries. The data came from questionnaires that were completed by study participants.

What the study showed: Most published analyses from this study have shown no statistically significant increases in brain or central nervous system cancers related to higher amounts of cell phone use. One analysis showed a statistically significant, although modest, increase in the risk of glioma among the small proportion of study participants who spent the most total time on cell phone calls. However, the researchers considered this finding inconclusive because they felt that the amount of use reported by some respondents was unlikely and because the participants who reported lower levels of use appeared to have a slightly reduced risk of brain cancer compared with people who did not use cell phones regularly. Another recent analysis from this study found no relationship between brain tumor locations and regions of the brain that were exposed to the highest level of radiofrequency energy from cell phones.

- **Danish Study**

  How the study was done: This cohort study, conducted in Denmark, linked billing information from more than 358,000 cell phone subscribers with brain tumor incidence data from the Danish Cancer Registry.

  What the study showed: No association was observed between cell phone use and the incidence of glioma, meningioma, or acoustic neuroma, even among people who had been cell phone subscribers for 13 or more years.

- **Million Women Study**

  How the study was done: This prospective cohort study conducted in the United Kingdom used data obtained from questionnaires that were completed by study participants.

  What the study showed: Self-reported cell phone use was not associated with an increased risk of glioma, meningioma, or noncentral nervous system tumors. Although the original published findings reported an association with an increased risk of acoustic neuroma, this association disappeared after additional follow up of the cohort.

In addition to these three large studies, other, smaller epidemiologic studies have looked for associations between cell phone use and cancer. These include:

- Two National Cancer Institute (NCI)-sponsored case-control studies, each conducted in multiple U.S. academic medical centers or hospitals between 1994 and 1998, that used data from questionnaires or computer-assisted personal interviews. Neither study showed a relationship between cell phone use and the risk of glioma, meningioma, or acoustic neuroma.

- The CERENAT study, another case-control study conducted in multiple areas in France from 2004–2006 using data collected in face-to-face interviews using standardized questionnaires. This study found no association for either gliomas or meningiomas when comparing regular cell phone users with nonusers. However, the heaviest users had significantly increased risks of both gliomas and meningiomas.

- A pooled analysis of two case-control studies conducted in Sweden that reported statistically significant trends of increasing brain cancer risk for the total amount of cell phone use and the years of use among people who began using cell phones before age 20.

- Another case-control study in Sweden, part of the Interphone pooled studies, did not find an increased risk of brain cancer among long-term cell phone users between the ages of 20 and 69.

- The CEFALO study, an international case-control study of children diagnosed with brain cancer between ages 7 and 19, which found no relationship between their cell phone use and risk for brain cancer.

Investigators have also conducted analyses of incidence trends to determine whether the incidence of brain or other cancers has changed during the time that cell phone use increased dramatically. These include:

- An analysis of data from NCI's Surveillance, Epidemiology, and End Results (SEER) Program evaluated trends in cancer incidence in the United States. This analysis found no increase in the incidence of brain or other central nervous system cancers between 1992 and 2006, despite the dramatic increase in cell phone use in this country during that time.

- An analysis of incidence data from Denmark, Finland, Norway, and Sweden for the period 1974–2008 similarly revealed no increase in age-adjusted incidence of brain tumors.

- A series of studies testing different scenarios (called simulations by the study authors) were carried out using incidence data from the Nordic countries to determine the likelihood of detecting various levels of risk as reported in studies of cell phone use and brain tumors between 1979 and 2008. The results were compatible with no increased risks from cell phones, as reported by most epidemiologic studies. The findings did suggest that the increase reported among the subset of heaviest regular users in the Interphone study could not be ruled out but was unlikely. The highly increased risks reported in the

Swedish pooled analysis were strongly inconsistent with the observed glioma rates in the Nordic countries.

- A study by NCI researchers compared observed glioma incidence rates in U.S. Surveillance, Epidemiology, and End Results (SEER) data with rates simulated from the small risks reported in the Interphone study and the greatly increased risk of brain cancer among cell phone users reported in the Swedish pooled analysis. The observed U.S. rates showed no increase, but a small increased risk among the subset of heaviest users in the Interphone study could not be ruled out. The observed incidence trends were inconsistent with the high risks reported in the Swedish pooled study. These findings suggest that the increased risks observed in the Swedish study are not reflected in U.S. incidence trends.

Why Are The Findings From Different Studies Of Cell Phone Use And Cancer Risk Inconsistent?

A limited number of studies have shown some evidence of statistical association of cell phone use and brain tumor risks, but most studies have found no association. Reasons for these discrepancies include the following:

- **Recall bias,** which can occur when data about prior habits and exposures are collected from study participants using questionnaires administered after diagnosis of a disease in some of the participants. It is possible that study participants who have brain tumors may remember their cell phone use differently from individuals without brain tumors. Many epidemiologic studies of cell phone use and brain cancer risk lack verifiable data about the total amount of cell phone use over time. In addition, people who develop a brain tumor may have a tendency to recall cell phone use mostly on the same side of the head where their tumor was found, regardless of whether they actually used their phone on that side of the head a lot or only a little.

- **Inaccurate reporting,** which can happen when people say that something has happened more or less often than it actually did. People may not remember how much they used cell phones in a given time period.

- **Morbidity and mortality** among study participants who have brain cancer. Gliomas are particularly difficult to study, for example, because of their high death rate and the short survival of people who develop these tumors. Patients who survive initial treatment are often impaired, which may affect their responses to questions. Furthermore, for people who have died, next-of-kin are often less familiar with the cell phone use patterns of their deceased family member and may not accurately describe their patterns of use to an interviewer.

- **Participation bias**, which can happen when people who are diagnosed with brain tumors are more likely than healthy people (known as controls) to enroll in a research study. Also, controls who did not or rarely used cell phones were less likely to participate in the Interphone study than controls who used cell phones regularly. For example, the Interphone study reported participation rates of 78 percent for meningioma patients (range 56–92 percent for the individual studies), 64 percent for glioma patients (range 36–92 percent), and 53 percent for control subjects (range 42–74 percent).

- **Changing technology and methods of use.** Older studies evaluated radiofrequency energy exposure from analog cell phones. However, most cell phones today use digital technology, which operates at a different frequency and a lower power level than analog phones. Digital cell phones have been in use for more than a decade in the United States, and cellular technology continues to change. Texting, for example, has become a popular way of using a cell phone to communicate that does not require bringing the phone close to the head. Furthermore, the use of hands-free technology, such as wired and wireless headsets, is increasing and may decrease radiofrequency energy exposure to the head and brain.

What Do Expert Organizations Conclude About The Cancer Risk From Cell Phone Use?

The International Agency for Research on Cancer (IARC), a component of the World Health Organization (WHO), appointed an expert Working Group to review all available evidence on the use of cell phones. The Working Group classified cell phone use as "possibly carcinogenic to humans," based on limited evidence from human studies, limited evidence from studies of radiofrequency energy and cancer in rodents, and inconsistent evidence from mechanistic studies.

The Working Group indicated that, although the human studies were susceptible to bias, the findings could not be dismissed as reflecting bias alone, and that a causal interpretation could not be excluded. The Working Group noted that any interpretation of the evidence should also consider that the observed associations could reflect chance, bias, or confounding rather than an underlying causal effect. In addition, the Working Group stated that the investigation of risk of cancer of the brain associated with cell phone use poses complex methodologic challenges in the conduct of the research and in the analysis and interpretation of findings.

The American Cancer Society (ACS) states that the IARC classification means that there could be some cancer risk associated with radiofrequency energy, but the evidence is not strong enough to be considered causal and needs to be investigated further. Individuals who are concerned about radiofrequency energy exposure can limit their exposure, including using an earpiece and limiting cell phone use, particularly among children.

The National Institute of Environmental Health Sciences (NIEHS) states that the weight of the current scientific evidence has not conclusively linked cell phone use with any adverse health problems, but more research is needed.

The U.S. Food and Drug Administration (FDA) notes that studies reporting biological changes associated with radiofrequency energy have failed to be replicated and that the majority of human epidemiologic studies have failed to show a relationship between exposure to radiofrequency energy from cell phones and health problems.

The Centers for Disease Control and Prevention (CDC) states that no scientific evidence definitively answers whether cell phone use causes cancer. The Federal Communications Commission (FCC) concludes that no scientific evidence establishes a causal link between wireless device use and cancer or other illnesses.

The European Commission Scientific Committee on Emerging and Newly Identified Health Risks (SCENIHR) concluded that, overall, the epidemiologic studies on cell phone radiofrequency electromagnetic radiation exposure do not show an increased risk of brain tumors or of other cancers of the head and neck region. The Committee also stated that epidemiologic studies do not indicate increased risk for other malignant diseases, including childhood cancer.

What Studies Are Underway That Will Help Further Our Understanding Of The Possible Health Effects Of Cell Phone Use?

A large prospective cohort study of cell phone use and its possible long-term health effects was launched in Europe. This study, known as Cohort Study of Mobile Phone Use and Health (COSMOS), has enrolled approximately 290,000 cell phone users aged 18 years or older to date and will follow them for 20–30 years.

Participants in COSMOS will complete a questionnaire about their health, lifestyle, and current and past cell phone use. This information will be supplemented with information from health records and cell phone records.

The challenge of this ambitious study is to continue following the participants for a range of health effects over many decades. Researchers will need to determine whether participants who leave the study are somehow different from those who remain throughout the follow up period. Although recall bias is minimized in studies such as COSMOS that link participants to their cell phone records, such studies face other problems. For example, it is impossible to know who is using the listed cell phone or whether that individual also places calls using other cell phones. To a lesser extent, it is not clear whether multiple users of a single phone will be represented on a single phone company account.

Do Children Have A Higher Risk Of Developing Cancer Due To Cell Phone Use Than Adults?

There are theoretical considerations as to why the possible risk should be investigated separately in children. Their nervous systems are still developing and, therefore, more vulnerable to factors that may cause cancer. Their heads are smaller than those of adults and consequently have a greater proportional exposure to the field of radiofrequency radiation that is emitted by cell phones. And, children have the potential of accumulating more years of cell phone exposure than adults do.

Thus far, the data from studies in children with cancer do not support this theory. The first published analysis came from a large case-control study called CEFALO, which was conducted in Denmark, Sweden, Norway, and Switzerland. The study included children who were diagnosed with brain tumors between 2004 and 2008, when their ages ranged from 7–19. Researchers did not find an association between cell phone use and brain tumor risk either by time since initiation of use, amount of use, or by the location of the tumor.

Several studies that will provide more information are under way. Researchers from the Centre for Research in Environmental Epidemiology (CREAL) in Spain are conducting another international case-control study—Mobi-Kids—that will include 2000 young people (aged 10–24 years) with newly diagnosed brain tumors and 4000 healthy young people. The goal of the study is to learn more about risk factors for childhood brain tumors.

What Can Cell Phone Users Do To Reduce Their Exposure To Radiofrequency Energy?

The FDA has suggested some steps that concerned cell phone users can take to reduce their exposure to radiofrequency energy:

- Reserve the use of cell phones for shorter conversations or for times when a landline phone is not available.

- Use a device with hands-free technology, such as wired headsets, which place more distance between the phone and the head of the user.

Hands-free kits reduce the amount of radiofrequency energy exposure to the head because the antenna, which is the source of energy, is not placed against the head. Exposures decline dramatically when cell phones are used hands-free.

Should People Stop Using Cell Phones?

At this time, we do not have the science to link health problems to cell phone use. Scientific studies are underway to determine whether cell phone use may cause health effects. It is also important to consider the benefits of cell phones. Their use can be valuable in an urgent or emergency situation—and even save lives.

To reduce radio frequency radiation near your body:

- Get a hands-free headset that connects directly to your phone.
- Use speaker-phone more often.
- In the past, radio frequency (RF) interfered with the operation of some pacemakers. If you have a pacemaker and are concerned about how your cell phone use may affect it, contact your healthcare provider.

(Source: "Radiation In Everyday Objects—Frequently Asked Questions About Cell Phones And Your Health," Centers for Disease Control and Prevention (CDC).)

Chapter 14

Cancer Prevention For Girls: Why See A Gynecologist?

Going to see a gynecologist—a doctor who focuses on women's reproductive health—means you're taking responsibility for your body in new ways. It can be very exciting to know you're making sure all is going well with puberty, your reproductive system, and more. Keep in mind that other doctors also can help with gynecological issues. For example, an adolescent medicine specialist, family doctor, or pediatrician can answer questions and may be able to examine your vagina, too. Of course, it can be stressful to deal with a whole new type of doctor's visit, but learning more can help you know what to expect.

Why See A Gynecologist?

Seeing a gynecologist can:

- Help you understand your body and how to care for it

- Give you and the doctor a sense of what is normal for you so you can notice any problem changes, like signs of a vaginal infection

- Let the doctor find problems early so they can be treated

- Explain what a normal vaginal discharge should look like and what could be a sign of a problem

- Teach you how to protect yourself if you have sex

About This Chapter: This chapter includes text excerpted from "Seeing The Doctor—Why See A Gynecologist?" girlshealth.gov, Office on Women's Health (OWH), April 15, 2014. Reviewed December 2017.

Your gynecologist can answer any questions you have about the many changes that may be happening to your body. It's great to build a relationship with your gynecologist over the years so he or she understands your health and what matters to you.

Gynecologic cancer is any cancer that starts in a woman's reproductive organs. Cancer is always named for the part of the body where it starts. Gynecologic cancers begin in different places within a woman's pelvis, which is the area below the stomach and in between the hip bones.

- Cervical cancer begins in the cervix, which is the lower, narrow end of the uterus. (The uterus is also called the womb.)
- Ovarian cancer begins in the ovaries, which are located on each side of the uterus.
- Uterine cancer begins in the uterus, the pear-shaped organ in a woman's pelvis where the baby grows when a woman is pregnant.
- Vaginal cancer begins in the vagina, which is the hollow, tube-like channel between the bottom of the uterus and the outside of the body.
- Vulvar cancer begins in the vulva, the outer part of the female genital organs.

Each gynecologic cancer is unique, with different signs and symptoms, different risk factors (things that may increase your chance of getting a disease), and different prevention strategies. All women are at risk for gynecologic cancers, and risk increases with age. When gynecologic cancers are found early, treatment is most effective.

(Source: "What Is Gynecologic Cancer?" Centers for Disease Control and Prevention (CDC).)

When Do I Need To Go?

The American College of Obstetricians and Gynecologists (ACOG) recommends that teenage girls start seeing a gynecologist between the ages of 13 and 15.

If you don't go at that time, you should make sure to visit a gynecologist, adolescent health specialist, or other health professional who can take care of women's reproductive health if:

- You have ever had sex (vaginal, oral, or anal) or intimate sexual contact

- It has been three months or more since your last period and you haven't gotten it again

- You have stomach pain, fever, and fluid coming from your vagina that is yellow, gray, or green with a strong smell—all of which are possible signs of a serious condition called pelvic inflammatory disease (PID) that needs immediate treatment

- You are having problems with your period, like a lot of pain, bleeding heavily, or bleeding for longer than usual, or it has stopped coming regularly

- You have not gotten your period by the age of 15 or within three years of when your breasts started to grow

- You've had your period for two years and it's still not regular or comes more than once a month

- You are having sex and missed your period

Preparing To Meet Gynecologist

Write down a list of questions. With a list, you won't walk out worrying about what you forgot to ask. Also, make sure you write down the name and dosage of all your medicines. If you have a complaint or concern, such as pain, abnormal bleeding, or recurring urinary infections, write it down and think about the answers to these questions:

- How long have you noticed it? What's the pattern?
- What makes it worse or better—activity, diet, position, sleep, sex, foods? Have you tried heat, rest, or over-the-counter (OTC) medicines?
- What else has changed during this time? Did you start a new job, try to lose weight, take a new dietary supplement? New soap or shampoo? New partner?

(Source: "What Your Gynecologist Wants You To Know," Office on Women's Health (OWH), U.S. Department of Health and Human Services (HHS).)

What Will Happen At The Visit?

It's understandable if you're nervous about your first visit. Keep in mind that part of the time will be spent just talking. Your doctor may ask questions about you and your family to learn if you have a history of illnesses. And you can ask the doctor any questions you might have. Don't worry—your doctor probably has already heard every question imaginable! You can talk about any concerns you have, including:

- Cramps and questions about periods

- Acne

- Weight issues

- Feeling depressed

- Sexually transmitted diseases or STDs (also known as sexually transmitted infections or STIs)

- Drinking, using drugs, or smoking

During your visit, your doctor will probably go through some of the usual items on a doctor's check up checklist, like weighing you and measuring your blood pressure. He or she also may check the outside of your genitals and do a breast exam. It's common for young women to have some lumpiness in their breasts, but your doctor may want to make sure you don't have problem lumps or pain.

You may have heard of Pap tests and pelvic exams and wonder if you need them. Most likely you won't need either of these until you're 21. If you are sexually active or have symptoms like an unusual vaginal fluid or a history of problems, there's a chance your doctor may choose to do one or both of these. It's helpful, then, to know what to expect.

A pelvic exam usually involves the doctor examining the outside of your genital area (the vulva). It may also involve the doctor using a tool called a speculum to look inside your vagina and check to make sure your cervix is healthy. Frequently, he or she also will feel inside to make sure organs like your ovaries and uterus feel okay. You probably will feel pressure, but it shouldn't hurt. Try to relax—breathing deeply can help.

A Pap test is done by gently taking some cells from your cervix. These cells are checked for changes that could be cancer or that could turn into cancer.

If you haven't already had the human papillomavirus (HPV) vaccine, ask your doctor about it. It helps guard against the human papillomavirus, which can cause genital warts and is the major cause of cervical cancer.

You have options to make your visit more comfortable:

- During the exam, if the doctor is a man, a female nurse or assistant should also be in the room. You can also ask if you can see a female doctor.

- You can ask to have your mom, sister, or a friend stay in the room with you during the visit if that would help.

- You can ask questions about what's going to happen so you know what to expect.

- You can ask the doctor about keeping things you discuss private.

Taking care of your health is a huge sign that you are growing up. Be proud of yourself for learning information that can protect your health.

Chapter 15

How To Perform A Breast Self-Exam

Breast self-examination is a technique people can use to visually and manually check their own breast tissue for lumps or other changes. Many healthcare practitioners and cancer-prevention organizations recommend performing monthly breast self-examinations beginning at age 18 as a method of early detection for breast cancer. People who conduct regular self-exams become familiar with the normal appearance and feel of their breast tissue, which enables them to recognize changes and discover lumps that may require medical attention. Some of the changes that should be checked by a doctor include:

- new lumps or areas of thickness, which may or may not be painful
- discharge of fluid from the nipples
- dimpling, puckering, rashes, or other changes to the skin
- changes to the size or shape of the breast

Finding lumps or noticing changes should not be a cause for alarm, however. An estimated 80 percent of lumps found in self-examinations are not cancerous, and most breast problems are caused by something other than cancer. In fact, some experts do not recommend self-examinations by people over 40 with no increased risk of breast cancer. They argue that the potential benefits of early detection are outweighed by the risks of undergoing tests and treatments that are unnecessary. Instead, they recommend regular checkups at a doctor's office as well as annual mammograms.

About This Chapter: "How To Perform A Breast Self-Exam," © 2016 Omnigraphics. Reviewed December 2017.

Self-Examination Procedures

Ideally, breast self-examinations should be performed on a monthly basis. For women who are menstruating, the best time is usually toward the end of the monthly period, when the breasts are less likely to be tender. For those who no longer have periods, experts recommend choosing a certain day of the month. Performing self-examinations on a regular schedule makes it easier to compare the results and recognize changes in breast tissue.

Visual Examination

The first part of the process involves a visual examination of the breasts. This examination should be conducted while standing in front of a mirror in three different positions: with your arms hanging naturally at your sides; with your arms raised above your head; and with your hands on your hips and your upper body leaning forward from the waist. Be sure to look from the right and left sides as well as from the front. Check carefully for any changes to the following:

- **Size and shape.** Make sure your breasts appear to be their usual size and shape, and that no sudden changes have occurred. Although one breast may normally be larger than the other, you should not see any visible swelling or bulging.

- **Skin and veins.** Check the skin on your breasts for anything that appears unusual, such as puckering, dimpling, or distortion. Also look for areas of redness, soreness, rashes, or texture changes. Make sure that the veins beneath the skin appear as they usually do. You should not see a noticeable increase in the size or number of veins in one breast as compared to the other breast.

- **Nipples.** Check for any physical changes to the appearance or position of the nipples, such as a sudden inversion. Also check the skin for redness, itching, scaliness, or swelling. Look for any fluid discharge, which may appear watery, milky, sticky, or bloody.

Manual Examination

The second part of the process involves a manual examination of each breast using the fingers of the opposite hand. It should cover the entire surface area of each breast, from the collarbone down to the abdomen, and from the armpit across to the cleavage. This examination should be conducted while lying down, and then again while standing up. The main steps are as follows:

1. Lie down on your back and place a pillow beneath your right shoulder.

2. Place your right arm on top of your head.

3. Use the pads of the three middle fingers on your left hand to examine your right breast.

4. Move your fingers in small circles, about the size of a quarter.

5. Vary the amount of pressure you apply in order to feel all levels of your breast tissue. Use light pressure to feel just beneath the skin, and firm pressure to feel the deep tissue against the ribcage.

6. Begin under the armpit and work from top to bottom along the outer part of your breast.

7. After completing one vertical strip, move over one finger width and begin a new strip, working from bottom to top. Do not lift the fingers between rows.

8. Check the entire breast area in an up-and-down pattern, as if mowing a lawn.

9. Repeat the process by using the left hand to examine the right breast.

10. Examine both breasts again while standing. Many women find it convenient to perform this part of the self-examination in the shower, while the skin is wet and soapy.

If you discover a lump in one breast, check to see if the same kind of lump exists in the other breast. If so, the lumps are probably normal. Many women have fibrocystic lumps that occur throughout both breasts, which may make self-examination difficult. By performing regular self-examinations, women can become familiar with the normal appearance of their breast tissue and consult with medical professionals if they notice any changes.

References

1. "Breast Self-Examination," Healthwise, February 20, 2015.

2. "The Five Steps Of A Breast Self-Exam," Breastcancer.org, 2016.

3. "How To Do A Breast Self-Exam," Maurer Foundation, March 26, 2016.

Part Two
Cancers Of Most Concern To Teens And Young Adults

Chapter 16

Bone Cancer

Cancer that starts in a bone is uncommon. Cancer that has spread to the bone from another part of the body is more common.

There are three types of bone cancer:

- **Osteosarcoma**—occurs most often between ages 10 and 19. It is more common in the knee and upper arm.

- **Chondrosarcoma**—starts in cartilage, usually after age 40

- **Ewing's sarcoma**—occurs most often in children and teens under 19. It is more common in boys than girls.

The most common symptom of bone cancer is pain. Other symptoms vary, depending on the location and size of the cancer. Surgery is often the main treatment for bone cancer. Other treatments may include amputation, chemotherapy, and radiation therapy. Because bone cancer can come back after treatment, regular follow-up visits are important.

Osteosarcoma And Malignant Fibrous Histiocytoma (MFH)

Osteosarcoma and malignant fibrous histiocytoma (MFH) of the bone are diseases in which malignant (cancer) cells form in bone. Osteosarcoma usually starts in osteoblasts,

About This Chapter: Text in this chapter begins with excerpts from "Bone Cancer," MedlinePlus, National Institutes of Health (NIH), August 12, 2016; Text under the heading "Osteosarcoma And Malignant Fibrous Histiocytoma" is excerpted from "Osteosarcoma And Malignant Fibrous Histiocytoma Of Bone Treatment (PDQ®)—Patient Version," National Cancer Institute (NCI), September 1, 2017; Text under the heading "Ewing Sarcoma" is excerpted from "Ewing Sarcoma Treatment (PDQ®)—Patient Version," National Cancer Institute (NCI), December 6, 2017.

which are a type of bone cell that becomes new bone tissue. Osteosarcoma is most common in adolescents. It commonly forms in the ends of the long bones of the body, which include bones of the arms and legs. In children and adolescents, it often forms in the bones near the knee. Rarely, osteosarcoma may be found in soft tissue or organs in the chest or abdomen.

Osteosarcoma is the most common type of bone cancer. MFH of bone is a rare tumor of the bone. It is treated like osteosarcoma.

What Are The Risks Factors Of Osteosarcoma?

Anything that increases your risk of getting a disease is called a risk factor. Having a risk factor does not mean that you will get cancer; not having risk factors doesn't mean that you will not get cancer. Talk with your child's doctor if you think your child may be at risk.

Having past treatment with radiation can increase the risk of osteosarcoma.

Risk factors for osteosarcoma include the following:

- Past treatment with radiation therapy.
- Past treatment with anticancer drugs called alkylating agents.
- Having a certain change in the retinoblastoma gene.
- Having certain conditions, such as the following:
  - Bloom syndrome
  - Diamond-Blackfan anemia
  - Li-Fraumeni syndrome
  - Paget disease
  - Hereditary retinoblastoma
  - Rothmund-Thomson syndrome
  - Werner syndrome

What Are The Signs And Symptoms Of Osteosarcoma?

Signs and symptoms of osteosarcoma and MFH include swelling over a bone or a bony part of the body and joint pain. These and other signs and symptoms may be caused by osteosarcoma or MFH or by other conditions. Check with a doctor if your child has any of the following:

- Swelling over a bone or bony part of the body.

- Pain in a bone or joint.

- A bone that breaks for no known reason.

How Is Osteosarcoma Diagnosed?

Imaging tests are used to detect (find) osteosarcoma and MFH. Imaging tests are done before the biopsy. The following tests and procedures may be used:

- Physical exam and history

- X-ray

- Computerized tomography scan (CAT scan)

- Magnetic resonance imaging (MRI)

How Does Biopsy Help In Diagnosing Osteosarcoma?

A biopsy is done to diagnose osteosarcoma. Cells and tissues are removed during a biopsy so they can be viewed under a microscope by a pathologist to check for signs of cancer. It is important that the biopsy be done by a surgeon who is an expert in treating cancer of the bone. It is best if that surgeon is also the one who removes the tumor. The biopsy and the surgery to remove the tumor are planned together. The way the biopsy is done affects which type of surgery can be done later.

The type of biopsy that is done will be based on the size of the tumor and where it is in the body. There are two types of biopsy that may be used:

- **Core biopsy.** The removal of tissue using a wide needle.

- **Incisional biopsy.** The removal of part of a lump or a sample of tissue that doesn't look normal.

The following test may be done on the tissue that is removed:

- **Light and electron microscopy.** A laboratory test in which cells in a sample of tissue are viewed under regular and high-powered microscopes to look for certain changes in the cells.

What Is The Prognosis For Osteosarcoma?

The prognosis of untreated osteosarcoma and MFH depends on the following:

- Where the tumor is in the body and whether tumors formed in more than one bone.

- The size of the tumor.

- Whether the cancer has spread to other parts of the body and where it has spread.

- The type of tumor (based on how the cancer cells look under a microscope).

- The patient's age and weight at diagnosis.

- Whether the tumor has caused a break in the bone.

- Whether the patient has certain genetic diseases.

After osteosarcoma or MFH is treated, prognosis also depends on the following:

- How much of the cancer was killed by chemotherapy.

- How much of the tumor was taken out by surgery.

- Whether chemotherapy is delayed for more than 3 weeks after surgery takes place.

- Whether the cancer has recurred (come back) within 2 years of diagnosis.

Treatment options for osteosarcoma and MFH depend on the following:

- Where the tumor is in the body.

- The size of the tumor.

- The stage of the cancer.

- Whether the bones are still growing.

- The patient's age and general health.

- The desire of the patient and family for the patient to be able to participate in activities such as sports or have a certain appearance.

- Whether the cancer is newly diagnosed or has recurred after treatment.

What Treatment Is Available For Patients With Osteosarcoma?

Different types of treatment are available for children with osteosarcoma or malignant fibrous histiocytoma MFH of bone. Some treatments are standard (the currently used treatment), and some are being tested in clinical trials. Because cancer in children is rare, taking part in a clinical trial should be considered.

Four types of standard treatment are used:

- **Surgery.** Surgery to remove the entire tumor will be done when possible. Chemotherapy may be given before surgery to make the tumor smaller. This is called neoadjuvant chemotherapy. Chemotherapy is given so less bone tissue needs to be removed and there are fewer problems after surgery. The following types of surgery may be done:

  - **Wide local excision.** Surgery to remove the cancer and some healthy tissue around it.

  - **Limb-sparing surgery.** Removal of the tumor in a limb (arm or leg) without amputation, so the use and appearance of the limb is saved. Most patients with osteosarcoma in a limb can be treated with limb-sparing surgery. The tumor is removed by wide local excision. Tissue and bone that are removed may be replaced with a graft using tissue and bone taken from another part of the patient's body, or with an implant such as artificial bone. If a fracture is found at diagnosis or during chemotherapy before surgery, limb-sparing surgery may still be possible in some cases. If the surgeon is not able to remove all of the tumor and enough healthy tissue around it, an amputation may be done.

  - **Amputation.** Surgery to remove part or all of an arm or leg. This may be done when it is not possible to remove all of the tumor in limb-sparing surgery. The patient may be fitted with a prosthesis (artificial limb) after amputation.

  - **Rotationplasty.** Surgery to remove the tumor and the knee joint. The part of the leg that remains below the knee is then attached to the part of the leg that remains above the knee, with the foot facing backward and the ankle acting as a knee. A prosthesis may then be attached to the foot.

Studies have shown that survival is the same whether the first surgery done is a limb-sparing surgery or an amputation.

Even if the doctor removes all the cancer that can be seen at the time of the surgery, patients are also given chemotherapy after surgery to kill any cancer cells that are left in the area where the tumor was removed or that have spread to other parts of the body. Treatment given after the surgery, to lower the risk that the cancer will come back, is called adjuvant therapy.

- **Chemotherapy.** Chemotherapy is a cancer treatment that uses drugs to stop the growth of cancer cells, either by killing the cells or by stopping them from dividing. When chemotherapy is taken by mouth or injected into a vein or muscle, the drugs enter the bloodstream and can reach cancer cells throughout the body (systemic chemotherapy). When chemotherapy is placed directly into the cerebrospinal fluid, an organ, or a body cavity such as the abdomen, the drugs mainly affect cancer cells in those areas (regional chemotherapy). Combination chemotherapy is the use of more than one anticancer drug. The way the chemotherapy is given depends on the type and stage of the cancer being treated. In the treatment of osteosarcoma and malignant fibrous histiocytosis of bone, chemotherapy is usually given before and after surgery to remove the primary tumor.

- **Radiation therapy.** Radiation therapy is a cancer treatment that uses high-energy X-rays or other types of radiation to kill cancer cells or keep them from growing. There are two types of radiation therapy:

  - **External radiation therapy** uses a machine outside the body to send radiation toward the cancer.

  - **Internal radiation therapy** uses a radioactive substance sealed in needles, seeds, wires, or catheters that are placed directly into or near the cancer.

The way the radiation therapy is given depends on the type and stage of the cancer being treated. Osteosarcoma and MFH cells are not killed easily by external radiation therapy. It may be used when a small amount of cancer is left after surgery or used together with other treatments.

- **Samarium.** Samarium is a radioactive drug that targets areas where bone cells are growing, such as tumor cells in bone. It helps relieve pain caused by cancer in the bone and it also kills blood cells in the bone marrow. It also is used to treat osteosarcoma that has come back after treatment in a different bone. Treatment with samarium may be followed by stem cell transplant. Before treatment with samarium, stem cells (immature blood cells) are removed from the blood or bone marrow of the patient and are frozen and stored. After treatment with samarium is complete, the stored stem cells are thawed and given back to the patient through an infusion. These reinfused stem cells grow into (and restore) the body's blood cells.

Side Effects Of Treatment

Treatment for osteosarcoma or malignant fibrous histiocytoma may cause side effects. Side effects from cancer treatment that begin after treatment and continue for months or years are called late effects. Late effects of cancer treatment may include the following:

- Physical problems

- Changes in mood, feelings, thinking, learning, or memory

- Second cancers (new types of cancer)

Some late effects may be treated or controlled. It is important to talk with your child's doctors about the effects cancer treatment can have on your child.

Ewing Sarcoma

Ewing sarcoma is a type of tumor that forms from a certain kind of cell in bone or soft tissue. Ewing sarcoma may be found in the bones of the legs, arms, feet, hands, chest, pelvis, spine, or skull. Ewing sarcoma also may be found in the soft tissue of the trunk, arms, legs, head and neck, abdominal cavity, or other areas. It is most common in adolescents and young adults.

Ewing sarcoma has also been called peripheral primitive neuroectodermal tumor, Askin tumor (Ewing sarcoma of the chest wall), extraosseous Ewing sarcoma (Ewing sarcoma in tissue other than bone), and Ewing sarcoma family of tumors.

What Are The Signs And Symptoms Of Ewing Sarcoma?

The signs and symptoms of Ewing sarcoma include swelling and pain near the tumor. These and other signs and symptoms may be caused by Ewing sarcoma or by other conditions. Check with your child's doctor if your child has any of the following:

- Pain and/or swelling, usually in the arms, legs, chest, back, or pelvis.

- A lump (which may feel soft and warm) in the arms, legs, chest, or pelvis.

- Fever for no known reason.

- A bone that breaks for no known reason.

How Is Ewing Sarcoma Diagnosed?

Procedures that make pictures of the bones and soft tissues and nearby areas help diagnose Ewing sarcoma and show how far the cancer has spread. The process used to find out if cancer cells have spread within and around the bones and soft tissues is called staging.

In order to plan treatment, it is important to know if the cancer is in the area where it first formed or if it has spread to other parts of the body. Tests and procedures to detect, diagnose, and stage Ewing sarcoma are usually done at the same time.

The following tests and procedures may be used to diagnose or stage Ewing sarcoma:

- Physical exam and history

- MRI

- CT scan (CAT scan)

- positron emission tomography (PET) scan

- Bone scan

- Bone marrow aspiration and biopsy

- X-ray

- Complete blood count (CBC)

- Blood chemistry studies

How Does Biopsy Help In Diagnosing Ewing Sarcoma?

A biopsy is done to diagnose Ewing sarcoma. Tissue samples are removed during a biopsy so they can be viewed under a microscope by a pathologist to check for signs of cancer. It is helpful if the biopsy is done at the same center where treatment will be given.

- **Needle biopsy.** For a needle biopsy, tissue is removed using a needle. This type of needle biopsy may be done if it's possible to remove tissue samples large enough to be used for testing.

- **Incisional biopsy.** For an incisional biopsy, a sample of tissue is removed through an incision in the skin.

- **Excisional biopsy.** The removal of an entire lump or area of tissue that doesn't look normal.

The specialists (pathologist, radiation oncologist, and surgeon) who will treat the patient usually work together to decide where the needle should be placed or the biopsy incision should be made. This is done so that the biopsy doesn't affect later treatment such as surgery to remove the tumor or radiation therapy.

If there is a chance that the cancer has spread to nearby lymph nodes, one or more lymph nodes may be removed and checked for signs of cancer.

The following tests may be done on the tissue that is removed:

- **Cytogenetic analysis.** A laboratory test in which cells in a sample of tissue are viewed under a microscope to look for certain changes in the chromosomes.

- **Immunohistochemistry.** A test that uses antibodies to check for certain antigens in a sample of tissue. The antibody is usually linked to a radioactive substance or a dye that causes the tissue to light up under a microscope. This type of test may be used to tell the difference between different types of cancer.

- **Flow cytometry.** A laboratory test that measures the number of cells in a sample, the percentage of live cells in a sample, and certain characteristics of cells, such as size, shape, and the presence of tumor markers on the cell surface. The cells are stained with a light-sensitive dye, placed in a fluid, and passed in a stream before a laser or other type of light. The measurements are based on how the light-sensitive dye reacts to the light.

What Is The Prognosis For Ewing Sarcoma?

The factors that affect prognosis (chance of recovery) are different before and after treatment.

Before treatment, prognosis depends on:

- Whether the tumor has spread to lymph nodes or distant parts of the body.
- Where in the body the tumor started.
- Whether the tumor formed in the bone or in soft tissue.
- How large the tumor is at when the tumor is diagnosed.
- Whether the lactic acid dehydrogenase (LDH) in the blood is higher than normal.
- How much radioactive glucose is taken up by the tumor during a PET scan.
- Whether the tumor has certain gene changes.
- Whether the child is younger than 15 years.
- The patient's sex.
- Whether the child has had treatment for a different cancer before Ewing sarcoma.
- Whether the tumor has just been diagnosed or has recurred (come back).

After treatment, prognosis is affected by:

- Whether the tumor was completely removed by surgery.
- Whether the tumor responds to chemotherapy or radiation therapy.

If the cancer recurs after initial treatment, prognosis depends on:

- Whether the cancer came back more than two years after the initial treatment.

- Where in the body the tumor came back.

- The type of initial treatment given.

What Treatment Is Available For Patients With Ewing Sarcoma?

Different types of treatments are available for children with Ewing sarcoma. Some treatments are standard (the currently used treatment), and some are being tested in clinical trials. A treatment clinical trial is a research study meant to help improve current treatments or obtain information on new treatments for patients with cancer. Because cancer in children is rare, taking part in a clinical trial should be considered. Some clinical trials are open only to patients who have not started treatment.

Five types of standard treatment are used:

- **Chemotherapy.** Chemotherapy is a cancer treatment that uses drugs to stop the growth of cancer cells, either by killing the cells or by stopping them from dividing. When chemotherapy is taken by mouth or injected into a vein or muscle, the drugs enter the bloodstream and can reach cancer cells throughout the body (systemic chemotherapy). When chemotherapy is placed directly into the cerebrospinal fluid, an organ, or a body cavity such as the abdomen, the drugs mainly affect cancer cells in those areas (regional chemotherapy). Combination chemotherapy is treatment using more than one anticancer drug. Systemic chemotherapy is part of the treatment for all patients with Ewing tumors. It is often the first treatment given and lasts for about 6–12 months. Chemotherapy is often given to shrink the tumor before surgery or radiation therapy and to kill any tumor cells that may have spread to other parts of the body.

- **Radiation therapy.** Radiation therapy is a cancer treatment that uses high-energy X-rays or other types of radiation to kill cancer cells or keep them from growing. There are two types of radiation therapy:

  - **External radiation therapy** uses a machine outside the body to send radiation toward the cancer.

  - **Internal radiation therapy** uses a radioactive substance sealed in needles, seeds, wires, or catheters that are placed directly into or near the cancer.

External radiation therapy is used to treat Ewing sarcoma. Radiation therapy is used when the tumor cannot be removed by surgery or when surgery to remove the tumor will affect important body functions or the way the child will look. It may be used to make the tumor smaller and decrease the amount of tissue that needs to be removed during surgery. It may also be used to treat any tumor that remains after surgery and tumors that have spread to other parts of the body.

- **Surgery.** Surgery is usually done to remove cancer that is left after chemotherapy or radiation therapy. When possible, the whole tumor is removed by surgery. Tissue and bone that are removed may be replaced with a graft, which uses tissue and bone taken from another part of the patient's body or a donor. Sometimes an implant, such as artificial bone, is used. Even if the doctor removes all of the cancer that can be seen at the time of the operation, chemotherapy or radiation therapy may be given after surgery to kill any cancer cells that are left. Chemotherapy or radiation therapy given after surgery to lower the risk that the cancer will come back is called adjuvant therapy.

- **Targeted therapy.** Targeted therapy is a type of treatment that uses drugs or other substances to identify and attack specific cancer cells without harming normal cells. Monoclonal antibody therapy is a type of targeted therapy used in the treatment of recurrent Ewing sarcoma. It is being studied for the treatment of metastatic Ewing sarcoma. Monoclonal antibodies are made in the laboratory from a single type of immune system cell. These antibodies can identify substances on cancer cells or normal substances that may help cancer cells grow. The antibodies attach to the substances and kill the cancer cells, block their growth, or keep them from spreading. Monoclonal antibodies are given by infusion. They may be used alone or to carry drugs, toxins, or radioactive material directly to cancer cells.

New types of targeted therapy are being studied.

- **Kinase inhibitor therapy** is another type of targeted therapy. Kinase inhibitors are drugs that block a protein needed for cancer cells to divide. They are being studied in the treatment of recurrent Ewing sarcoma.

- **PARP (Poly ADP (Adenosine Diphosphate)-Ribose Polymerase) inhibitor therapy** is another type of targeted therapy. PARP inhibitors are drugs that block DNA repair and may cause cancer cells to die. They are being studied in the treatment of recurrent Ewing sarcoma.

- **High-dose chemotherapy with stem cell rescue.** High-dose chemotherapy with stem cell rescue is a way of giving high doses of chemotherapy to treat Ewing sarcoma and then replacing blood-forming cells destroyed by cancer treatment. Stem cells (immature blood cells) are removed from the blood or bone marrow of the patient and are frozen and stored. After chemotherapy is completed, the stored stem cells are thawed and given back to the patient through an infusion. These reinfused stem cells grow into (and restore) the body's blood cells. Chemotherapy with stem cell rescue is used to treat recurrent Ewing sarcoma.

Side Effects Of Treatment For Ewing Sarcoma

Treatment for Ewing sarcoma may cause side effects. Side effects from cancer treatment that begin after treatment and continue for months or years are called late effects. Late effects of cancer treatment may include the following:

- Physical problems

- Changes in mood, feelings, thinking, learning, or memory

- Second cancers (new types of cancer). Patients treated for Ewing sarcoma have an increased risk of acute myeloid leukemia and myelodysplastic syndrome. There is also an increased risk of sarcoma in the area treated with radiation therapy.

Some late effects may be treated or controlled. It is important to talk with your child's doctors about the effects cancer treatment can have on your child.

Chapter 17

Brain And Spinal Cord Tumors

General Information About Childhood Brain And Spinal Cord Tumors

A childhood brain or spinal cord tumor is a disease in which abnormal cells form in the tissues of the brain or spinal cord. There are many types of childhood brain and spinal cord tumors. The tumors are formed by the abnormal growth of cells and may begin in different areas of the brain or spinal cord. The tumors may be benign (not cancer) or malignant (cancer). Benign brain tumors (BBT) grow and press on nearby areas of the brain. They rarely spread into other tissues. Malignant brain tumors (MBT) are likely to grow quickly and spread into other brain tissue. When a tumor grows into or presses on an area of the brain, it may stop that part of the brain from working the way it should. Both benign and malignant brain tumors can cause signs or symptoms and need treatment.

Together, the brain and spinal cord make up the central nervous system (CNS).

Brain And Its Functions

The brain controls many important body functions.

The brain has three major parts:

- The **cerebrum** is the largest part of the brain. It is at the top of the head. The cerebrum controls thinking, learning, problem solving, emotions, speech, reading, writing, and voluntary movement.

About This Chapter: This chapter includes text excerpted from "Childhood Brain And Spinal Cord Tumors Treatment Overview (PDQ®)—Patient Version," National Cancer Institute (NCI), August 18, 2017.

- The **cerebellum** is in the lower back of the brain (near the middle of the back of the head). It controls movement, balance, and posture.

- The **brainstem** connects the brain to the spinal cord. It is in the lowest part of the brain (just above the back of the neck). The brainstem controls breathing, heart rate, and the nerves, and muscles used in seeing, hearing, walking, talking, and eating.

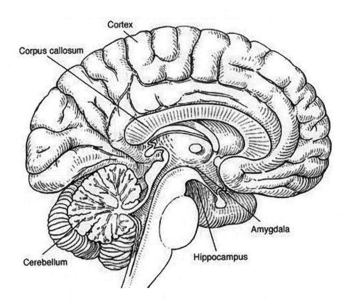

Figure 17.1. Structure Of Brain

(Source: "Alcohol And The Adolescent Brain—Human Studies," National Institute on Alcohol Abuse and Alcoholism (NIAAA).)

The Spinal Cord And Its Role

The spinal cord connects the brain with nerves in most parts of the body. It is a column of nerve tissue that runs from the brain stem down the center of the back. It is covered by three thin layers of tissue called membranes. These membranes are surrounded by the vertebrae (back bones). Spinal cord nerves carry messages between the brain and the rest of the body, such as a message from the brain to cause muscles to move or a message from the skin to the brain to feel touch.

Brain And Spinal Cord Tumors

Brain and spinal cord tumors are a common type of childhood cancer. Although cancer is rare in children, brain and spinal cord tumors are the third most common type of childhood cancer, after leukemia and lymphoma. Brain tumors can occur in both children and adults. Treatment for children is usually different than treatment for adults.

Metastatic tumors are formed by cancer cells that begin in other parts of the body and spread to the brain or spinal cord. The cause of most childhood brain and spinal cord tumors is unknown.

Signs And Symptoms Of Childhood Brain And Spinal Cord Tumors

The signs and symptoms of childhood brain and spinal cord tumors are not the same in every child.

Signs and symptoms depend on the following:

- Where the tumor forms in the brain or spinal cord

- The size of the tumor

- How fast the tumor grows

- The child's age and development

Signs and symptoms may be caused by childhood brain and spinal cord tumors or by other conditions, including cancer that has spread to the brain. Check with your child's doctor if your child has any of the following:

The signs and symptoms of brain tumor include:

- Morning headache or headache that goes away after vomiting.

- Frequent nausea and vomiting.

- Vision, hearing, and speech problems.

- Loss of balance and trouble walking.

- Unusual sleepiness or change in activity level.

- Unusual changes in personality or behavior.

- Seizures.

- Increase in the head size (in infants).

The signs and symptoms of spinal cord tumor include:

- Back pain or pain that spreads from the back towards the arms or legs.

- A change in bowel habits or trouble urinating.

- Weakness in the legs.

- Trouble walking.

In addition to these signs and symptoms of brain and spinal cord tumors, some children are unable to reach certain growth and development milestones such as sitting up, walking, and talking in sentences.

Diagnosis Of Childhood Brain And Spinal Cord Tumors

The following tests and procedures may be used:

- **Physical exam and history.** An exam of the body to check general signs of health, including checking for signs of disease, such as lumps or anything else that seems unusual. A history of the patient's health habits and past illnesses and treatments will also be taken.

- **Neurological exam.** A series of questions and tests to check the brain, spinal cord, and nerve function. The exam checks a person's mental status, coordination, and ability to walk normally, and how well the muscles, senses, and reflexes work. This may also be called a neuro exam or a neurologic exam.

- **Magnetic resonance imaging (MRI) with gadolinium.** A procedure that uses a magnet, radio waves, and a computer to make a series of detailed pictures of the brain and spinal cord. A substance called gadolinium is injected into a vein. The gadolinium collects around the cancer cells so they show up brighter in the picture. This procedure is also called nuclear magnetic resonance imaging (NMRI).

- **Serum tumor marker test.** A procedure in which a sample of blood is examined to measure the amounts of certain substances released into the blood by organs, tissues, or tumor cells in the body. Certain substances are linked to specific types of cancer when found in increased levels in the blood. These are called tumor markers.

Most Childhood Brain Tumors Are Diagnosed And Removed In Surgery

If doctors think there might be a brain tumor, a biopsy may be done to remove a sample of tissue. For tumors in the brain, the biopsy is done by removing part of the skull and using a needle to remove a sample of tissue. A pathologist views the tissue under a microscope to look for cancer cells. If cancer cells are found, the doctor may remove as much tumor as safely possible during the same surgery. The pathologist checks the cancer cells to find out the type and grade of brain tumor. The grade of the tumor is based on how abnormal the cancer cells look under a microscope and how quickly the tumor is likely to grow and spread.

The following test may be done on the sample of tissue that is removed:

- **Immunohistochemistry.** A test that uses antibodies to check for certain antigens in a sample of tissue. The antibody is usually linked to a radioactive substance or a dye that causes the tissue to light up under a microscope. This type of test may be used to tell the difference between different types of cancer.

Some Childhood Brain And Spinal Cord Tumors Are Diagnosed By Imaging Tests

Sometimes a biopsy or surgery cannot be done safely because of where the tumor formed in the brain or spinal cord. These tumors are diagnosed based on the results of imaging tests and other procedures.

Certain Factors Affect Prognosis (Chance Of Recovery)

The prognosis (chance of recovery) depends on the following:

- Whether there are any cancer cells left after surgery.
- The type of tumor.
- Where the tumor is in the body.
- The child's age.
- Whether the tumor has just been diagnosed or has recurred (come back).

Treatment Options Overview

Different types of treatment are available for children with brain and spinal cord tumors. Some treatments are standard (the currently used treatment), and some are being tested in clinical trials. Because cancer in children is rare, taking part in a clinical trial should be considered.

Three types of standard treatment are used.

- **Surgery.** Surgery may be used to diagnose and treat childhood brain and spinal cord tumors.

- **Radiation Therapy.** Radiation therapy is a cancer treatment that uses high-energy X-rays or other types of radiation to kill cancer cells or keep them from growing. There are two types of radiation therapy:

  - **External radiation therapy** uses a machine outside the body to send radiation toward the cancer.

  - **Internal radiation therapy** uses a radioactive substance sealed in needles, seeds, wires, or catheters that are placed directly into or near the cancer.

The way the radiation therapy is given depends on the type of cancer being treated. External radiation therapy is used to treat childhood brain and spinal cord tumors.

- **Chemotherapy.** Chemotherapy is a cancer treatment that uses drugs to stop the growth of cancer cells, either by killing the cells or by stopping them from dividing. When chemotherapy is taken by mouth or injected into a vein or muscle, the drugs enter the bloodstream and can reach cancer cells throughout the body (systemic chemotherapy). When chemotherapy is placed directly in the cerebrospinal fluid, an organ, or a body cavity such as the abdomen, the drugs mainly affect cancer cells in those areas (regional chemotherapy). The way the chemotherapy is given depends on the type and stage of the cancer being treated. Anticancer drugs given by mouth or vein to treat brain and spinal cord tumors cannot cross the blood-brain barrier and enter the fluid that surrounds the brain and spinal cord. Instead, an anticancer drug is injected into the fluid-filled space to kill cancer cells there. This is called intrathecal chemotherapy.

High Dose Chemotherapy With Stem Cell Transplant

High dose chemotherapy with stem cell transplant is a way of giving high doses of chemotherapy and replacing blood forming cells destroyed by the cancer treatment. Stem cells (immature blood cells) are removed from the blood or bone marrow of the patient or a donor and are frozen and stored. After the chemotherapy is completed, the stored stem cells are thawed and given back to the patient through an infusion. These reinfused stem cells grow into (and restore) the body's blood cells.

Side Effects Of Treatment

Some cancer treatments cause side effects months or years after treatment has ended. These are called late effects. Late effects of cancer treatment may include the following:

- Physical problems.

- Changes in mood, feelings, thinking, learning, or memory.

- Second cancers (new types of cancer).

Some late effects may be treated or controlled. It is important to talk with your child's doctors about the effects cancer treatment can have on your child.

Chapter 18

Breast Cancer

What Is Breast Cancer?

Breast cancer is a disease in which cells in the breast grow out of control. There are different kinds of breast cancer. The kind of breast cancer depends on which cells in the breast turn into cancer.

Breast cancer can begin in different parts of the breast. A breast is made up of three main parts: lobules, ducts, and connective tissue. The lobules are the glands that produce milk. The

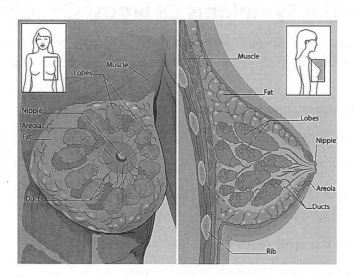

Figure 18.1. Anterior View And Cross-Section View Of The Breast

About This Chapter: This chapter includes text excerpted from "Breast Cancer—Basic Information," Centers for Disease Control and Prevention (CDC), July 25, 2017.

ducts are tubes that carry milk to the nipple. The connective tissue (which consists of fibrous and fatty tissue) surrounds and holds everything together. Most breast cancers begin in the ducts or lobules.

Breast cancer can spread outside the breast through blood vessels and lymph vessels. When breast cancer spreads to other parts of the body, it is said to have metastasized.

Kinds Of Breast Cancer

The most common kinds of breast cancer are:

- **Invasive ductal carcinoma.** The cancer cells grow outside the ducts into other parts of the breast tissue. Invasive cancer cells can also spread, or metastasize, to other parts of the body.

- **Invasive lobular carcinoma.** Cancer cells spread from the lobules to the breast tissues that are close by. These invasive cancer cells can also spread to other parts of the body.

There are several other less common kinds of breast cancer, such as Paget disease, medullary, mucinous, and inflammatory breast cancer.

Ductal carcinoma in situ (DCIS) is a breast disease that may lead to breast cancer. The cancer cells are only in the lining of the ducts, and have not spread to other tissues in the breast.

What Are The Symptoms Of Breast Cancer?

Different people have different symptoms of breast cancer. Some people do not have any signs or symptoms at all. A person may find out they have breast cancer after a routine mammogram.

Some warning signs of breast cancer are:

- New lump in the breast or underarm (armpit).

- Thickening or swelling of part of the breast.

- Irritation or dimpling of breast skin.

- Redness or flaky skin in the nipple area or the breast.

- Pulling in of the nipple or pain in the nipple area.

- Nipple discharge other than breast milk, including blood.

- Any change in the size or the shape of the breast.

- Pain in any area of the breast.

Keep in mind that these symptoms can happen with other conditions that are not cancer.

If you have any signs or symptoms that worry you, be sure to see your doctor right away.

What Is A Normal Breast?

No breast is typical. What is normal for you may not be normal for another woman. Most women say their breasts feel lumpy or uneven. The way your breasts look and feel can be affected by getting your period, having children, losing or gaining weight, and taking certain medications. Breasts also tend to change as you age.

What Do Lumps In My Breast Mean?

Many conditions can cause lumps in the breast, including cancer. But most breast lumps are caused by other medical conditions. The two most common causes of breast lumps are fibrocystic breast condition and cysts. Fibrocystic condition causes noncancerous changes in the breast that can make them lumpy, tender, and sore. Cysts are small fluid-filled sacs that can develop in the breast.

Breast Cancer In Young Women

Most breast cancers are found in women who are 50 years old or older, but breast cancer also affects younger women. About 11 percent of all new cases of breast cancer in the United States are found in women younger than 45 years of age. While breast cancer diagnosis and treatment are difficult for women of any age, young survivors may find it overwhelming.

Risk Factors For Breast Cancer In Young Women

Some young women are at a higher risk for getting breast cancer at an early age compared with other women their age. If you are a woman under age 45, you may have a higher risk if:

- You have close relatives (parents, siblings, or children) who were diagnosed with breast or ovarian cancer when they were younger than 45, especially if more than one relative was diagnosed or if a male relative had breast cancer.

- You have changes in certain breast cancer genes (*BRCA1* and *BRCA2*), or have close relatives with these changes.

- You have an Ashkenazi Jewish heritage.

- You were treated with radiation therapy to the breast or chest during childhood or early adulthood.

- You have had breast cancer or certain other breast health problems such as lobular carcinoma in situ (LCIS), ductal carcinoma in situ (DCIS), atypical ductal hyperplasia, or atypical lobular hyperplasia.

- You have been told that you have dense breasts on a mammogram.

Breast Density

A term used to describe the amount of dense tissue compared to the amount of fatty tissue in the breast on a mammogram. Dense breast tissue has more fibrous and glandular tissue than fat. There are different levels of breast density, ranging from little or no dense tissue to very dense tissue. The more density, the harder it may be to find tumors or other changes on a mammogram.

(Source: "NCI Dictionary Of Cancer Terms," National Cancer Institute (NCI).)

What Can I Do To Reduce My Risk?

Breast cancer in a woman under the age of 45 is relatively rare compared to older women, but some women have higher risk for this disease. If you're a woman in this age group, it is important that you:

- **Know how your breasts normally look and feel.** If you notice a change in the size or shape of your breast, feel pain in your breast, have nipple discharge other than breast milk (including blood), or other symptoms, talk to a doctor right away.

- **Talk to your doctor if you have a higher risk.** If you have a family history of breast or ovarian cancer or other risk factors, you should talk to your doctor about ways to manage your risk. If your risk is high, your doctor may suggest that you get genetic counseling and be tested for changes, called mutations, in your *BRCA1* and *BRCA2* genes. Your doctor may also talk to you about getting mammograms earlier and more often than other women, whether other screening tests might be right for you, and medicines or surgeries that can lower your risk.

Aside from genetics, little is known about what causes breast cancer in women under age 45, but you can do the following things to reduce your risk for breast cancer.

- Keep a healthy weight.

- Exercise regularly (at least four hours a week).

- Research shows that lack of nighttime sleep can be a risk factor.

- Don't drink alcohol, or limit alcoholic drinks to no more than one per day.

- Avoid exposure to chemicals that can cause cancer (carcinogens) and chemicals that interfere with the normal function of the body.

- Limit exposure to radiation from medical imaging tests like X-rays, computed tomography (CT) scans, and positron emission tomography (PET) scans if not medically necessary.

- If you are taking, or have been told to take, hormone replacement therapy or oral contraceptives (birth control pills), ask your doctor about the risks and find out if it is right for you.

- Breastfeed any children you may have, if possible.

If you have a family history of breast cancer or inherited changes in your *BRCA1* and *BRCA2* genes, you may be at high risk for getting breast cancer. Talk to your doctor about more ways to lower your risk.

Staying healthy throughout your life will lower your risk of developing cancer, and improve your chances of surviving cancer if it occurs.

How Is Breast Cancer Treated?

Breast cancer is treated in several ways. It depends on the kind of breast cancer and how far it has spread. People with breast cancer often get more than one kind of treatment.

- **Surgery.** An operation where doctors cut out cancer tissue.

- **Chemotherapy.** Using special medicines to shrink or kill the cancer cells. The drugs can be pills you take or medicines given in your veins, or sometimes both.

- **Hormonal therapy.** Blocks cancer cells from getting the hormones they need to grow.

- **Biological therapy.** Works with your body's immune system to help it fight cancer cells or to control side effects from other cancer treatments.

- **Radiation therapy.** Using high-energy rays (similar to X-rays) to kill the cancer cells.

Doctors from different specialties often work together to treat breast cancer. Surgeons are doctors who perform operations. Medical oncologists are doctors who treat cancer with medicine. Radiation oncologists are doctors who treat cancer with radiation.

Chapter 19

Cervical Cancer

When cancer starts in the cervix, it is called cervical cancer. The cervix is the lower, narrow end of the uterus. Also known as the womb, the uterus is where a baby grows when a woman is pregnant. The cervix connects the upper part of the uterus to the vagina (the birth canal).

All women are at risk for cervical cancer. It occurs most often in women over age 30. Each year, about 12,000 women in the United States get cervical cancer and about 4,000 women die from it.

Human papillomavirus (HPV) is the main cause of cervical cancer. HPV is a common virus that is passed from one person to another during sex. At least half of sexually active people will have HPV at some point in their lives, but few women will get cervical cancer.

Risk Factors

Almost all cervical cancers are caused by HPV, a common virus that can be passed from one person to another during sex. There are many types of HPV. Some HPV types can cause changes on a woman's cervix that can lead to cervical cancer over time, while other types can cause genital or skin warts.

HPV is so common that most people get it at some time in their lives. HPV usually causes no symptoms so you can't tell that you have it. For most women, HPV will go away on its own; however, if it does not, there is a chance that over time it may cause cervical cancer.

About This Chapter: This chapter includes text excerpted from "Gynecologic Cancers—Cervical Cancer," Centers for Disease Control and Prevention (CDC), February 13, 2017.

Other things can increase your risk of cervical cancer:

- Smoking.

- Having human immunodeficiency virus (HIV) (the virus that causes acquired immuno-deficiency syndrome (AIDS)) or another condition that makes it hard for your body to fight off health problems.

- Using birth control pills for a long time (five or more years).

- Having given birth to three or more children.

- Having several sexual partners.

Signs And Symptoms

Early on, cervical cancer may not cause signs and symptoms. Advanced cervical cancer may cause bleeding or discharge from the vagina that is not normal for you, such as bleeding after sex. If you have any of these signs, see your doctor. They may be caused by something other than cancer, but the only way to know is to see your doctor.

Screening

Cervical cancer is the easiest gynecologic cancer to prevent, with regular screening tests and follow up. Two screening tests can help prevent cervical cancer or find it early:

- The **Pap test** (or Pap smear) looks for precancers, cell changes on the cervix that might become cervical cancer if they are not treated appropriately.

- The **HPV test** looks for the virus (human papillomavirus) that can cause these cell changes.

The Pap test is recommended for all women between the ages of 21 and 65 years old, and can be done in a doctor's office or clinic. During the Pap test, the doctor will use a plastic or metal instrument, called a speculum, to widen your vagina. This helps the doctor examine the vagina and the cervix, and collect a few cells and mucus from the cervix and the area around it. The cells are then placed on a slide or in a bottle of liquid and sent to a laboratory. The laboratory will check to be sure that the cells are normal.

How To Prepare For Your Pap Test

You should not schedule your Pap test for a time when you are having your period. If you are going to have a Pap test in the next two days:

- You should not douche (rinse the vagina with water or another fluid).

- You should not use a tampon.

- You should not have sex.

- You should not use a birth control foam, cream, or jelly.

- You should not use a medicine or cream in your vagina.

If you get the HPV test along with the Pap test, the cells collected during the Pap test will be tested for HPV at the laboratory. Talk with your doctor, nurse, or other healthcare professional about whether the HPV test is right for you.

When you have a Pap test, the doctor may also perform a pelvic exam, checking your uterus, ovaries, and other organs to make sure there are no problems. There are times when your doctor may perform a pelvic exam without giving you a Pap test. Ask your doctor which tests you are having, if you are unsure.

If you have a low income or do not have health insurance, you may be able to get a free or low cost Pap test through the National Breast and Cervical Cancer Early Detection Program (NBCCEDP).

Pap Test Versus HPV Test

The Pap test and the HPV test look for different things.

A Pap test checks the cervix for abnormal cell changes that, if not found and treated, can lead to cervical cancer. Your doctor takes cells from your cervix to examine under a microscope. How often you need a Pap test depends on your age and health history. Talk with your doctor about what is best for you.

An HPV test looks for HPV on a woman's cervix. Certain types of HPV can lead to cervical cancer. Your doctor will swab the cervix for cells. An HPV test is not the same as the HPV vaccine.

According to the U.S. Preventive Services Task Force (USPSTF), women ages 30–65 can combine the HPV test with a Pap test every 5 years. The USPSTF does not recommend the HPV test for women under age 30.

(Source: "Cancer—Cervical Cancer," Office on Women's Health (OWH), U.S. Department of Health and Human Services (HHS).)

When To Get Screened

You should start getting regular Pap tests at age 21. The Pap test, which screens for cervical cancer, is one of the most reliable and effective cancer screening tests available.

The only cancer for which the Pap test screens is cervical cancer. It does not screen for ovarian, uterine, vaginal, or vulvar cancers. So even if you have a Pap test regularly, if you notice any signs or symptoms that are unusual for you, see a doctor to find out why you're having them. If your Pap test results are normal, your doctor may tell you that you can wait three years until your next Pap test.

If you are 30 years old or older, you may choose to have an HPV test along with the Pap test. Both tests can be performed by your doctor at the same time. When both tests are performed together, it is called cotesting. If your test results are normal, your chance of getting cervical cancer in the next few years is very low. Your doctor may then tell you that you can wait as long as five years for your next screening. But you should still go to the doctor regularly for a checkup.

If you are 21–65 years old, it is important for you to continue getting a Pap test as directed by your doctor—even if you think you are too old to have a child or are not having sex anymore. If you have had your cervix removed as part of a total hysterectomy for noncancerous conditions, like fibroids, your doctor may tell you that you do not need to have a Pap test anymore.

Test Results

It can take as long as three weeks to receive your test results. If your test shows that something might not be normal, your doctor will contact you and figure out how best to follow up. There are many reasons why test results might not be normal. It usually does not mean you have cancer.

If your test results show cells that are not normal and may become cancer, your doctor will let you know if you need to be treated. In most cases, treatment prevents cervical cancer from developing. It is important to follow up with your doctor right away to learn more about your test results and receive any treatment that may be needed.

Diagnosis And Treatment

If your doctor says that you have cervical cancer, ask to be referred to a gynecologic oncologist—a doctor who has been trained to treat cancers of a woman's reproductive system. This doctor will work with you to create a treatment plan.

The extent of disease is referred to as the stage. Information about the size of the cancer or how far it has spread is often used to determine the stage. Doctors use this information to plan treatment and to monitor progress.

Types Of Treatment

Cervical cancer is treated in several ways. It depends on the kind of cervical cancer and how far it has spread. Treatments include surgery, chemotherapy, and radiation therapy.

- **Surgery.** Doctors remove cancer tissue in an operation.

- **Chemotherapy.** Using special medicines to shrink or kill the cancer. The drugs can be pills you take or medicines given in your veins, or sometimes both.

- **Radiation.** Using high-energy rays (similar to X-rays) to kill the cancer.

Different treatments may be provided by different doctors on your medical team.

- Gynecologic oncologists are doctors who have been trained to treat cancers of a woman's reproductive system.

- Surgeons are doctors who perform operations.

- Medical oncologists are doctors who treat cancer with medicine.

- Radiation oncologists are doctors who treat cancer with radiation.

Complementary And Alternative Medicine

Complementary and alternative medicine (CAM) are medicines and health practices that are not standard cancer treatments. Complementary medicine is used in addition to standard treatments, and alternative medicine is used instead of standard treatments. Meditation, yoga, and supplements like vitamins and herbs are some examples.

Many kinds of complementary and alternative medicine have not been tested scientifically and may not be safe. Talk to your doctor about the risks and benefits before you start any kind of complementary or alternative medicine.

Which Treatment Is Right For Me?

Choosing the treatment that is right for you may be hard. Talk to your cancer doctor about the treatment options available for your type and stage of cancer. Your doctor can explain the risks and benefits of each treatment and their side effects. Side effects are how your body reacts to drugs or other treatments.

Sometimes people get an opinion from more than one cancer doctor. This is called a "second opinion." Getting a second opinion may help you choose the treatment that is right for you.

Prevention

Getting An HPV Vaccine

The HPV vaccine protects against the types of HPV that most often cause cervical, vaginal, and vulvar cancers. It is recommended for preteens (both boys and girls) aged 11–12 years, but can be given as early as age 9 and until age 26. The vaccine is given in a series of either two or three shots, depending on age. It is important to note that even women who are vaccinated against HPV need to have regular Pap tests to screen for cervical cancer.

Additional Steps To Help Prevent Cervical Cancer

These things may also help lower your risk for cervical cancer:

- Don't smoke.

- Use condoms during sex.*

- Limit your number of sexual partners.

*HPV infection can occur in both male and female genital areas that are covered or protected by a latex condom, as well as in areas that are not covered. While the effect of condoms in preventing HPV infection is unknown, condom use has been associated with a lower rate of cervical cancer.

Chapter 20

Colorectal Cancer

The colon is part of the body's digestive system. The digestive system removes and processes nutrients (vitamins, minerals, carbohydrates, fats, proteins, and water) from foods and helps pass waste material out of the body. The digestive system is made up of the mouth, throat, esophagus, stomach, and the small and large intestines. The colon (large bowel) is the first part of the large intestine and is about 5 feet long. Together, the rectum and anal canal make up the last part of the large intestine and are 6–8 inches long. The anal canal ends at the anus (the opening of the large intestine to the outside of the body).

Cancer that begins in the colon is called colon cancer, and cancer that begins in the rectum is called rectal cancer. Cancer that affects either of these organs may also be called colorectal cancer.

Colorectal cancer is the second leading cause of death from cancer in the United States. The number of new colorectal cancer cases and the number of deaths from colorectal cancer are both decreasing a little bit each year. However, in adults younger than 50 years, the number of new colorectal cancer cases has slowly increased since 1998. The number of new colorectal cancers and deaths from colorectal cancer are higher in African Americans than in other races.

Finding and treating colorectal cancer early may prevent death from colorectal cancer. Screening tests may be used to help find colorectal cancer.

About This Chapter: Text in this chapter begins with excerpts from "Colorectal Cancer Prevention (PDQ®)— Patient Version," National Cancer Institute (NCI), February 8, 2017; Text beginning with the heading "What Are The Risk Factors For Colorectal Cancer?" is excerpted from "Colorectal (Colon) Cancer—Basic Information About Colorectal Cancer," Centers for Disease Control and Prevention (CDC), April 25, 2016; Text under the heading "Colon Cancer Treatment" is excerpted from "Colon Cancer Treatment (PDQ®)—Patient Version," National Cancer Institute (NCI), December 7, 2017; Text under the heading "Rectal Cancer Treatment" is excerpted from "Rectal Cancer Treatment (PDQ®)—Patient Version," National Cancer Institute (NCI), May 19, 2017.

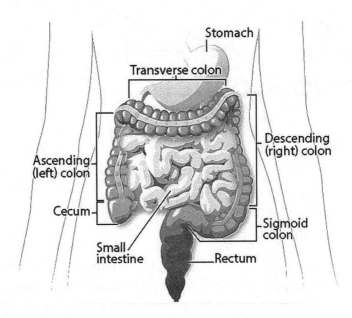

Figure 20.1. Digestive System

(Source: "Colorectal (Colon) Cancer—Basic Information About Colorectal Cancer," Centers for Disease Control and Prevention (CDC).)

What Are The Risk Factors For Colorectal Cancer?

Your risk of getting colorectal cancer increases as you get older. Other risk factors include having:

- Inflammatory bowel disease such as Crohn's disease or ulcerative colitis.

- A personal or family history of colorectal cancer or colorectal polyps.

- A genetic syndrome such as familial adenomatous polyposis (FAP) or hereditary non-polyposis colorectal cancer (Lynch syndrome).

Lifestyle factors that may contribute to an increased risk of colorectal cancer include:

- Lack of regular physical activity.

- A diet low in fruit and vegetables.

- A low-fiber and high-fat diet.

- Overweight and obesity.

- Alcohol consumption.

- Tobacco use.

What Can I Do To Reduce My Risk Of Colorectal Cancer?

Almost all colorectal cancers begin as precancerous polyps (abnormal growths) in the colon or rectum. Such polyps can be present in the colon for years before invasive cancer develops. They may not cause any symptoms. Colorectal cancer screening can find precancerous polyps so they can be removed before they turn into cancer. In this way, colorectal cancer is prevented. Screening can also find colorectal cancer early, when there is a greater chance that treatment will be most effective and lead to a cure.

Research is underway to find out if changes to your diet can reduce your colorectal cancer risk. Medical experts don't agree on the role of diet in preventing colorectal cancer, but often recommend a diet low in animal fats and high in fruits, vegetables, and whole grains to reduce the risk of other chronic diseases, such as coronary artery disease and diabetes. This diet also may reduce the risk of colorectal cancer. Also, researchers are examining the role of certain medicines and supplements in preventing colorectal cancer.

The U.S. Preventive Services Task Force (USPSTF) found that taking low-dose aspirin can help prevent cardiovascular disease and colorectal cancer in some adults, depending on age and risk factors.

Some studies suggest that people may reduce their risk of developing colorectal cancer by increasing physical activity, limiting alcohol consumption, and avoiding tobacco.

What Are The Symptoms Of Colorectal Cancer?

Colorectal polyps and colorectal cancer don't always cause symptoms, especially at first. Someone could have polyps or colorectal cancer and not know it. That is why getting screened regularly for colorectal cancer is so important.

If you have symptoms, they may include:

- Blood in or on your stool (bowel movement).

- Stomach pain, aches, or cramps that don't go away.

- Losing weight and you don't know why.

If you have any of these symptoms, talk to your doctor. They may be caused by something other than cancer. The only way to know what is causing them is to see your doctor.

What Is Colorectal Cancer Screening?

A screening test is used to look for a disease when a person doesn't have symptoms. (When a person has symptoms, diagnostic tests are used to find out the cause of the symptoms.)

Colorectal cancer almost always develops from precancerous polyps (abnormal growths) in the colon or rectum. Screening tests can find precancerous polyps, so that they can be removed before they turn into cancer. Screening tests can also find colorectal cancer early, when treatment works best.

When Should I Begin To Get Screened?

You should begin screening for colorectal cancer soon after turning 50, then continue getting screened at regular intervals. However, you may need to be tested earlier than 50, or more often than other people, if:

- You or a close relative have had colorectal polyps or colorectal cancer.

- You have an inflammatory bowel disease such as Crohn's disease or ulcerative colitis.

- You have a genetic syndrome such as familial adenomatous polyposis (FAP) or hereditary nonpolyposis colorectal cancer (Lynch syndrome).

If you think you are at increased risk for colorectal cancer, speak with your doctor about:

- When to begin screening.

- Which test is right for you.

- How often to get tested.

Free Or Low-Cost Screening

Six states in Centers for Disease Control and Prevention's (CDC) Colorectal Cancer Control Program (CRCCP) provide colorectal cancer screening to some people. Those eligible are low-income men and women aged 50–64 years who are underinsured or uninsured for screening, when resources are available and there is no other payment option.

Colorectal cancer screening tests may be covered by your health insurance policy without a deductible or copay.

Colon Cancer Treatment

Six types of standard treatment are used:

Surgery

Surgery (removing the cancer in an operation) is the most common treatment for all stages of colon cancer. A doctor may remove the cancer using one of the following types of surgery:

- **Local excision:** If the cancer is found at a very early stage, the doctor may remove it without cutting through the abdominal wall. Instead, the doctor may put a tube with a cutting tool through the rectum into the colon and cut the cancer out. This is called a local excision. If the cancer is found in a polyp (a small bulging area of tissue), the operation is called a polypectomy.

- **Resection of the colon with anastomosis:** If the cancer is larger, the doctor will perform a partial colectomy (removing the cancer and a small amount of healthy tissue around it). The doctor may then perform an anastomosis (sewing the healthy parts of the colon together). The doctor will also usually remove lymph nodes near the colon and examine them under a microscope to see whether they contain cancer.

- **Resection of the colon with colostomy:** If the doctor is not able to sew the 2 ends of the colon back together, a stoma (an opening) is made on the outside of the body for waste to pass through. This procedure is called a colostomy. A bag is placed around the stoma to collect the waste. Sometimes the colostomy is needed only until the lower colon has healed, and then it can be reversed. If the doctor needs to remove the entire lower colon, however, the colostomy may be permanent.

Even if the doctor removes all the cancer that can be seen at the time of the operation, some patients may be given chemotherapy or radiation therapy after surgery to kill any cancer cells that are left. Treatment given after the surgery, to lower the risk that the cancer will come back, is called adjuvant therapy.

Radiofrequency Ablation

Radiofrequency ablation is the use of a special probe with tiny electrodes that kill cancer cells. Sometimes the probe is inserted directly through the skin and only local anesthesia is needed. In other cases, the probe is inserted through an incision in the abdomen. This is done in the hospital with general anesthesia.

Cryosurgery

Cryosurgery is a treatment that uses an instrument to freeze and destroy abnormal tissue. This type of treatment is also called cryotherapy.

Chemotherapy

Chemotherapy is a cancer treatment that uses drugs to stop the growth of cancer cells, either by killing the cells or by stopping them from dividing. When chemotherapy is taken by mouth or injected into a vein or muscle, the drugs enter the bloodstream and can reach cancer cells throughout the body (systemic chemotherapy). When chemotherapy is placed directly into the cerebrospinal fluid, an organ, or a body cavity such as the abdomen, the drugs mainly affect cancer cells in those areas (regional chemotherapy).

Chemoembolization of the hepatic artery may be used to treat cancer that has spread to the liver. This involves blocking the hepatic artery (the main artery that supplies blood to the liver) and injecting anticancer drugs between the blockage and the liver. The liver's arteries then deliver the drugs throughout the liver. Only a small amount of the drug reaches other parts of the body. The blockage may be temporary or permanent, depending on what is used to block the artery. The liver continues to receive some blood from the hepatic portal vein, which carries blood from the stomach and intestine.

The way the chemotherapy is given depends on the type and stage of the cancer being treated.

Radiation Therapy

Radiation therapy is a cancer treatment that uses high-energy X-rays or other types of radiation to kill cancer cells or keep them from growing. There are two types of radiation therapy:

- External radiation therapy uses a machine outside the body to send radiation toward the cancer.

- Internal radiation therapy uses a radioactive substance sealed in needles, seeds, wires, or catheters that are placed directly into or near the cancer.

The way the radiation therapy is given depends on the type and stage of the cancer being treated. External radiation therapy is used as palliative therapy to relieve symptoms and improve quality of life.

Targeted Therapy

Targeted therapy is a type of treatment that uses drugs or other substances to identify and attack specific cancer cells without harming normal cells.

Types of targeted therapies used in the treatment of colon cancer include the following:

- **Monoclonal antibodies:** Monoclonal antibodies are made in the laboratory from a single type of immune system cell. These antibodies can identify substances on cancer cells or normal substances that may help cancer cells grow. The antibodies attach to the substances and kill the cancer cells, block their growth, or keep them from spreading. Monoclonal antibodies are given by infusion. They may be used alone or to carry drugs, toxins, or radioactive material directly to cancer cells.

  - Bevacizumab and ramucirumab are types of monoclonal antibodies that bind to a protein called vascular endothelial growth factor (VEGF). This may prevent the growth of new blood vessels that tumors need to grow.

  - Cetuximab and panitumumab are types of monoclonal antibodies that bind to a protein called epidermal growth factor receptor (EGFR) on the surface of some types of cancer cells. This may stop cancer cells from growing and dividing.

- **Angiogenesis inhibitors:** Angiogenesis inhibitors stop the growth of new blood vessels that tumors need to grow.

  - Ziv-aflibercept is a vascular endothelial growth factor trap that blocks an enzyme needed for the growth of new blood vessels in tumors.

  - Regorafenib is used to treat colorectal cancer that has spread to other parts of the body and has not gotten better with other treatment. It blocks the action of certain proteins, including vascular endothelial growth factor. This may help keep cancer cells from growing and may kill them. It may also prevent the growth of new blood vessels that tumors need to grow.

Rectal Cancer Treatment

Five types of standard treatment are used:

Surgery

Surgery is the most common treatment for all stages of rectal cancer. The cancer is removed using one of the following types of surgery:

- Polypectomy: If the cancer is found in a polyp (a small piece of bulging tissue), the polyp is often removed during a colonoscopy.

- Local excision: If the cancer is found on the inside surface of the rectum and has not spread into the wall of the rectum, the cancer and a small amount of surrounding healthy tissue is removed.

- Resection: If the cancer has spread into the wall of the rectum, the section of the rectum with cancer and nearby healthy tissue is removed. Sometimes the tissue between the rectum and the abdominal wall is also removed. The lymph nodes near the rectum are removed and checked under a microscope for signs of cancer.

- Radiofrequency ablation: The use of a special probe with tiny electrodes that kill cancer cells. Sometimes the probe is inserted directly through the skin and only local anesthesia is needed. In other cases, the probe is inserted through an incision in the abdomen. This is done in the hospital with general anesthesia.

- Cryosurgery: A treatment that uses an instrument to freeze and destroy abnormal tissue. This type of treatment is also called cryotherapy.

- Pelvic exenteration: If the cancer has spread to other organs near the rectum, the lower colon, rectum, and bladder are removed. In women, the cervix, vagina, ovaries, and nearby lymph nodes may be removed. In men, the prostate may be removed. Artificial openings (stoma) are made for urine and stool to flow from the body to a collection bag.

After the cancer is removed, the surgeon will either:

- do an anastomosis (sew the healthy parts of the rectum together, sew the remaining rectum to the colon, or sew the colon to the anus);

  or

- make a stoma (an opening) from the rectum to the outside of the body for waste to pass through. This procedure is done if the cancer is too close to the anus and is called a colostomy. A bag is placed around the stoma to collect the waste. Sometimes the colostomy is needed only until the rectum has healed, and then it can be reversed. If the entire rectum is removed, however, the colostomy may be permanent.

Radiation therapy and/or chemotherapy may be given before surgery to shrink the tumor, make it easier to remove the cancer, and help with bowel control after surgery. Treatment given before surgery is called neoadjuvant therapy. Even if all the cancer that can be seen at the time of the operation is removed, some patients may be given radiation therapy and/or chemotherapy after surgery to kill any cancer cells that are left. Treatment given after the surgery, to lower the risk that the cancer will come back, is called adjuvant therapy.

Radiation Therapy

Radiation therapy is a cancer treatment that uses high-energy X-rays or other types of radiation to kill cancer cells or keep them from growing. There are two types of radiation therapy:

- External radiation therapy uses a machine outside the body to send radiation toward the cancer.

- Internal radiation therapy uses a radioactive substance sealed in needles, seeds, wires, or catheters that are placed directly into or near the cancer.

The way the radiation therapy is given depends on the type and stage of the cancer being treated. External radiation therapy is used to treat rectal cancer.

Short-course preoperative radiation therapy is used in some types of rectal cancer. This treatment uses fewer and lower doses of radiation than standard treatment, followed by surgery several days after the last dose.

Chemotherapy

Chemotherapy is a cancer treatment that uses drugs to stop the growth of cancer cells, either by killing the cells or by stopping the cells from dividing. When chemotherapy is taken by mouth or injected into a vein or muscle, the drugs enter the bloodstream and can reach cancer cells throughout the body (systemic chemotherapy). When chemotherapy is placed directly in the cerebrospinal fluid, an organ, or a body cavity such as the abdomen, the drugs mainly affect cancer cells in those areas (regional chemotherapy).

Chemoembolization of the hepatic artery is a type of regional chemotherapy that may be used to treat cancer that has spread to the liver. This is done by blocking the hepatic artery (the main artery that supplies blood to the liver) and injecting anticancer drugs between the blockage and the liver. The liver's arteries then carry the drugs into the liver. Only a small amount of the drug reaches other parts of the body. The blockage may be temporary or permanent, depending on what is used to block the artery. The liver continues to receive some blood from the hepatic portal vein, which carries blood from the stomach and intestine.

The way the chemotherapy is given depends on the type and stage of the cancer being treated.

Active Surveillance

Active surveillance is closely following a patient's condition without giving any treatment unless there are changes in test results. It is used to find early signs that the condition is getting worse. In active surveillance, patients are given certain exams and tests to check if the cancer is growing. When the cancer begins to grow, treatment is given to cure the cancer. Tests include the following:

- Digital rectal exam.

- MRI.

- Endoscopy.

- Sigmoidoscopy.

- CT scan.

- Carcinoembryonic antigen (CEA) assay.

Targeted Therapy

Targeted therapy is a type of treatment that uses drugs or other substances to identify and attack specific cancer cells without harming normal cells.

Types of targeted therapies used in the treatment of rectal cancer include the following:

- Monoclonal antibodies: Monoclonal antibody therapy is a type of targeted therapy being used for the treatment of rectal cancer. Monoclonal antibody therapy uses antibodies made in the laboratory from a single type of immune system cell. These antibodies can identify substances on cancer cells or normal substances that may help cancer cells grow. The antibodies attach to the substances and kill the cancer cells, block their growth, or keep them from spreading. Monoclonal antibodies are given by infusion. They may be used alone or to carry drugs, toxins, or radioactive material directly to cancer cells.

  - Bevacizumab and ramucirumab are types of monoclonal antibodies that bind to a protein called vascular endothelial growth factor (VEGF). This may prevent the growth of new blood vessels that tumors need to grow.

  - Cetuximab and panitumumab are types of monoclonal antibodies that bind to a protein called epidermal growth factor receptor (EGFR) on the surface of some types of cancer cells. This may stop cancer cells from growing and dividing.

- Angiogenesis inhibitors: Angiogenesis inhibitors stop the growth of new blood vessels that tumors need to grow.

  - Ziv-aflibercept is a vascular endothelial growth factor trap that blocks an enzyme needed for the growth of new blood vessels in tumors.

  - Regorafenib is used to treat colorectal cancer that has spread to other parts of the body and has not gotten better with other treatment. It blocks the action of certain proteins, including vascular endothelial growth factor. This may help keep cancer cells from growing and may kill them. It may also prevent the growth of new blood vessels that tumors need to grow.

Chapter 21

Childhood Extracranial Germ Cell Tumors

What Are Childhood Extracranial Germ Cell Tumors?

Childhood extracranial germ cell tumors form from germ cells in parts of the body other than the brain.

A germ cell is a type of cell that forms as a fetus (unborn baby) develops. These cells later become sperm in the testicles or eggs in the ovaries. Sometimes while the fetus is forming, germ cells travel to parts of the body where they should not be and grow into a germ cell tumor. The tumor may form before or after birth.

Extracranial germ cell tumors usually form in the following areas of the body:

- Testicles
- Ovaries
- Sacrum or coccyx (bottom part of the spine)
- Retroperitoneum (the back wall of the abdomen)
- Mediastinum (area between the lungs)

Extracranial germ cell tumors are most common in adolescents 15–19 years of age. It may be benign (noncancer) or malignant (cancer).

About This Chapter: This chapter includes text excerpted from "Childhood Extracranial Germ Cell Tumors Treatment (PDQ®)–Patient Version," National Cancer Institute (NCI), August 12, 2016.

What Are The Types Of Childhood Extracranial Germ Cell Tumors?

There are three types of extracranial germ cell tumors. Extracranial germ cell tumors are grouped into mature teratomas, immature teratomas, and malignant germ cell tumors:

Mature teratomas. Mature teratomas are the most common type of extracranial germ cell tumor. Mature teratomas are benign tumors and not likely to become cancer. They usually occur in the sacrum or coccyx (bottom part of the spine) in newborns or in the ovaries of girls at the start of puberty. The cells of mature teratomas look almost like normal cells under a microscope. Some mature teratomas release enzymes or hormones that cause signs and symptoms of disease.

Immature teratomas. Immature teratomas also usually occur in the sacrum or coccyx (bottom part of the spine) in newborns or the ovaries of girls at the start of puberty. Immature teratomas have cells that look very different from normal cells under a microscope. Immature teratomas may be cancer. They often have several different types of tissue in them, such as hair, muscle, and bone. Some immature teratomas release enzymes or hormones that cause signs and symptoms of disease.

Malignant germ cell tumors. Malignant germ cell tumors are cancer. There are two main types of malignant germ cell tumors:

- Germinomas. Tumors that make a hormone called beta-human chorionic gonadotropin (β-hCG). There are three types of germinomas:

  - Dysgerminomas form in the ovary in girls.

  - Seminomas form in the testicle in boys.

  - Germinomas form in areas of the body that are not the ovary or testicle.

- Nongerminomas. There are four types of nongerminomas:

  - Yolk sac tumors make a hormone called alpha-fetoprotein (AFP). They can form in the ovary, testicle, or other areas of the body.

  - Choriocarcinomas make a hormone called beta-human chorionic gonadotropin (β-hCG). They can form in the ovary, testicle, or other areas of the body.

  - Embryonal carcinomas may make a hormone called β-hCG and/or a hormone called AFP. They can form in the testicle or other parts of the body, but not in the ovary.

- Mixed germ cell tumors are made up of both malignant germ cell tumor and teratoma. They can form in the ovary, testicle, or other areas of the body.

Childhood extracranial germ cell tumors are grouped as gonadal or extragonadal. Malignant extracranial germ cell tumors are gonadal or extragonadal.

- Gonadal germ cell tumors. Gonadal germ cell tumors form in the testicles in boys or ovaries in girls.

  - Testicular germ cell tumors. Testicular germ cell tumors are divided into two main types, seminoma, and nonseminoma.

    - Seminomas make a hormone called beta-human chorionic gonadotropin (β-hCG).

    - Nonseminomas are usually large and cause signs or symptoms. They tend to grow and spread more quickly than seminomas.

Testicular germ cell tumors usually occur before the age of 4 years or in adolescents and young adults. Testicular germ cell tumors in adolescents and young adults are different from those that form in early childhood. Boys older than 14 years with testicular germ cell tumors are treated in pediatric cancer centers, but the treatment is much like the treatment used in adults.

- Ovarian germ cell tumors. Ovarian germ cell tumors are more common in adolescent girls and young women. Most ovarian germ cell tumors are benign teratomas. Sometimes immature teratomas, dysgerminomas, yolk sac tumors, and mixed germ cell tumors (cancer) occur.

- Extragonadal extracranial germ cell tumors. Extragonadal extracranial germ cell tumors form in areas other than the brain, testicles, or ovaries. Most extragonadal extracranial germ cell tumors form along the midline of the body. This includes the following:

  - Sacrum (the large, triangle shaped bone in the lower spine that forms part of the pelvis).

  - Coccyx (the small bone at the bottom of the spine, also called the tailbone).

  - Mediastinum (the area between the lungs).

  - Back of the abdomen.

  - Neck.

In younger children, extragonadal extracranial germ cell tumors usually occur at birth or in early childhood. Most of these tumors are teratomas in the sacrum or coccyx. In older children, adolescents, and young adults, extragonadal extracranial germ cell tumors are often in the mediastinum.

The cause of most childhood extracranial germ cell tumors is unknown.

What Are The Risks Of Childhood Extracranial Germ Cell Tumors?

Having certain inherited disorders can increase the risk of an extracranial germ cell tumor. Anything that increases your risk of getting a disease is called a risk factor. Having a risk factor does not mean that you will get cancer; not having risk factors doesn't mean that you will not get cancer. Talk with your child's doctor if you think your child may be at risk.

Possible risk factors for extracranial germ cell tumors include the following:

- Having certain genetic syndromes:

  - Klinefelter syndrome may increase the risk of germ cell tumors in the mediastinum.

  - Swyer syndrome may increase the risk of germ cell tumors in the testicles or ovaries.

  - Turner syndrome may increase the risk of germ cell tumors in the ovaries.

- Having an undescended testicle may increase the risk of developing a testicular germ cell tumor.

What Are The Signs Of Childhood Extracranial Germ Cell Tumors?

The signs of childhood extracranial germ cell tumors depend on the type of tumor and where it is in the body. Different tumors may cause the following signs and symptoms. Other conditions may cause these same signs and symptoms. Check with a doctor if your child has any of the following:

- A lump in the abdomen or lower back

- A painless lump in the testicle

- Pain in the abdomen

- Fever

- Constipation

- In females, no menstrual periods

- In females, unusual vaginal bleeding

How Are Childhood Extracranial Germ Cell Tumors Diagnosed?

Imaging studies and blood tests are used to detect (find) and diagnose childhood extracranial germ cell tumors. The following tests and procedures may be used:

- **Physical exam and history.** An exam of the body to check general signs of health, including checking for signs of disease, such as lumps or anything else that seems unusual. The testicles may be checked for lumps, swelling, or pain. A history of the patient's health habits and past illnesses and treatments will also be taken.

- **Serum tumor marker test.** A procedure in which a sample of blood is checked to measure the amounts of certain substances released into the blood by organs, tissues, or tumor cells in the body. Certain substances are linked to specific types of cancer when found in increased levels in the blood. These are called tumor markers. Most malignant germ cell tumors release tumor markers. The following tumor markers are used to detect extracranial germ cell tumors:

  - Alpha-fetoprotein (AFP).

  - Beta-human chorionic gonadotropin (β-hCG).

For testicular germ cell tumors, blood levels of the tumor markers help show if the tumor is a seminoma or nonseminoma.

- **Blood chemistry studies.** A procedure in which a blood sample is checked to measure the amounts of certain substances released into the blood by organs and tissues in the body. An unusual (higher or lower than normal) amount of a substance can be a sign of disease.

- **Chest X-ray.** An X-ray of the organs and bones inside the chest. An X-ray is a type of energy beam that can go through the body and onto film, making a picture of areas inside the body.

- **Computed tomography (CT) scan (Computerized axial tomography (CAT) scan).** A procedure that makes a series of detailed pictures of areas inside the body, taken from different angles. The pictures are made by a computer linked to an X-ray machine. A

145

dye may be injected into a vein or swallowed to help the organs or tissues show up more clearly. This procedure is also called computed tomography, computerized tomography, or computerized axial tomography.

- **Magnetic resonance imaging (MRI).** A procedure that uses a magnet, radio waves, and a computer to make a series of detailed pictures of areas inside the body. This procedure is also called nuclear magnetic resonance imaging (NMRI).

- **Ultrasound exam.** A procedure in which high-energy sound waves (ultrasound) are bounced off internal tissues or organs and make echoes. The echoes form a picture of body tissues called a sonogram. The picture can be printed to be looked at later.

- **Biopsy.** The removal of cells or tissues so they can be viewed under a microscope by a pathologist to check for signs of cancer. In some cases, the tumor is removed during surgery and then a biopsy is done.

The following tests may be done on the sample of tissue that is removed:

- **Cytogenetic analysis.** A laboratory test in which cells in a sample of tissue are viewed under a microscope to look for certain changes in the chromosomes.

- **Immunohistochemistry.** A test that uses antibodies to check for certain antigens in a sample of tissue. The antibody is usually linked to a radioactive substance or a dye that causes the tissue to light up under a microscope. This type of test may be used to tell the difference between different types of cancer.

What Is The Prognosis For Childhood Extracranial Germ Cell Tumors?

Certain factors affect prognosis (chance of recovery) and treatment options.

- The type of germ cell tumor.

- Where the tumor first began to grow.

- The stage of the cancer (whether it has spread to nearby areas or to other places in the body).

- How well the tumor responds to treatment (lower AFP and β-hCG levels).

- Whether the tumor can be completely removed by surgery.

- The patient's age and general health.

- Whether the cancer has just been diagnosed or has recurred (come back).

The prognosis for childhood extracranial germ cell tumors, especially ovarian germ cell tumors, is good.

What Are The Treatment Options For Childhood Extracranial Germ Cell Tumors?

Three types of standard treatment are used:

Surgery

Surgery to completely remove the tumor is done whenever possible. If the tumor is very large, chemotherapy may be given first, to make the tumor smaller and decrease the amount of tissue that needs to be removed during surgery. A goal of surgery is to keep reproductive function. The following types of surgery may be used:

- **Resection.** Surgery to remove tissue or part or all of an organ.
- **Radical inguinal orchiectomy.** Surgery to remove one or both testicles through an incision (cut) in the groin.
- **Unilateral salpingo-oophorectomy.** Surgery to remove one ovary and one fallopian tube on the same side.

Even if the doctor removes all the cancer that can be seen at the time of the surgery, some patients may be given chemotherapy after surgery to kill any cancer cells that are left. Treatment given after the surgery, to lower the risk that the cancer will come back, is called adjuvant therapy.

Observation

Observation is closely monitoring a patient's condition without giving any treatment until signs or symptoms appear or change. For childhood extracranial germ cell tumors, this includes:

- physical exams
- imaging tests and
- tumor marker tests

Chemotherapy

Chemotherapy is a cancer treatment that uses drugs to stop the growth of cancer cells, either by killing the cells or by stopping them from dividing. When chemotherapy is taken by mouth or injected into a vein or muscle, the drugs enter the bloodstream and can reach cancer cells throughout the body (systemic chemotherapy). When chemotherapy is placed directly into the cerebrospinal fluid, an organ, or a body cavity such as the abdomen, the drugs mainly affect cancer cells in those areas (regional chemotherapy). Combination chemotherapy is treatment using more than one anticancer drug.

The way the chemotherapy is given depends on the type and stage of the cancer being treated.

High Dose Chemotherapy With Stem Cell Transplant

High dose chemotherapy with stem cell transplant is a way of giving high doses of chemotherapy and replacing blood forming cells destroyed by the cancer treatment. Stem cells (immature blood cells) are removed from the blood or bone marrow of the patient or a donor and are frozen and stored. After the chemotherapy is completed, the stored stem cells are thawed and given back to the patient through an infusion. These reinfused stem cells grow into (and restore) the body's blood cells.

Radiation Therapy

Radiation therapy is a cancer treatment that uses high-energy X-rays or other types of radiation to kill cancer cells or keep them from growing. There are two types of radiation therapy:

- **External radiation therapy** uses a machine outside the body to send radiation toward the cancer.

- **Internal radiation therapy** uses a radioactive substance sealed in needles, seeds, wires, or catheters that are placed directly into or near the cancer.

The way the radiation therapy is given depends on the type of cancer and whether it has come back. External radiation therapy is being studied for the treatment of childhood extracranial germ cell tumors that have come back.

Side Effects Of Treatment

Some cancer treatments cause side effects months or years after treatment has ended. Side effects from cancer treatment that begin during or after treatment and continue for months or years are called late effects. Late effects of cancer treatment may include the following:

- Physical problems.

- Changes in mood, feelings, thinking, learning, or memory.

- Second cancers (new types of cancer).

For example, late effects of surgery to remove tumors in the sacrum or coccyx include:

- Constipation

- Loss of bowel and bladder control

- Scars

Some late effects may be treated or controlled. It is important to talk with your child's doctors about the effects cancer treatment can have on your child.

Chapter 22

Childhood Acute Lymphoblastic Leukemia

What Is Childhood Acute Lymphoblastic Leukemia (ALL)?

Childhood acute lymphoblastic leukemia (also called ALL or acute lymphocytic leukemia) is a cancer of the blood and bone marrow. This type of cancer usually gets worse quickly if it is not treated. ALL is the most common type of cancer in children.

Leukemia may affect red blood cells, white blood cells, and platelets. In a healthy child, the bone marrow makes blood stem cells (immature cells) that become mature blood cells over time. A blood stem cell may become a myeloid stem cell or a lymphoid stem cell.

A myeloid stem cell becomes one of three types of mature blood cells:

- Red blood cells that carry oxygen and other substances to all tissues of the body.

- Platelets that form blood clots to stop bleeding.

- White blood cells that fight infection and disease.

A lymphoid stem cell becomes a lymphoblast cell and then one of three types of lymphocytes (white blood cells):

- B lymphocytes that make antibodies to help fight infection.

- T lymphocytes that help B lymphocytes make the antibodies that help fight infection.

- Natural killer cells that attack cancer cells and viruses.

About This Chapter: This chapter includes text excerpted from "Childhood Acute Lymphoblastic Leukemia Treatment (PDQ®)—Patient Version," National Cancer Institute (NCI), October 26, 2017.

In a child with ALL, too many stem cells become lymphoblasts, B lymphocytes, or T lymphocytes. The cells do not work like normal lymphocytes and are not able to fight infection very well. These cells are cancer (leukemia) cells. Also, as the number of leukemia cells increases in the blood and bone marrow, there is less room for healthy white blood cells, red blood cells, and platelets. This may lead to infection, anemia, and easy bleeding.

What Are The Risk Factors For Childhood Acute Lymphoblastic Leukemia?

Past treatment for cancer and certain genetic conditions affect the risk of having childhood ALL. Anything that increases your risk of getting a disease is called a risk factor. Having a risk factor does not mean that you will get cancer; not having risk factors doesn't mean that you will not get cancer. Talk with your child's doctor if you think your child may be at risk.

Possible risk factors for ALL include the following:

- Being exposed to X-rays before birth.

- Being exposed to radiation.

- Past treatment with chemotherapy.

- Having certain genetic conditions, such as:

  - Down syndrome.

  - Neurofibromatosis type 1.

  - Bloom syndrome.

  - Fanconi anemia.

  - Ataxia-telangiectasia.

  - Li-Fraumeni syndrome.

  - Constitutional mismatch repair deficiency (mutations in certain genes that stop deoxyribonucleic acid (DNA) from repairing itself, which leads to the growth of cancers at an early age).

- Having certain changes in the chromosomes or genes.

What Are The Signs And Symptoms Of Childhood Acute Lymphoblastic Leukemia?

The signs of childhood ALL include fever and bruising. These and other signs and symptoms may be caused by childhood ALL or by other conditions. Check with your child's doctor if your child has any of the following:

- Bleeding.

- Petechiae (flat, pinpoint, dark-red spots under the skin caused by bleeding).

- Bone or joint pain.

- Painless lumps in the neck, underarm, stomach, or groin.

- Pain or feeling of fullness below the ribs.

- Weakness, feeling tired, or looking pale.

- Loss of appetite.

How Is Childhood Acute Lymphoblastic Leukemia Diagnosed?

The tests that examine the blood and bone marrow are used to detect (find) and diagnose childhood ALL. The following tests and procedures may be used to diagnose childhood ALL and find out if leukemia cells have spread to other parts of the body such as the brain or testicles:

- **Physical exam and history.** An exam of the body to check general signs of health, including checking for signs of disease, such as lumps or anything else that seems unusual. A history of the patient's health habits and past illnesses and treatments will also be taken.

- **Complete blood count (CBC) with differential.** A procedure in which a sample of blood is drawn and checked for the following:

  - The number of red blood cells and platelets.

  - The number and type of white blood cells.

  - The amount of hemoglobin (the protein that carries oxygen) in the red blood cells.

  - The portion of the sample made up of red blood cells.

- **Blood chemistry studies.** A procedure in which a blood sample is checked to measure the amounts of certain substances released into the blood by organs and tissues in the body. An unusual (higher or lower than normal) amount of a substance can be a sign of disease.

- **Bone marrow aspiration and biopsy.** The removal of bone marrow and a small piece of bone by inserting a hollow needle into the hipbone or breastbone. A pathologist views the bone marrow and bone under a microscope to look for signs of cancer.

The following tests are done on blood or the bone marrow tissue that is removed:

- **Cytogenetic analysis.** A laboratory test in which the cells in a sample of blood or bone marrow are viewed under a microscope to look for certain changes in the chromosomes of lymphocytes. For example, in Philadelphia chromosome—positive ALL, part of one chromosome switches places with part of another chromosome. This is called the "Philadelphia chromosome."

- **Immunophenotyping.** A laboratory test in which the antigens or markers on the surface of a blood or bone marrow cell are checked to see if they are lymphocytes or myeloid cells. If the cells are malignant lymphocytes (cancer) they are checked to see if they are B lymphocytes or T lymphocytes.

- **Lumbar puncture.** A procedure used to collect a sample of cerebrospinal fluid (CSF) from the spinal column. This is done by placing a needle between two bones in the spine and into the CSF around the spinal cord and removing a sample of the fluid. The sample of CSF is checked under a microscope for signs that leukemia cells have spread to the brain and spinal cord. This procedure is also called an LP or spinal tap.

This procedure is done after leukemia is diagnosed to find out if leukemia cells have spread to the brain and spinal cord. Intrathecal chemotherapy is given after the sample of fluid is removed to treat any leukemia cells that may have spread to the brain and spinal cord.

- **Chest X-ray.** An X-ray of the organs and bones inside the chest. An X-ray is a type of energy beam that can go through the body and onto film, making a picture of areas inside the body. The chest X-ray is done to see if leukemia cells have formed a mass in the middle of the chest.

What Is The Prognosis For Childhood Acute Lymphoblastic Leukemia?

Certain factors affect prognosis (chance of recovery) and treatment options. The prognosis (chance of recovery) depends on:

- How quickly and how low the leukemia cell count drops after the first month of treatment.

- Age at the time of diagnosis, sex, race, and ethnic background.

- The number of white blood cells in the blood at the time of diagnosis.

- Whether the leukemia cells began from B lymphocytes or T lymphocytes.

- Whether there are certain changes in the chromosomes or genes of the lymphocytes with cancer.

- Whether the child has Down syndrome.

- Whether leukemia cells are found in the cerebrospinal fluid.

- The child's weight at the time of diagnosis and during treatment.

Treatment options depend on:

- Whether the leukemia cells began from B lymphocytes or T lymphocytes.

- Whether the child has standard-risk, high-risk, or very high–risk ALL.

- The age of the child at the time of diagnosis.

- Whether there are certain changes in the chromosomes of lymphocytes, such as the Philadelphia chromosome.

- Whether the child was treated with steroids before the start of induction therapy.

- How quickly and how low the leukemia cell count drops during treatment.

For leukemia that relapses (comes back) after treatment, the prognosis and treatment options depend partly on the following:

- How long it is between the time of diagnosis and when the leukemia comes back.

- Whether the leukemia comes back in the bone marrow or in other parts of the body.

What Are The Treatment Options For Childhood Acute Lymphoblastic Leukemia?

Different types of treatment are available for children with acute lymphoblastic leukemia (ALL). Some treatments are standard (the currently used treatment), and some are being tested in clinical trials. A treatment clinical trial is a research study meant to help improve current treatments or obtain information on new treatments for patients with cancer. When clinical trials show that a new treatment is better than the standard treatment, the new treatment may become the standard treatment.

Because cancer in children is rare, taking part in a clinical trial should be considered. Some clinical trials are open only to patients who have not started treatment.

Treatment Phase

The treatment of childhood ALL usually has three phases. The treatment of childhood ALL is done in phases:

- **Remission induction.** This is the first phase of treatment. The goal is to kill the leukemia cells in the blood and bone marrow. This puts the leukemia into remission.

- **Consolidation/intensification.** This is the second phase of treatment. It begins once the leukemia is in remission. The goal of consolidation/intensification therapy is to kill any leukemia cells that remain in the body and may cause a relapse.

- **Maintenance.** This is the third phase of treatment. The goal is to kill any remaining leukemia cells that may regrow and cause a relapse. Often the cancer treatments are given in lower doses than those used during the remission induction and consolidation/intensification phases. Not taking medication as ordered by the doctor during maintenance therapy increases the chance the cancer will come back. This is also called the continuation therapy phase.

Standard Treatment

Four types of standard treatment are used:

Chemotherapy

Chemotherapy is a cancer treatment that uses drugs to stop the growth of cancer cells, either by killing the cells or by stopping them from dividing. When chemotherapy is taken by mouth or injected into a vein or muscle, the drugs enter the bloodstream and can reach cancer cells throughout the body (systemic chemotherapy). When chemotherapy is placed directly into the cerebrospinal fluid (intrathecal), an organ, or a body cavity such as the abdomen, the drugs mainly affect cancer cells in those areas (regional chemotherapy). Combination chemotherapy is treatment using more than one anticancer drug.

The way the chemotherapy is given depends on the child's risk group. Children with high-risk ALL receive more anticancer drugs and higher doses of anticancer drugs than children with standard-risk ALL. Intrathecal chemotherapy may be used to treat childhood ALL that has spread, or may spread, to the brain and spinal cord.

Radiation Therapy

Radiation therapy is a cancer treatment that uses high-energy X-rays or other types of radiation to kill cancer cells or keep them from growing. There are two types of radiation therapy:

- **External radiation therapy** uses a machine outside the body to send radiation toward the cancer.

- **Internal radiation therapy** uses a radioactive substance sealed in needles, seeds, wires, or catheters that are placed directly into or near the cancer.

The way the radiation therapy is given depends on the type of cancer being treated. External radiation therapy may be used to treat childhood ALL that has spread, or may spread, to the brain, spinal cord, or testicles. It may also be used to prepare the bone marrow for a stem cell transplant.

Chemotherapy With Stem Cell Transplant

Stem cell transplant is a method of giving high doses of chemotherapy and sometimes total-body irradiation, and then replacing the blood-forming cells destroyed by the cancer treatment. Stem cells (immature blood cells) are removed from the blood or bone marrow of a donor. After the patient receives treatment, the donor's stem cells are given to the patient through an infusion. These reinfused stem cells grow into (and restore) the patient's blood cells. The stem cell donor doesn't have to be related to the patient.

Stem cell transplant is rarely used as initial treatment for children and adolescents with ALL. It is used more often as part of treatment for ALL that relapses (comes back after treatment).

Targeted Therapy

Targeted therapy is a treatment that uses drugs or other substances to identify and attack specific cancer cells without harming normal cells.

Tyrosine kinase inhibitors (TKIs) are targeted therapy drugs that block the enzyme, tyrosine kinase, which causes stem cells to become more white blood cells or blasts than the body needs. Imatinib mesylate is a TKI used in the treatment of children with Philadelphia chromosome—positive ALL. Dasatinib and ruxolitinib are TKIs that are being studied in the treatment of newly diagnosed high-risk ALL.

Monoclonal antibody therapy is a cancer treatment that uses antibodies made in the laboratory, from a single type of immune system cell. These antibodies can identify substances on cancer cells or normal substances that may help cancer cells grow. The antibodies attach to the substances and kill the cancer cells, block their growth, or keep them from spreading. Monoclonal antibodies are given by infusion. They may be used alone or to carry drugs, toxins, or radioactive material directly to cancer cells. Blinatumomab and inotuzumab are monoclonal antibodies being studied in the treatment of refractory childhood ALL.

CNS-Directed Therapy

Treatment to kill leukemia cells or prevent the spread of leukemia cells to the brain and spinal cord (central nervous system; CNS) is called CNS-directed therapy. Chemotherapy may be used to treat leukemia cells that have spread, or may spread, to the brain and spinal cord. Because standard doses of chemotherapy may not reach leukemia cells in the CNS, the cells are able to hide in the CNS. Systemic chemotherapy given in high doses or intrathecal chemotherapy (into the cerebrospinal fluid) is able to reach leukemia cells in the CNS. Sometimes external radiation therapy to the brain is also given.

These treatments are given in addition to treatment that is used to kill leukemia cells in the rest of the body. All children with ALL receive CNS-directed therapy as part of induction therapy and consolidation/intensification therapy and sometimes during maintenance therapy.

If the leukemia cells spread to the testicles, treatment includes high doses of systemic chemotherapy and sometimes radiation therapy.

Chimeric Antigen Receptor (CAR) T-Cell Therapy

CAR T-cell therapy is a type of immunotherapy that changes the patient's T cells (a type of immune system cell) so they will attack certain proteins on the surface of cancer cells. T cells are taken from the patient and special receptors are added to their surface in the laboratory.

The changed cells are called chimeric antigen receptor (CAR) T cells. The CAR T cells are grown in the laboratory and given to the patient by infusion. The CAR T cells multiply in the patient's blood and attack cancer cells. CAR T-cell therapy is being studied in the treatment of childhood ALL that has relapsed (come back) a second time.

What Are The Side Effects Of Childhood Acute Lymphoblastic Leukemia?

Children and adolescents may have treatment-related side effects that appear months or years after treatment for acute lymphoblastic leukemia. Regular follow up exams are very important. Treatment can cause side effects long after it has ended. These are called late effects.

Late effects of cancer treatment may include:

- Physical problems, including problems with the heart, blood vessels, liver, or bones, and fertility. When dexrazoxane is given with chemotherapy drugs called anthracyclines, the risk of late heart effects is lessened.

- Changes in mood, feelings, thinking, learning, or memory. Children younger than 4 years who have received radiation therapy to the brain have a higher risk of these effects.

- Second cancers (new types of cancer) or other conditions, such as brain tumors, thyroid cancer, acute myeloid leukemia, and myelodysplastic syndrome.

Some late effects may be treated or controlled. It is important to talk with your child's doctors about the possible late effects caused by some treatments.

Chapter 23

Lymphoma

There are two general types of lymphoma: Hodgkin lymphoma and non-Hodgkin lymphoma.

Hodgkin lymphoma often occurs in adolescents 15–19 years of age.

Childhood Hodgkin Lymphoma

What Is Childhood Hodgkin Lymphoma?

Childhood Hodgkin lymphoma is a type of cancer that develops in the lymph system, which is part of the body's immune system. The immune system protects the body from foreign substances, infection, and diseases.

The Lymph System

The lymph system is made up of the following:

- **Lymph.** Colorless, watery fluid that carries white blood cells called lymphocytes through the lymph system. Lymphocytes protect the body against infections and the growth of tumors.

- **Lymph vessels.** A network of thin tubes that collect lymph from different parts of the body and return it to the bloodstream.

About This Chapter: Text in this chapter begins with excerpts from "Childhood Hodgkin Lymphoma Treatment (PDQ®)—Patient Version," National Cancer Institute (NCI), September 1, 2017; Text under the heading "Childhood Non-Hodgkin Lymphoma Treatment" is excerpted from "Childhood Non-Hodgkin Lymphoma Treatment (PDQ®)—Patient Version," National Cancer Institute (NCI), August 18, 2017.

- **Lymph nodes.** Small, bean-shaped structures that filter lymph and store white blood cells that help fight infection and disease. Lymph nodes are located along the network of lymph vessels found throughout the body. Clusters of lymph nodes are found in the neck, underarm, abdomen, pelvis, and groin.

- **Spleen.** An organ that makes lymphocytes, filters the blood, stores blood cells, and destroys old blood cells. The spleen is on the left side of the abdomen near the stomach.

- **Thymus.** An organ in which lymphocytes grow and multiply. The thymus is in the chest behind the breastbone.

- **Tonsils.** Two small masses of lymph tissue at the back of the throat. The tonsils make lymphocytes.

- **Bone marrow.** The soft, spongy tissue in the center of large bones. Bone marrow makes white blood cells, red blood cells, and platelets.

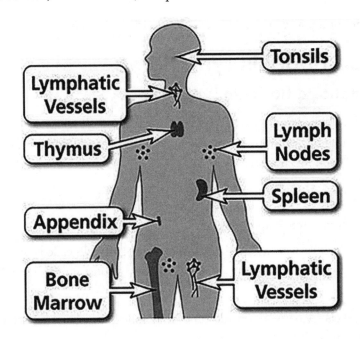

Figure 23.1. Immune System

(Source: "HIV/AIDS Glossary—Immune System," AIDSinfo, U.S. Department of Health and Human Services (HHS).)

Lymph tissue is also found in other parts of the body such as the stomach, thyroid gland, brain, and skin.

What Are The Risk Factors For Childhood Hodgkin Lymphoma?

Anything that increases your risk of getting a disease is called a risk factor. Having a risk factor does not mean that you will get cancer; not having risk factors doesn't mean that you will not get cancer. Talk with your child's doctor if you think your child may be at risk. *Epstein-Barr* virus infection increases the risk of childhood Hodgkin lymphoma.

Other risk factors for childhood Hodgkin lymphoma include the following:

- Being infected with the human immunodeficiency virus (HIV).

- Having certain diseases of the immune system.

- Having a personal history of mononucleosis ("mono").

- Having a parent or sibling with a personal history of Hodgkin lymphoma.

Being exposed to common infections in early childhood may decrease the risk of Hodgkin lymphoma in children because of the effect it has on the immune system.

What Are The Signs And Symptoms For Childhood Hodgkin Lymphoma?

Signs of childhood Hodgkin lymphoma include swollen lymph nodes, fever, night sweats, and weight loss. These and other signs and symptoms may be caused by childhood Hodgkin lymphoma or by other conditions. Check with your child's doctor if your child has any of the following:

- Painless, swollen lymph nodes near the collarbone or in the neck, chest, underarm, or groin.

- Fever for no known reason.

- Weight loss for no known reason.

- Night sweats.

- Fatigue.

- Anorexia.

- Itchy skin.

- Pain in the lymph nodes after drinking alcohol.

Fever, weight loss, and night sweats are called B symptoms.

How Is Childhood Hodgkin Lymphoma Diagnosed?

The following tests and procedures may be used to detect (find) and diagnose childhood Hodgkin lymphoma:

- **Physical exam and history.** An exam of the body to check general signs of health, including checking for signs of disease, such as lumps or anything else that seems unusual. A history of the patient's health habits and past illnesses and treatments will also be taken.

- **Computerized tomography (CT) scan.** A procedure that makes a series of detailed pictures of areas inside the body, such as the neck, chest, abdomen, or pelvis, taken from different angles. The pictures are made by a computer linked to an X-ray machine. A dye may be injected into a vein or swallowed to help the organs or tissues show up more clearly. This procedure is also called computed tomography, computerized tomography, or computerized axial tomography.

- **PET scan (positron emission tomography scan).** A procedure to find malignant tumor cells in the body. A small amount of radioactive glucose (sugar) is injected into a vein. The PET scanner rotates around the body and makes a picture of where glucose is being used in the body. Malignant tumor cells show up brighter in the picture because they are more active and take up more glucose than normal cells do. Sometimes a PET scan and a CT scan are done at the same time. If there is any cancer, this increases the chance that it will be found.

- **Chest X-ray.** An X-ray of the organs and bones inside the chest. An X-ray is a type of energy beam that can go through the body and onto film, making a picture of areas inside the body.

- **Complete blood count (CBC).** A procedure in which a sample of blood is drawn and checked for the following:

  - The number of red blood cells, white blood cells, and platelets.

  - The amount of hemoglobin (the protein that carries oxygen) in the red blood cells.

  - The portion of the blood sample made up of red blood cells.

- **Blood chemistry studies.** A procedure in which a blood sample is checked to measure the amounts of certain substances released into the blood by organs and tissues in the body. An unusual (higher or lower than normal) amount of a substance can be a sign of disease.

- **Sedimentation rate.** A procedure in which a sample of blood is drawn and checked for the rate at which the red blood cells settle to the bottom of the test tube. The sedimentation rate is a measure of how much inflammation is in the body. A higher than normal sedimentation rate may be a sign of lymphoma. Also called erythrocyte sedimentation rate, sed rate, or ESR.

- **Lymph node biopsy.** The removal of all or part of a lymph node. The lymph node may be removed during an image-guided CT scan or a thoracoscopy, mediastinoscopy, or laparoscopy. One of the following types of biopsies may be done:

  - **Excisional biopsy.** The removal of an entire lymph node.

  - **Incisional biopsy.** The removal of part of a lymph node.

  - **Core biopsy.** The removal of tissue from a lymph node using a wide needle.

  - **Fine-needle aspiration (FNA) biopsy.** The removal of tissue from a lymph node using a thin needle.

A pathologist views the tissue under a microscope to look for cancer cells, especially Reed-Sternberg cells. Reed-Sternberg cells are common in classical Hodgkin lymphoma.

The following test may be done on tissue that was removed:

- **Immunophenotyping.** A laboratory test used to identify cells, based on the types of antigens or markers on the surface of the cell. This test is used to diagnose the specific type of lymphoma by comparing the cancer cells to normal cells of the immune system.

What Is The Prognosis For Childhood Hodgkin Lymphoma?

The prognosis (chance of recovery) and treatment options depend on the following:

- The stage of the cancer.

- The size of the tumor.

- Whether there are B symptoms at diagnosis.

- The type of Hodgkin lymphoma.

- Certain features of the cancer cells.

- Whether there are too many white blood cells or too few red blood cells at the time of diagnosis.

- How well the tumor responds to initial treatment with chemotherapy.

- Whether the cancer is newly diagnosed or has recurred (come back).

The treatment options also depend on:

- The child's age and sex.
- The risk of long-term side effects.

Most children and adolescents with newly diagnosed Hodgkin lymphoma can be cured.

What Is The Treatment For Childhood Hodgkin Lymphoma?

Different types of treatment are available for children with Hodgkin lymphoma. Some treatments are standard and some are being tested in clinical trials. A treatment clinical trial is a research study meant to help improve current treatments or obtain information on new treatments for patients with cancer. Because cancer in children is rare, taking part in a clinical trial should be considered. Some clinical trials are open only to patients who have not started treatment.

The treatment of Hodgkin lymphoma in adolescents and young adults may be different than the treatment for children. Some adolescents and young adults are treated with an adult treatment regimen.

Five types of standard treatment are used:

Chemotherapy. Chemotherapy is a cancer treatment that uses drugs to stop the growth of cancer cells, either by killing the cells or by stopping them from dividing. When chemotherapy is taken by mouth or injected into a vein or muscle, the drugs enter the bloodstream and can reach cancer cells throughout the body (systemic chemotherapy). When chemotherapy is placed directly into the cerebrospinal fluid, an organ, or a body cavity such as the abdomen, the drugs mainly affect cancer cells in those areas (regional chemotherapy). Combination chemotherapy is treatment using more than one anticancer drug.

The way the chemotherapy is given depends on the risk group. For example, children with low-risk Hodgkin lymphoma receive fewer cycles of treatment, fewer anticancer drugs, and lower doses of anticancer drugs than children with high-risk lymphoma.

Radiation therapy. Radiation therapy is a cancer treatment that uses high-energy X-rays or other types of radiation to kill cancer cells or keep them from growing. There are two types of radiation therapy:

- **External radiation therapy** uses a machine outside the body to send radiation toward the cancer. Certain ways of giving radiation therapy can help keep radiation from damaging nearby healthy tissue. These types of external radiation therapy include the following:

- **Conformal radiation therapy.** Conformal radiation therapy is a type of external radiation therapy that uses a computer to make a 3-dimensional (3-D) picture of the tumor and shapes the radiation beams to fit the tumor.

- **Intensity-modulated radiation therapy (IMRT).** IMRT is a type of 3-dimensional (3-D) radiation therapy that uses a computer to make pictures of the size and shape of the tumor. Thin beams of radiation of different intensities (strengths) are aimed at the tumor from many angles.

- **Internal radiation therapy** uses a radioactive substance sealed in needles, seeds, wires, or catheters that are placed directly into or near the cancer.

Radiation therapy may be given, based on the child's risk group and chemotherapy regimen. External radiation therapy is used to treat childhood Hodgkin lymphoma. The radiation is given only to the lymph nodes or other areas with cancer. Internal radiation therapy is not used to treat Hodgkin lymphoma.

Targeted therapy. Targeted therapy is a type of treatment that uses drugs or other substances to identify and attack specific cancer cells without harming normal cells. Monoclonal antibody therapy and proteasome inhibitor therapy are being used in the treatment of childhood Hodgkin lymphoma.

Monoclonal antibody therapy is a cancer treatment that uses antibodies made in the laboratory from a single type of immune system cell. These antibodies can identify substances on cancer cells or normal substances that may help cancer cells grow. The antibodies attach to the substances and kill the cancer cells, block their growth, or keep them from spreading. Monoclonal antibodies are given by infusion. They may be used alone or to carry drugs, toxins, or radioactive material directly to cancer cells.

In children, rituximab may be used to treat refractory or recurrent Hodgkin lymphoma. Brentuximab, nivolumab, pembrolizumab, and atezolizumab are monoclonal antibodies being studied to treat children.

Proteasome inhibitor therapy is a type of targeted therapy that blocks the action of proteasomes (proteins that remove other proteins the body no longer needs) in cancer cells and may prevent the growth of tumors. Bortezomib is a proteasome inhibitor used to treat refractory or recurrent childhood Hodgkin lymphoma.

Surgery. Surgery may be done to remove as much of the tumor as possible for localized nodular lymphocyte-predominant childhood Hodgkin lymphoma.

High-dose chemotherapy with stem cell transplant. High-dose chemotherapy with stem cell transplant is a way of giving high doses of chemotherapy and replacing blood-forming cells destroyed by the cancer treatment. Stem cells (immature blood cells) are removed from the blood or bone marrow of the patient or a donor and are frozen and stored. After the chemotherapy is completed, the stored stem cells are thawed and given back to the patient through an infusion. These reinfused stem cells grow into (and restore) the body's blood cells.

Proton beam radiation therapy. Proton-beam therapy is a type of high-energy, external radiation therapy that uses streams of protons (small, positively-charged particles of matter) to make radiation. This type of radiation therapy may help lessen the damage to healthy tissue near the tumor.

Side Effects Of The Treatment

Children and adolescents may have treatment-related side effects that appear months or years after treatment for Hodgkin lymphoma. Some cancer treatments cause side effects that continue or appear months or years after cancer treatment has ended. These are called late effects. Because late effects affect health and development, regular follow-up exams are important.

Late effects of cancer treatment may include:

- Physical problems that affect the following:

    - Development of sex and reproductive organs.

    - Fertility (ability to have children).

    - Bone and muscle growth and development.

    - Thyroid, heart, or lung function.

    - Teeth, gums, and salivary gland function.

    - Spleen function (increased risk of infection).

- Changes in mood, feelings, thinking, learning, or memory.

- Second cancers (new types of cancer).

For female survivors of Hodgkin lymphoma, there is an increased risk of breast cancer. This risk depends on the amount of radiation therapy they received to the breast during treatment and the chemotherapy regimen used. The risk of breast cancer is decreased if these female survivors also received radiation therapy to the ovaries.

It is suggested that female survivors who received radiation therapy to the breast have a mammogram once a year starting 8 years after treatment or at age 25 years, whichever is later.

Female survivors of childhood Hodgkin lymphoma who have breast cancer have an increased risk of dying from the disease compared to patients with no history of Hodgkin lymphoma who have breast cancer.

Some late effects may be treated or controlled. It is important to talk with your child's doctors about the possible late effects caused by some treatments.

Childhood Non-Hodgkin Lymphoma

What Is Childhood Non-Hodgkin Lymphoma?

Childhood non-Hodgkin lymphoma is a type of cancer that forms in the lymph system, which is part of the body's immune system. Non-Hodgkin lymphoma can begin in B lymphocytes, T lymphocytes, or natural killer cells. Lymphocytes can also be found in the blood and collect in the lymph nodes, spleen, and thymus.

Non-Hodgkin lymphoma can occur in both adults and children. Treatment for children is different than treatment for adults.

What Are The Major Types Of Childhood Non-Hodgkin Lymphoma?

The type of lymphoma is determined by how the cells look under a microscope. The three major types of childhood non-Hodgkin lymphoma are:

Mature B-Cell Non-Hodgkin Lymphoma

Mature B-cell non-Hodgkin lymphomas include:

- **Burkitt and Burkitt-like lymphoma/leukemia**. Burkitt lymphoma and Burkitt leukemia are different forms of the same disease. Burkitt lymphoma/leukemia is an aggressive (fast-growing) disorder of B lymphocytes that is most common in children and young adults. It may form in the abdomen, Waldeyer's ring, testicles, bone, bone marrow, skin, or central nervous system (CNS). Burkitt leukemia may start in the lymph nodes as Burkitt lymphoma and then spread to the blood and bone marrow, or it may start in the blood and bone marrow without forming in the lymph nodes first. Both Burkitt leukemia and Burkitt lymphoma have been linked to infection with the *Epstein-Barr virus* (EBV), although EBV infection is more likely to occur in patients in Africa than in the United States. Burkitt and Burkitt-like lymphoma/leukemia are diagnosed when a sample of tissue is checked and a certain change to the c-myc gene is found.

- **Diffuse large B-cell lymphoma.** Diffuse large B-cell lymphoma is the most common type of non-Hodgkin lymphoma. It is a type of B-cell non-Hodgkin lymphoma that grows quickly in the lymph nodes. The spleen, liver, bone marrow, or other organs are also often affected. Diffuse large B-cell lymphoma occurs more often in adolescents than in children.

- **Primary mediastinal B-cell lymphoma.** A type of lymphoma that develops from B cells in the mediastinum (the area behind the breastbone). It may spread to nearby organs including the lungs and the sac around the heart. It may also spread to lymph nodes and distant organs including the kidneys. In children and adolescents, primary mediastinal B-cell lymphoma occurs more often in older adolescents.

Lymphoblastic Lymphoma

Lymphoblastic lymphoma is a type of lymphoma that mainly affects T-cell lymphocytes. It usually forms in the mediastinum (the area behind the breastbone). This causes trouble breathing, wheezing, trouble swallowing, or swelling of the head and neck. It may spread to lymph nodes, bone, bone marrow, skin, the CNS, abdominal organs, and other areas. Lymphoblastic lymphoma is a lot like acute lymphoblastic leukemia (ALL).

Anaplastic Large Cell Lymphoma

Anaplastic large cell lymphoma is a type of lymphoma that mainly affects T-cell lymphocytes. It usually forms in the lymph nodes, skin, or bone, and sometimes forms in the gastrointestinal tract, lung, tissue that covers the lungs, and muscle. Patients with anaplastic large cell lymphoma have a receptor, called CD30, on the surface of their T cells. In many children, anaplastic large cell lymphoma is marked by changes in the *ALK* gene that makes a protein called anaplastic lymphoma kinase. A pathologist checks for these cell and gene changes to help diagnose anaplastic large cell lymphoma.

Rare Types Of Non-Hodgkin Lymphoma

Some types of childhood non-Hodgkin lymphoma are less common. These include:

- **Pediatric-type follicular lymphoma.** In children, follicular lymphoma occurs mainly in males. It is more likely to be found in one area and does not spread to other places in the body. It usually forms in the tonsils and lymph nodes in the neck, but may also form in the testicles, kidney, gastrointestinal tract, and salivary gland.

- **Marginal zone lymphoma.** Marginal zone lymphoma is a type of lymphoma that tends to grow and spread slowly and is usually found at an early stage. It may be found in the lymph nodes or in areas outside the lymph nodes. Marginal zone lymphoma found outside the lymph nodes in children is called mucosa-associated lymphoid tissue (MALT) lymphoma and may be linked to *Helicobacter pylori* infection of the gastrointestinal tract and Chlamydophila psittaci infection of the conjunctival membrane which lines the eye.

- **Primary central nervous system (CNS) lymphoma.** Primary CNS lymphoma is extremely rare in children.

- **Peripheral T-cell lymphoma.** Peripheral T-cell lymphoma is an aggressive (fast-growing) non-Hodgkin lymphoma that begins in mature T lymphocytes. The T lymphocytes mature in the thymus gland and travel to other parts of the lymph system, such as the lymph nodes, bone marrow, and spleen.

- **Cutaneous T-cell lymphoma.** Cutaneous T-cell lymphoma begins in the skin and can cause the skin to thicken or form a tumor. It is very rare in children, but is more common in adolescents and young adults. There are different types of cutaneous T-cell lymphoma, such as cutaneous anaplastic large cell lymphoma, subcutaneous panniculitis-like T-cell lymphoma, gamma-delta T-cell lymphoma, and mycosis fungoides. Mycosis fungoides rarely occurs in children and adolescents.

What Are The Risk Factors For Childhood Non-Hodgkin Lymphoma?

Past treatment for cancer and having a weakened immune system affect the risk of having childhood non-Hodgkin lymphoma. Anything that increases your risk of getting a disease is called a risk factor. Having a risk factor does not mean that you will get cancer; not having risk factors doesn't mean that you will not get cancer. Talk with your child's doctor if you think your child may be at risk.

Possible risk factors for childhood non-Hodgkin lymphoma include the following:

- Past treatment for cancer.

- Being infected with the *Epstein-Barr* virus or human immunodeficiency virus (HIV).

- Having a weakened immune system after a transplant or from medicines given after a transplant.

- Having certain inherited diseases of the immune system.

If lymphoma or lymphoproliferative disease is linked to a weakened immune system from certain inherited diseases, HIV infection, a transplant or medicines given after a transplant, the condition is called lymphoproliferative disease associated with immunodeficiency. The different types of lymphoproliferative disease associated with immunodeficiency include:

- Lymphoproliferative disease associated with primary immunodeficiency.

- HIV-associated non-Hodgkin lymphoma.

- Post-transplant lymphoproliferative disease.

What Are The Signs And Symptoms For Childhood Non-Hodgkin Lymphoma?

These and other signs may be caused by childhood non-Hodgkin lymphoma or by other conditions. Check with a doctor if your child has any of the following:

- Trouble breathing.

- Wheezing.

- Coughing.

- High-pitched breathing sounds.

- Swelling of the head, neck, upper body, or arms.

- Trouble swallowing.

- Painless swelling of the lymph nodes in the neck, underarm, stomach, or groin.

- Painless lump or swelling in a testicle.

- Fever for no known reason.

- Weight loss for no known reason.

- Night sweats.

How Is Childhood Non-Hodgkin Lymphoma Diagnosed?

The following tests and procedures may be used to detect (find) and diagnose childhood non-Hodgkin lymphoma:

- **Physical exam and history**. An exam of the body to check general signs of health, including checking for signs of disease, such as lumps or anything else that seems unusual. A history of the patient's health habits and past illnesses and treatments will also be taken.

- **Blood chemistry studies.** A procedure in which a blood sample is checked to measure the amounts of certain substances released into the blood by organs and tissues in the body, including electrolytes, uric acid, blood urea nitrogen (BUN), creatinine, and liver function values. An unusual (higher or lower than normal) amount of a substance can be a sign of disease.

- **Liver function tests.** A procedure in which a blood sample is checked to measure the amounts of certain substances released into the blood by the liver. A higher than normal amount of a substance can be a sign of cancer.

- **Computerized tomography (CT) scan.** A procedure that makes a series of detailed pictures of areas inside the body, taken from different angles. The pictures are made by a computer linked to an X-ray machine. A dye may be injected into a vein or swallowed to help the organs or tissues show up more clearly. This procedure is also called computed tomography, computerized tomography, or computerized axial tomography (CAT) scan.

- **PET scan (positron emission tomography scan).** A procedure to find malignant tumor cells in the body. A small amount of radioactive glucose (sugar) is injected into a vein. The PET scanner rotates around the body and makes a picture of where glucose is being used in the body. Malignant tumor cells show up brighter in the picture because they are more active and take up more glucose than normal cells do. Sometimes a PET scan and a CT scan are done at the same time. If there is any cancer, this increases the chance that it will be found.

- **MRI (magnetic resonance imaging).** A procedure that uses a magnet, radio waves, and a computer to make a series of detailed pictures of areas inside the body. This procedure is also called nuclear magnetic resonance imaging (NMRI).

- **Lumbar puncture.** A procedure used to collect cerebrospinal fluid (CSF) from the spinal column. This is done by placing a needle between two bones in the spine and into the CSF around the spinal cord and removing a sample of the fluid. The sample of CSF is checked under a microscope for signs that the cancer has spread to the brain and spinal cord. This procedure is also called an LP or spinal tap.

- **Chest X-ray.** An X-ray of the organs and bones inside the chest. An X-ray is a type of energy beam that can go through the body and onto film, making a picture of areas inside the body.

- **Ultrasound exam.** A procedure in which high-energy sound waves (ultrasound) are bounced off internal tissues or organs and make echoes. The echoes form a picture of body tissues called a sonogram. The picture can be printed to be looked at later.

Biopsy

Cells and tissues are removed during a biopsy so they can be viewed under a microscope by a pathologist to check for signs of cancer. Because treatment depends on the type of non-Hodgkin lymphoma, biopsy samples should be checked by a pathologist who has experience in diagnosing childhood non-Hodgkin lymphoma.

One of the following types of biopsies may be done:

- **Excisional biopsy.** The removal of an entire lymph node or lump of tissue.

- **Incisional biopsy.** The removal of part of a lump, lymph node, or sample of tissue.

- **Core biopsy.** The removal of tissue or part of a lymph node using a wide needle.

- **Fine-needle aspiration (FNA) biopsy.** The removal of tissue or part of a lymph node using a thin needle.

The procedure used to remove the sample of tissue depends on where the tumor is in the body:

- **Bone marrow aspiration and biopsy.** The removal of bone marrow and a small piece of bone by inserting a hollow needle into the hipbone or breastbone.

- **Mediastinoscopy.** A surgical procedure to look at the organs, tissues, and lymph nodes between the lungs for abnormal areas. An incision (cut) is made at the top of the breastbone and a mediastinoscope is inserted into the chest. A mediastinoscope is a thin, tube-like instrument with a light and a lens for viewing. It also has a tool to remove tissue or lymph node samples, which are checked under a microscope for signs of cancer.

- **Anterior mediastinotomy.** A surgical procedure to look at the organs and tissues between the lungs and between the breastbone and heart for abnormal areas. An incision (cut) is made next to the breastbone and a mediastinoscope is inserted into the chest. A mediastinoscope is a thin, tube-like instrument with a light and a lens for viewing. It also has a tool to remove tissue or lymph node samples, which are checked under a microscope for signs of cancer. This is also called the Chamberlain procedure.

- **Thoracentesis.** The removal of fluid from the space between the lining of the chest and the lung, using a needle. A pathologist views the fluid under a microscope to look for cancer cells.

If cancer is found, the following tests may be done to study the cancer cells:

- **Immunohistochemistry.** A laboratory test that uses antibodies to check for certain antigens in a sample of tissue. The antibody is usually linked to a radioactive substance or a dye that causes the tissue to light up under a microscope. This type of test may be used to tell the difference between different types of cancer.

- **Flow cytometry.** A laboratory test that measures the number of cells in a sample, the percentage of live cells in a sample, and certain characteristics of cells, such as size, shape, and the presence of tumor markers on the cell surface. The cells are stained with a light-sensitive dye, placed in a fluid, and passed in a stream before a laser or other type of light. The measurements are based on how the light-sensitive dye reacts to the light.

- **Cytogenetic analysis.** A laboratory test in which cells in a sample of tissue are viewed under a microscope to look for certain changes in the chromosomes.

- **FISH (fluorescence in situ hybridization).** A laboratory test used to look at genes or chromosomes in cells and tissues. Pieces of deoxyribonucleic acid (DNA) that contain a fluorescent dye are made in the laboratory and added to cells or tissues on a glass slide. When these pieces of DNA attach to certain genes or areas of chromosomes on the slide, they light up when viewed under a microscope with a special light. This type of test is used to find certain gene changes.

- **Immunophenotyping.** A laboratory test used to identify cells, based on the types of antigens or markers on the surface of the cell. This test is used to diagnose specific types of lymphoma by comparing the cancer cells to normal cells of the immune system.

What Is The Prognosis For Childhood Non-Hodgkin Lymphoma?

Certain factors affect prognosis (chance of recovery) and treatment options. The prognosis (chance of recovery) and treatment options depend on:

- The type of lymphoma.
- Where the tumor is in the body when the tumor is diagnosed.
- The stage of the cancer.
- Whether there are certain changes in the chromosomes.
- The type of initial treatment.
- Whether the lymphoma responded to initial treatment.

- The patient's age and general health.

What Is The Treatment For Childhood Non-Hodgkin Lymphoma?

Different types of treatment are available for children with non-Hodgkin lymphoma. Some treatments are standard (the currently used treatment), and some are being tested in clinical trials. Taking part in a clinical trial should be considered for all children with non-Hodgkin lymphoma. Some clinical trials are open only to patients who have not started treatment.

Healthcare Treatment

Treatment will be overseen by a pediatric oncologist, a doctor who specializes in treating children with cancer. The pediatric oncologist works with other healthcare providers who are experts in treating children with non-Hodgkin lymphoma and who specialize in certain areas of medicine. These may include the following specialists:

- Pediatrician
- Radiation oncologist
- Pediatric hematologist
- Pediatric surgeon
- Pediatric nurse specialist
- Rehabilitation specialist
- Psychologist
- Social worker

Standard Treatment For Childhood Non-Hodgkin Lymphoma

Chemotherapy. Chemotherapy is a cancer treatment that uses drugs to stop the growth of cancer cells, either by killing the cells or by stopping them from dividing. When chemotherapy is taken by mouth or injected into a vein or muscle, the drugs enter the bloodstream and can reach cancer cells throughout the body (systemic chemotherapy). When chemotherapy is placed directly into the cerebrospinal fluid (intrathecal chemotherapy), an organ, or a body cavity such as the abdomen, the drugs mainly affect cancer cells in those areas. Combination chemotherapy is treatment using two or more anticancer drugs.

The way the chemotherapy is given depends on the type and stage of the cancer being treated.

Intrathecal chemotherapy may be used to treat childhood non-Hodgkin lymphoma that has spread, or may spread, to the brain. When used to lessen the chance cancer will spread to the brain, it is called CNS prophylaxis. Intrathecal chemotherapy is given in addition to chemotherapy by mouth or vein. Higher than usual doses of chemotherapy may also be used as CNS prophylaxis.

Radiation therapy. Radiation therapy is a cancer treatment that uses high-energy X-rays or other types of radiation to kill cancer cells or keep them from growing. There are two types of radiation therapy:

- **External radiation therapy** uses a machine outside the body to send radiation toward the cancer.

- **Internal radiation therapy** uses a radioactive substance sealed in needles, seeds, wires, or catheters that are placed directly into or near the cancer.

The way the radiation therapy is given depends on the type of non-Hodgkin lymphoma being treated. External radiation therapy may be used to treat childhood non-Hodgkin lymphoma that has spread, or may spread, to the brain and spinal cord. Internal radiation therapy is not used to treat non-Hodgkin lymphoma.

High-dose chemotherapy with stem cell transplant. This treatment is a way of giving high doses of chemotherapy and then replacing blood-forming cells destroyed by the cancer treatment. Stem cells (immature blood cells) are removed from the bone marrow or blood of the patient or a donor and are frozen and stored. After the chemotherapy is completed, the stored stem cells are thawed and given back to the patient through an infusion. These reinfused stem cells grow into (and restore) the body's blood cells.

Targeted therapy. Targeted therapy is a type of treatment that uses drugs or other substances to identify and attack specific cancer cells without harming normal cells. Monoclonal antibodies, tyrosine kinase inhibitors, and immunotoxins are three types of targeted therapy being used or studied in the treatment of childhood non-Hodgkin lymphoma.

Monoclonal antibody therapy is a cancer treatment that uses antibodies made in the laboratory from a single type of immune system cell. These antibodies can identify substances on cancer cells or normal substances that may help cancer cells grow. The antibodies attach to the substances and kill the cancer cells, block their growth, or keep them from spreading. Monoclonal antibodies are given by infusion. They may be used alone or to carry drugs, toxins, or radioactive material directly to cancer cells.

- Rituximab is used to treat several types of childhood non-Hodgkin lymphoma.

- Brentuximab vedotin is a monoclonal antibody combined with an anticancer drug that is used to treat anaplastic large cell lymphoma.

A bispecific monoclonal antibody is made up of two different monoclonal antibodies that bind to two different substances and kills cancer cells. Bispecific monoclonal antibody therapy is used in the treatment of Burkitt and Burkitt-like lymphoma /leukemia and diffuse large B-cell lymphoma.

Tyrosine kinase inhibitors (TKIs) block signals that tumors need to grow. Some TKIs also keep tumors from growing by preventing the growth of new blood vessels to the tumors. Other types of kinase inhibitors, such as crizotinib, are being studied for childhood non-Hodgkin lymphoma.

Immunotoxins can bind to cancer cells and kill them. Denileukin diftitox is an immunotoxin used to treat cutaneous T-cell lymphoma.

Targeted therapy is being studied for the treatment of childhood non-Hodgkin lymphoma that has recurred (come back).

Other drug therapy. Retinoids are drugs related to vitamin A. Retinoid therapy with bexarotene is used to treat several types of cutaneous T-cell lymphoma. Steroids are hormones made naturally in the body. They can also be made in a laboratory and used as drugs. Steroid therapy is used to treat cutaneous T-cell lymphoma.

Phototherapy. Phototherapy is a cancer treatment that uses a drug and a certain type of laser light to kill cancer cells. A drug that is not active until it is exposed to light is injected into a vein. The drug collects more in cancer cells than in normal cells. For skin cancer in the skin, laser light is shined onto the skin and the drug becomes active and kills the cancer cells. Phototherapy is used in the treatment of cutaneous T-cell lymphoma.

Side Effects Of The Treatment

Some cancer treatments cause side effects months or years after treatment has ended.

Side effects from cancer treatment that begin during or after treatment and continue for months or years are called late effects. Late effects of cancer treatment may include the following:

- Physical problems.
- Changes in mood, feelings, thinking, learning, or memory.
- Second cancers (new types of cancer).

Some late effects may be treated or controlled. It is important to talk with your child's doctors about the effects cancer treatment can have on your child.

Chapter 24

Esthesioneuroblastoma

Esthesioneuroblastoma (olfactory neuroblastoma) is a tumor that begins in the olfactory bulb in the brain. The olfactory bulb connects to the nerve that is important to the sense of smell. Even though it is very rare, esthesioneuroblastoma is the most common tumor of the nasal cavity in children.

Respiratory System

The nose opens into the nasal cavity, which is divided into two nasal passages. Air moves through these passages during breathing. The nasal cavity lies above the bone that forms the roof of the mouth and curves down at the back to join the throat. The area just inside the nostrils is called the nasal vestibule. A small area of special cells in the roof of each nasal passage sends signals to the brain to give the sense of smell.

Together the paranasal sinuses and the nasal cavity filter and warm the air, and make it moist before it goes into the lungs.

(Source: "Paranasal Sinus And Nasal Cavity Cancer Treatment (PDQ®)—Patient Version," National Cancer Institute (NCI).)

Most children have a tumor in the nose or nasal sinus at the time of diagnosis. The tumor may spread into the bone around the eyes, sinuses, and the front part of the brain. The disease rarely spreads to other parts of the body. Esthesioneuroblastoma usually appears during the teen years.

About This Chapter: This chapter includes text excerpted from "Unusual Cancers Of Childhood Treatment (PDQ®)–Patient Version—Unusual Cancers Of The Head And Neck," National Cancer Institute (NCI), November 16, 2017.

Signs And Symptoms And Staging Tests

Esthesioneuroblastoma may cause any of the following signs and symptoms. Check with your child's doctor if your child has any of the following:

- Headache

- Blocked nose

- Nosebleeds

- Change in or loss of the sense of smell

- Bulging of the eye

- Frequent sinus infections

Other conditions that are not esthesioneuroblastoma may cause these same signs and symptoms.

Esthesioneuroblastoma has usually spread by the time it is diagnosed. Tests to stage esthesioneuroblastoma may include the following:

- Positron emission tomography-computed tomography (PET-CT) scan: Sometimes a PET scan and a CT scan are done at the same time. If there is any cancer, this increases the chance that it will be found.

Cause

The cause of olfactory neuroblastoma is not well understood. No specific environmental or genetic causes have been confirmed, although comprehensive genetic testing of affected individuals has identified regions within chromosomes 2, 5, 6, 7, and 20 that may be involved.

(Source: "Olfactory Neuroblastoma," Genetic and Rare Diseases Information Center (GARD), National Center for Advancing Translational Sciences (NCATS).)

Treatment

Treatment of esthesioneuroblastoma in children may include the following:

- Surgery for tumors that are in the nose only. External radiation therapy may also be given if the tumor was not completely removed.

- Surgery followed by radiation therapy for tumors that have spread to the nasal sinus.

- Chemotherapy and radiation therapy given alone or at the same time followed by surgery to remove the tumor for tumors that have spread outside the nose and nasal sinus but not to other parts of the body.

- Chemotherapy, radiation therapy, and surgery for tumors that have spread to other parts of the body.

Diagnosis

A diagnosis of olfactory neuroblastoma may be suspected based on presenting signs and symptoms and imaging studies such as magnetic resonance imaging (MRI) and CT scans. The diagnosis is confirmed through biopsy of the tumor.

(Source: "Olfactory Neuroblastoma," Genetic and Rare Diseases Information Center (GARD), National Center for Advancing Translational Sciences (NCATS).)

Prognosis

The prognosis (chance of recovery) depends on the following:

- Whether the tumor was completely removed by surgery.

- Whether the cancer is only in the nose or if it has spread to nearby nasal sinuses, lymph nodes, or to other parts of the body.

Chapter 25

Melanoma And Other Skin Cancers

Skin cancer is the most common cancer in the United States. Some people are at higher risk of skin cancer than others, but anyone can get it. The most preventable cause of skin cancer is overexposure to ultraviolet (UV) light, either from the sun or from artificial sources like tanning beds.

What Is Skin Cancer?

Skin cancer is the most common form of cancer in the United States. The two most common types of skin cancer—basal cell and squamous cell carcinomas (SCC)—are highly curable, but can be disfiguring and costly to treat. Melanoma, the third most common skin cancer, is more dangerous and causes the most deaths. The majority of these three types of skin cancer are caused by overexposure to ultraviolet (UV) light.

Ultraviolet (UV) Light

Ultraviolet (UV) rays are an invisible kind of radiation that comes from the sun, tanning beds, and sunlamps. UV rays can penetrate and change skin cells.

The three types of UV rays are ultraviolet A (UVA), ultraviolet B (UVB), and ultraviolet C (UVC):

- More UVA rays reach the earth's surface than the other types of UV rays. UVA rays can reach deep into human skin, UVA rays can damaging connective tissue and the skin's deoxyribonucleic acid (DNA).

About This Chapter: Text in this chapter begins with excerpts from "Skin Cancer—Basic Information About Skin Cancer," Centers for Disease Control and Prevention (CDC), April 25, 2017; Text under the heading "Skin Cancer Treatment" is excerpted from "Skin Cancer Treatment (PDQ®)—Patient Version," National Cancer Institute (NCI), August 28, 2017.

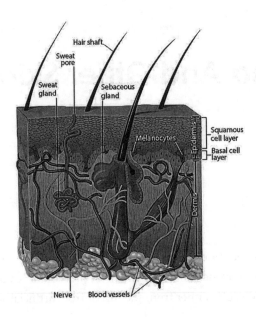

Figure 25.1. Basal Cell Layer Of The Skin

Basal cell carcinoma begins in the basal cell layer of the skin. Squamous cell carcinoma begins in the squamous layer of the skin. Melanoma begins in the melanocytes, which are the cells that make melanin, the pigment that gives skin its color.

- Most UVB rays are absorbed by the ozone layer, so fewer of them reach the earth's surface compared to UVA rays. UVB rays, which help produce vitamin D in the skin, don't reach as far into the skin as UVA rays, but they can still cause sunburn and damage DNA.

- UVC rays are very dangerous, but they are absorbed completely by the ozone layer and do not reach the earth's surface.

In addition to causing sunburn, too much exposure to UV rays can change skin texture, cause the skin to age prematurely, and can lead to skin cancer. UV rays also have been linked to eye conditions such as cataracts.

The National Weather Service (NWS) and the Environmental Protection Agency (EPA) developed the UV Index to forecast the risk of overexposure to UV rays. It lets you know how much caution you should take when spending time outdoors.

The UV Index predicts exposure levels on a 0–15 scale; higher levels indicate a higher risk of overexposure. Calculated on a next-day basis for dozens of cities across the United States, the UV Index takes into account clouds and other local conditions that affect the amount of UV rays reaching the ground.

What Are The Risk Factors For Skin Cancer?

People with certain risk factors are more likely than others to develop skin cancer. Risk factors vary for different types of skin cancer, but some general risk factors are having:

- A lighter natural skin color.
- Family history of skin cancer.
- A personal history of skin cancer.
- Exposure to the sun through work and play.
- A history of sunburns, especially early in life.
- A history of indoor tanning.
- Skin that burns, freckles, reddens easily, or becomes painful in the sun.
- Blue or green eyes.
- Blond or red hair.
- Certain types and a large number of moles.

Tanning And Burning

Ultraviolet (UV) rays come from the sun or from indoor tanning (using a tanning bed, booth, or sunlamp to get tan). When UV rays reach the skin's inner layer, the skin makes more melanin. Melanin is the pigment that colors the skin. It moves toward the outer layers of the skin and becomes visible as a tan.

A tan does not indicate good health. A tan is a response to injury, because skin cells signal that they have been hurt by UV rays by producing more pigment.

People burn or tan depending on their skin type, the time of year, and how long they are exposed to UV rays. The six types of skin, based on how likely it is to tan or burn, are:

- Always burns, never tans.
- Burns easily, tans minimally.
- Burns moderately, tans gradually to light brown.
- Burns minimally, always tans well to moderately brown.

- Rarely burns, tans profusely to dark.

- Never burns, deeply pigmented, least sensitive.

Although everyone's skin can be damaged by UV exposure, people with skin types I and II are at the highest risk.

What Are The Symptoms Of Skin Cancer?

A change in your skin is the most common sign of skin cancer. This could be a new growth, a sore that doesn't heal, or a change in a mole. Not all skin cancers look the same.

A simple way to remember the signs of melanoma is to remember the A-B-C-D-Es of melanoma:

- "A" stands for asymmetrical. Does the mole or spot have an irregular shape with two parts that look very different?

- "B" stands for border. Is the border irregular or jagged?

- "C" is for color. Is the color uneven?

- "D" is for diameter. Is the mole or spot larger than the size of a pea?

- "E" is for evolving. Has the mole or spot changed during the past few weeks or months?

Talk to your doctor if you notice changes in your skin such as a new growth, a sore that doesn't heal, a change in an old growth, or any of the A-B-C-D-Es of melanoma.

What Can I Do To Reduce My Risk Of Skin Cancer?

Protection from ultraviolet (UV) radiation is important all year round, not just during the summer or at the beach. UV rays from the sun can reach you on cloudy and hazy days, as well as bright and sunny days. UV rays also reflect off of surfaces like water, cement, sand, and snow. Indoor tanning (using a tanning bed, booth, or sunlamp to get tan) exposes users to UV radiation.

The hours between 10 a.m. and 4 p.m. Daylight Saving Time (DST) (9 a.m. to 3 p.m. standard time) are the most hazardous for UV exposure outdoors in the continental United States. UV rays from sunlight are the greatest during the late spring and early summer in North America.

The centers for disease control and prevention (CDC) recommends easy options for protection from UV radiation:

- Stay in the shade, especially during midday hours

- Wear clothing that covers your arms and legs

- Wear a hat with a wide brim to shade your face, head, ears, and neck

- Wear sunglasses that wrap around and block both UVA and UVB rays

- Use sunscreen with a sun protection factor (SPF) of 15 or higher, and both UVA and UVB (broad spectrum) protection

- Avoid indoor tanning

What Screening Tests Are There?

The U.S. Preventive Services Task Force (USPSTF) has concluded there is not enough evidence to recommend for or against routine screening (total body examination by a doctor) to find skin cancers early. This recommendation is for people who do not have a history of skin cancer and who do not have any suspicious moles or other spots. Report any unusual moles or changes in your skin to your doctor. Also talk to your doctor if you are at increased risk of skin cancer.

Treatment For Skin Cancer

Treatment is more likely to work well when cancer is found early. If not treated, some types of skin cancer cells can spread to other tissues and organs. Treatments include surgery, radiation therapy, chemotherapy, photodynamic therapy (PDT), and biologic therapy. PDT uses a drug and a type of laser light to kill cancer cells. Biologic therapy boosts your body's own ability to fight cancer.

(Source: "Skin Cancer," MedlinePlus, National Institutes of Health (NIH).)

Skin Cancer Treatment

Six types of standard treatment are used:

Surgery

One or more of the following surgical procedures may be used to treat nonmelanoma skin cancer or actinic keratosis:

- Mohs micrographic surgery: The tumor is cut from the skin in thin layers. During surgery, the edges of the tumor and each layer of tumor removed are viewed through a microscope to check for cancer cells. Layers continue to be removed until no more cancer cells are seen. This type of surgery removes as little normal tissue as possible and is often used to remove skin cancer on the face.

- Simple excision: The tumor is cut from the skin along with some of the normal skin around it.

- Shave excision: The abnormal area is shaved off the surface of the skin with a small blade.

- Electrodesiccation and curettage: The tumor is cut from the skin with a curette (a sharp, spoon-shaped tool). A needle-shaped electrode is then used to treat the area with an electric current that stops the bleeding and destroys cancer cells that remain around the edge of the wound. The process may be repeated one to three times during the surgery to remove all of the cancer.

- Cryosurgery: A treatment that uses an instrument to freeze and destroy abnormal tissue, such as carcinoma in situ. This type of treatment is also called cryotherapy.

- Laser surgery: A surgical procedure that uses a laser beam (a narrow beam of intense light) as a knife to make bloodless cuts in tissue or to remove a surface lesion such as a tumor.

- Dermabrasion: Removal of the top layer of skin using a rotating wheel or small particles to rub away skin cells.

Radiation Therapy

Radiation therapy is a cancer treatment that uses high-energy x-rays or other types of radiation to kill cancer cells or keep them from growing. There are two types of radiation therapy:

- External radiation therapy uses a machine outside the body to send radiation toward the cancer.

- Internal radiation therapy uses a radioactive substance sealed in needles, seeds, wires, or catheters that are placed directly into or near the cancer.

The way the radiation therapy is given depends on the type of cancer being treated. External radiation therapy is used to treat skin cancer.

Chemotherapy

Chemotherapy is a cancer treatment that uses drugs to stop the growth of cancer cells, either by killing the cells or by stopping them from dividing. When chemotherapy is taken by mouth or injected into a vein or muscle, the drugs enter the bloodstream and can reach cancer cells throughout the body (systemic chemotherapy). When chemotherapy is placed directly into the cerebrospinal fluid, an organ, or a body cavity such as the abdomen, the drugs mainly affect cancer cells in those areas (regional chemotherapy). Chemotherapy for nonmelanoma skin cancer and actinic keratosis is usually topical (applied to the skin in a cream or lotion). The way the chemotherapy is given depends on the condition being treated.

Retinoids (drugs related to vitamin A) are sometimes used to treat squamous cell carcinoma of the skin.

Photodynamic Therapy

Photodynamic therapy (PDT) is a cancer treatment that uses a drug and a certain type of laser light to kill cancer cells. A drug that is not active until it is exposed to light is injected into a vein. The drug collects more in cancer cells than in normal cells. For skin cancer, laser light is shined onto the skin and the drug becomes active and kills the cancer cells. Photodynamic therapy causes little damage to healthy tissue.

Biologic Therapy

Biologic therapy is a treatment that uses the patient's immune system to fight cancer. Substances made by the body or made in a laboratory are used to boost, direct, or restore the body's natural defenses against cancer. This type of cancer treatment is also called biotherapy or immunotherapy.

Interferon and imiquimod are biologic agents used to treat skin cancer. Interferon (by injection) may be used to treat squamous cell carcinoma of the skin. Topical imiquimod therapy (a cream applied to the skin) may be used to treat some small basal cell carcinomas.

Targeted Therapy

Targeted therapy is a type of treatment that uses drugs or other substances to attack cancer cells. Targeted therapies usually cause less harm to normal cells than chemotherapy or radiation therapy do.

Targeted therapy with a signal transduction inhibitor is used to treat basal cell carcinoma. Signal transduction inhibitors block signals that are passed from one molecule to another inside a cell. Blocking these signals may kill cancer cells. Vismodegib and sonidegib are signal transduction inhibitors used to treat basal cell carcinoma.

Chapter 26

Nasopharyngeal Cancer

Nasopharyngeal cancer is a disease in which malignant (cancer) cells form in the lining of the nasal cavity (inside of the nose) and throat. It is rare in children younger than 10 and more common in adolescents.

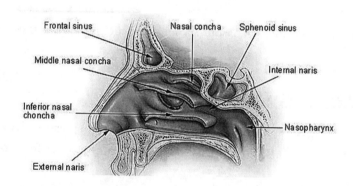

Figure 26.1. Nose And Nasal Cavity

(Source: "Respiratory System—Nose, Nasal Cavities, And Paranasal Sinuses," National Cancer Institute (NCI).)

Risk Factors

The risk of nasopharyngeal cancer is greatly increased by having an infection with the *Epstein-Barr* virus (EBV), which infects cells of the immune system. The risk of nasopharyngeal cancer is also increased by having a certain marker on cells.

About This Chapter: This chapter includes text excerpted from "Unusual Cancers Of Childhood Treatment (PDQ®)—Patient Version," National Cancer Institute (NCI), November 16, 2017.

Signs And Symptoms

Nasopharyngeal cancer may cause any of the following signs and symptoms. Check with your child's doctor if your child has any of the following:

- Painless lumps in the neck

- Nosebleeds

- Blocked or stuffy nose

- Headache

- Pain in the ear

- Ear infection

- Problems moving the jaw

- Hearing loss

- Double vision

Other conditions that are not nasopharyngeal cancer may cause these same signs and symptoms.

Diagnostic And Staging Tests

When nasopharyngeal is diagnosed, it usually has already spread to lymph nodes in the neck and bones of the skull. It may also spread to the nose, mouth, throat, bones, lung, and/or liver.

Tests to diagnose and stage nasopharyngeal cancer may include the following:

- Physical exam and history.

- Magnetic resonance imaging (MRI) of the head and neck.

- Computed tomography (CT) scan of the chest and abdomen. Sometimes a Positron emission tomography (PET) scan and a CT scan are done at the same time. If there is any cancer, this increases the chance that it will be found.

- Endoscopy.

- Bone scan.

- Biopsy.

Other tests used to diagnose or stage nasopharyngeal cancer include the following:

- **Neurological exam.** A series of questions and tests to check the brain, spinal cord, and nerve function. The exam checks a person's mental status, coordination, and ability to walk normally, and how well the muscles, senses, and reflexes work. This may also be called a neuro exam or a neurologic exam.

- **Nasoscopy.** A procedure in which a doctor inserts a nasoscope (a thin, lighted tube) into the patient's nose to look for abnormal areas.

- *Epstein-Barr* **virus (EBV) tests.** Blood tests to check for antibodies to the *Epstein-Barr* virus and deoxyribonucleic acid (DNA) markers of the *Epstein-Barr* virus. These are found in the blood of patients who have been infected with EBV.

Treatment

Treatment of nasopharyngeal cancer in children may include the following:

- Chemotherapy given before or at the same time as external radiation therapy.

- Interferon given with external radiation therapy alone or with chemotherapy and external radiation therapy.

- Chemotherapy and external radiation therapy (ERT) given with internal radiation therapy (IRT).

- External radiation therapy.

- Surgery.

- A clinical trial of chemotherapy followed by immunotherapy (EBV-specific cytotoxic T-lymphocytes).

Young patients are more likely than adults to have problems caused by treatment, including second cancers.

Prognosis

The prognosis (chance of recovery) for most young patients with nasopharyngeal cancer is very good.

Chapter 27

Neuroblastoma: Cancer Of The Nervous System

What Is Neuroblastoma?

Neuroblastoma is a disease in which malignant (cancer) cells form in neuroblasts (immature nerve tissue) in the adrenal gland, neck, chest, or spinal cord.

Neuroblastoma often begins in the nerve tissue of the adrenal glands. There are two adrenal glands, one on top of each kidney in the back of the upper abdomen. The adrenal glands make important hormones that help control heart rate, blood pressure, blood sugar, and the way the body reacts to stress.

Neuroblastoma may also begin in nerve tissue in the neck, chest, abdomen or pelvis. Neuroblastoma most often begins in infancy and may be diagnosed in the first month of life. It is found when the tumor begins to grow and cause signs or symptoms. Sometimes it forms before birth and is found during a fetal ultrasound.

By the time neuroblastoma is diagnosed, the cancer has usually metastasized (spread). Neuroblastoma spreads most often to the lymph nodes, bones, bone marrow, and liver. In infants, it also spreads to the skin.

What Is The Cause Of Neuroblastoma?

Gene mutations that increase the risk of neuroblastoma are sometimes inherited (passed from the parent to the child). In children with a gene mutation, neuroblastoma usually occurs at a younger age and more than one tumor may form in the adrenal glands.

About This Chapter: This chapter includes text excerpted from "Neuroblastoma Treatment (PDQ®)—Patient Version," National Cancer Institute (NCI), October 6, 2017.

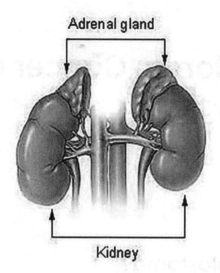

Figure 27.1. Adrenal Gland

(Source: "Endocrine Glands And Their Hormones—Adrenal Gland," National Cancer Institute (NCI).)

What Are The Signs And Symptoms Of Neuroblastoma?

The most common signs and symptoms of neuroblastoma are caused by the tumor pressing on nearby tissues as it grows or by cancer spreading to the bone. These and other signs and symptoms may be caused by neuroblastoma or by other conditions.

Check with your child's doctor if your child has any of the following:

- Lump in the abdomen, neck, or chest

- Bulging eyes

- Dark circles around the eyes ("black eyes")

- Bone pain

- Swollen stomach and trouble breathing (in infants)

- Painless, bluish lumps under the skin (in infants)

- Weakness or paralysis (loss of ability to move a body part)

Less common signs and symptoms of neuroblastoma include the following:

- Fever

- Shortness of breath

- Feeling tired

- Easy bruising or bleeding

- Petechiae (flat, pinpoint spots under the skin caused by bleeding)

- High blood pressure

- Severe watery diarrhea

- Horner syndrome (droopy eyelid, smaller pupil, and less sweating on one side of the face)

- Jerky muscle movements

- Uncontrolled eye movements

How Is Neuroblastoma Diagnosed?

The following tests and procedures may be used:

- **Physical exam and history.** An exam of the body to check general signs of health, including checking for signs of disease, such as lumps or anything else that seems unusual. A history of the patient's health habits and past illnesses and treatments will also be taken.

- **Neurological exam.** A series of questions and tests to check the brain, spinal cord, and nerve function. The exam checks a person's mental status, coordination, and ability to walk normally, and how well the muscles, senses, and reflexes work. This may also be called a neuro exam or a neurologic exam.

- **Urine catecholamine studies.** A procedure in which a urine sample is checked to measure the amount of certain substances, vanillylmandelic acid (VMA) and homovanillic acid (HVA), that are made when catecholamines break down and are released into the urine. A higher than normal amount of VMA or HVA can be a sign of neuroblastoma.

- **Blood chemistry studies.** A procedure in which a blood sample is checked to measure the amounts of certain substances released into the blood by organs and tissues in the body. An unusual (higher or lower than normal) amount of a substance can be a sign of disease.

- **X-ray.** An X-ray is a type of energy beam that can go through the body and onto film, making a picture of areas inside the body.

- **Computed tomography (CT) scan (Computerized axial tomography (CAT) scan).** A procedure that makes a series of detailed pictures of areas inside the body, take from different angles. The pictures are made by a computer linked to an X-ray machine. A dye may be injected into a vein or swallowed to help the organs or tissues show up more clearly. This procedure is also called computed tomography (CT), computerized tomography, or computerized axial tomography (CAT).

- **Magnetic resonance imaging (MRI) with gadolinium.** A procedure that uses a magnet, radio waves, and a computer to make a series of detailed pictures of areas inside the body. A substance called gadolinium is injected into a vein. The gadolinium collects around the cancer cells so they show up brighter in the picture. This procedure is also called nuclear magnetic resonance imaging (NMRI).

- **Metaiodobenzylguanidine (MIBG) scan.** A procedure used to find neuroendocrine tumors, such as neuroblastoma. A very small amount of a substance called radioactive MIBG is injected into a vein and travels through the bloodstream. Neuroendocrine tumor cells take up the radioactive MIBG and are detected by a scanner. Scans may be taken over 1–3 days. An iodine solution may be given before or during the test to keep the thyroid gland from absorbing too much of the MIBG. This test is also used to find out how well the tumor is responding to treatment. MIBG is used in high doses to treat neuroblastoma.

- **Bone marrow aspiration and biopsy.** The removal of bone marrow, blood, and a small piece of bone by inserting a hollow needle into the hipbone or breastbone. A pathologist views the bone marrow, blood, and bone under a microscope to look for signs of cancer.

- **Ultrasound exam.** A procedure in which high-energy sound waves (ultrasound) are bounced off internal tissues or organs and make echoes. The echoes form a picture of body tissues called a sonogram. The picture can be printed to be looked at later. An ultrasound exam is not done if a CT/MRI has been done.

Biopsy

Cells and tissues are removed during a biopsy so they can be viewed under a microscope by a pathologist to check for signs of cancer. The way the biopsy is done depends on where the tumor is in the body. Sometimes the whole tumor is removed at the same time the biopsy is done.

The following tests may be done on the tissue that is removed:

- **Cytogenetic analysis.** A laboratory test in which cells in a sample of tissue are viewed under a microscope to look for certain changes in the chromosomes.

- **Light microscopy.** A laboratory test in which cells in a sample of tissue are viewed under regular and high powered microscopes to look for certain changes in the cells.

- **Immunohistochemistry.** A test that uses antibodies to check for certain antigens in a sample of tissue. The antibody is usually linked to a radioactive substance or a dye that causes the tissue to light up under a microscope. This type of test may be used to tell the difference between different types of cancer.

- **MYCN amplification study.** A laboratory study in which tumor or bone marrow cells are checked for the level of *MYCN*. *MYCN* is important for cell growth. A higher level of *MYCN* (more than 10 copies of the gene) is called *MYCN* amplification. Neuroblastoma with *MYCN* amplification is more likely to spread in the body and less likely to respond to treatment.

Children up to 6 months old may not need a biopsy or surgery to remove the tumor because the tumor may disappear without treatment.

What Is The Prognosis For Neuroblastoma?

The prognosis (chance of recovery) and treatment options depend on the following:

- Age of the child at the time of diagnosis

- The child's risk group

- Whether there are certain changes in the genes

- Where in the body the tumor started

- Tumor histology (the shape, function, and structure of the tumor cells)

- Whether there is cancer in the lymph nodes on the same side of the body as the primary cancer or whether there is cancer in the lymph nodes on the opposite side of the body

- How the tumor responds to treatment

- How much time passed between diagnosis and when the cancer recurred (for recurrent cancer)

Prognosis and treatment options for neuroblastoma are also affected by tumor biology, which includes:

- The patterns of the tumor cells
- How different the tumor cells are from normal cells
- How fast the tumor cells are growing
- Whether the tumor shows *MYCN* amplification
- Whether the tumor has changes in the anaplastic lymphoma kinase (*ALK*) gene

The tumor biology is said to be favorable or unfavorable, depending on these factors. A favorable tumor biology means there is a better chance of recovery.

In some children up to 6 months old, neuroblastoma may disappear without treatment. This is called spontaneous regression. The child is closely watched for signs or symptoms of neuroblastoma. If signs or symptoms occur, treatment may be needed.

What Treatment Options Are Available For Neuroblastoma?

Different types of treatment are available for patients with neuroblastoma. Some treatments are standard (the currently used treatment), and some are being tested in clinical trials. A treatment clinical trial is a research study meant to help improve current treatments or obtain information on new treatments for patients with cancer. When clinical trials show that a new treatment is better than the standard treatment, the new treatment may become the standard treatment.

Because cancer in children is rare, taking part in a clinical trial should be considered. Some clinical trials are open only to patients who have not started treatment.

Seven types of standard treatment are used:

Observation

Observation is closely monitoring a patient's condition without giving any treatment until signs or symptoms appear or change.

Surgery

Surgery is used to treat neuroblastoma unless it has spread to other parts of the body. Depending on where the tumor is, as much of the tumor as is safely possible will be removed. If the tumor cannot be removed, a biopsy may be done instead.

Radiation Therapy

Radiation therapy is a cancer treatment that uses high-energy X-rays or other types of radiation to kill cancer cells or keep them from growing. There are two types of radiation therapy:

- **External radiation therapy** uses a machine outside the body to send radiation toward the cancer.

- **Internal radiation therapy** uses a radioactive substance sealed in needles, seeds, wires, or catheters that are placed directly into or near the cancer.

The way the radiation therapy is given depends on the type of cancer being treated and the child's risk group. External radiation therapy is used to treat neuroblastoma.

Iodine 131-MIBG Therapy

Iodine 131-MIBG therapy is a treatment with radioactive iodine. The radioactive iodine is given through an intravenous (IV) line and enters the bloodstream which carries radiation directly to tumor cells. Radioactive iodine collects in neuroblastoma cells and kills them with the radiation that is given off. Iodine 131-MIBG therapy is sometimes used to treat high risk neuroblastoma that comes back after initial treatment.

Chemotherapy

Chemotherapy is a cancer treatment that uses drugs to stop the growth of cancer cells, either by killing the cells or by stopping them from dividing. When chemotherapy is taken by mouth or injected into a vein or muscle, the drugs enter the bloodstream and can reach cancer cells throughout the body (systemic chemotherapy). When chemotherapy is placed directly into the cerebrospinal fluid, an organ, or a body cavity such as the abdomen, the drugs mainly affect cancer cells in those areas (regional chemotherapy). The way the chemotherapy is given depends on the type of cancer being treated and the child's risk group.

The use of two or more anticancer drugs is called combination chemotherapy.

High Dose Chemotherapy (HDC) And Radiation Therapy With Stem Cell Rescue

High dose chemotherapy (HDC) and radiation therapy with stem cell rescue is a way of giving high doses of chemotherapy and radiation therapy and replacing blood forming cells destroyed by cancer treatment for high risk neuroblastoma. Stem cells (immature blood cells) are removed from the blood or bone marrow of the patient and are frozen and stored. After chemotherapy and radiation therapy are completed, the stored stem cells are thawed and given back to the patient through an infusion. These reinfused stem cells grow into (and restore) the body's blood cells.

Maintenance therapy is given after high dose chemotherapy and radiation therapy with stem cell rescue to kill any cancer cells that may regrow and cause the disease to come back. Maintenance therapy is given for 6 months and includes the following treatments:

- **Isotretinoin.** A vitamin like drug that slows the cancer's ability to make more cancer cells and changes how these cells look and act. This drug is taken by mouth.

- **Dinutuximab.** A type of monoclonal antibody therapy that uses an antibody made in the laboratory from a single type of immune system cell. Dinutuximab identifies and attaches to a substance, called GD2, on the surface of neuroblastoma cells. Once dinutuximab attaches to the GD2, a signal is sent to the immune system that a foreign substance has been found and needs to be killed. Then the body's immune system kills the neuroblastoma cell. Dinutuximab is given by infusion. It is a type of targeted therapy.

- **Granulocyte macrophage colony stimulating factor (GM-CSF).** A cytokine that helps make more immune system cells, especially granulocytes and macrophages (white blood cells), which can attack and kill cancer cells.

- **Interleukin 2 (IL-2).** A type of immunotherapy that boosts the growth and activity of many immune cells, especially lymphocytes (a type of white blood cell). Lymphocytes can attack and kill cancer cells.

Targeted Therapy

Targeted therapy is a type of treatment that uses drugs or other substances to identify and attack cancer cells with less harm to normal cells.

Tyrosine kinase inhibitors (TKI) are small molecule drugs that go through the cell membrane and work inside cancer cells to block signals that cancer cells need to grow and divide. Crizotinib is used to treat neuroblastoma that has come back after treatment.

Side Effects Of Treatment

Children who are treated for neuroblastoma may have late effects, including an increased risk of second cancers. Some cancer treatments cause side effects that continue or appear years after cancer treatment has ended. These are called late effects. Late effects of cancer treatment may include:

- Physical problems

- Changes in mood, feelings, thinking, learning, or memory

- Second cancers (new types of cancer)

Some late effects may be treated or controlled. It is important that parents of children who are treated for neuroblastoma talk with their doctors about the possible late effects caused by some treatments.

Chapter 28

Oral Cavity Cancer

What Is Oral Cavity Cancer?

Oral cavity cancer is a disease in which malignant (cancer) cells form in the tissues of the mouth.

The oral cavity includes the following:

- The front two thirds of the tongue.

- The gingiva (gums).

- The buccal mucosa (the lining of the inside of the cheeks).

- The floor (bottom) of the mouth under the tongue.

- The hard palate (the roof of the mouth).

- The retromolar trigone (the small area behind the wisdom teeth).

Most tumors in the oral cavity are benign (not cancer). The most common type of oral cavity cancer in adults, squamous cell carcinoma (cancer of the thin, flat cells lining the mouth), is very rare in children. Malignant tumors in children include lymphomas and sarcomas.

About This Chapter: This chapter includes text excerpted from "Unusual Cancers Of Childhood Treatment (PDQ®)—Patient Version," National Cancer Institute (NCI), November 16, 2017.

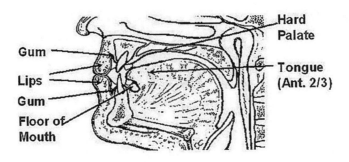

Figure 28.1. Lip And Oral Cavity

(Source: "Head And Neck Cancer—Anatomy—Lip And Oral Cavity," National Cancer Institute (NCI).)

Oral Cancer: Facts

- Oral cancer includes cancers of the mouth and pharynx (the back of the throat).
- Oral cancer accounts for roughly 3 percent of all cancers diagnosed annually in the United States. Approximately 48,000 people will be diagnosed with oral cancer each year and about 9,600 will die from the disease.
- On average, 64 percent of those with the disease will survive more than 5 years.

(Source: "Oral Cancer," National Institute of Dental and Craniofacial Research (NIDCR).)

What Are The Signs And Symptoms Of Oral Cavity Cancer?

Oral cavity cancer may cause any of the following signs and symptoms. Check with your child's doctor if your child has any of the following:

- A sore in the mouth that does not heal.
- A lump or thickening in the oral cavity.
- A white or red patch on the gums, tongue, or lining of the mouth.
- Bleeding, pain, or numbness in the mouth.

Other conditions that are not oral cavity cancer may cause these same signs and symptoms.

How Is Oral Cavity Cancer Diagnosed?

Tests to diagnose and stage oral cavity cancer may include the following:

- Physical exam and history

- X-ray

- Magnetic resonance imaging (MRI) of the head and neck

- Computed tomography (CT) scan

- Positron emission tomography (PET) scan

- Biopsy

How Is Oral Cavity Cancer Treated?

Treatment of oral cavity cancer in children may include the following:

- Surgery for benign tumors.

- Surgery, chemotherapy, and radiation therapy for malignant tumors.

Importance Of Early Detection

It is important to find oral cancer as early as possible when it can be treated more successfully.

An oral cancer examination can detect early signs of cancer. The exam is painless and takes only a few minutes.

Your regular dental check-up is an excellent opportunity to have the exam. During the exam, your dentist or dental hygienist will check your face, neck, lips, and entire mouth for possible signs of cancer.

Some parts of the pharynx are not visible during an oral cancer exam. Talk to your dentist about whether a specialist should check your pharynx.

(Source: "Oral Cancer," National Institute of Dental and Craniofacial Research (NIDCR).)

Chapter 29

Soft Tissue Sarcomas

Soft tissue sarcoma is a cancer that starts in soft tissues of the body, including muscle, tendons, fat, lymph vessels, blood vessels, nerves, and tissue around joints. The tumors can be found anywhere in the body but often form in the arms, legs, chest, or abdomen.

Signs of soft tissue sarcoma include a lump or swelling in soft tissue. Sometimes there are no signs or symptoms until the tumor is big and presses on nearby nerves or other parts of the body.

Both children and adults can develop soft tissue sarcoma. Treatment often works better in children and they may have a better chance of being cured than adults.

There are many types of soft tissue sarcoma, based on the type of soft tissue cell in which the cancer formed. Different types may be treated differently.

Rhabdomyosarcoma is the most common type of soft tissue sarcoma in children. It begins in muscles that are attached to bones and help the body move. Most rhabdomyosarcomas are diagnosed in children younger than 10 years. Rhabdomyosarcomas usually form lumps near the surface of the body and are found early.

Ewing sarcoma, Kaposi sarcoma, and uterine sarcoma are other types of soft tissue sarcoma.

Radiation therapy and certain diseases and inherited conditions can increase the risk of soft tissue sarcoma.

About This Chapter: Text in this chapter begins with excerpts from "Soft Tissue Sarcoma—Patient Version," National Cancer Institute (NCI), May 15, 2015; Text under the heading "Childhood Rhabdomyosarcoma" is excerpted from "Childhood Rhabdomyosarcoma Treatment (PDQ®)—Patient Version," National Cancer Institute (NCI), September 1, 2017; Text under the heading "Childhood Soft Tissue Sarcoma" is excerpted from "Childhood Soft Tissue Sarcoma Treatment (PDQ®)—Patient Version," National Cancer Institute (NCI), August 18, 2017.

Childhood Rhabdomyosarcoma

Rhabdomyosarcoma is a type of sarcoma. Sarcoma is cancer of soft tissue (such as muscle), connective tissue (such as tendon or cartilage), or bone. Rhabdomyosarcoma usually begins in muscles that are attached to bones and that help the body move. Rhabdomyosarcoma is the most common type of soft tissue sarcoma in children. It can begin in many places in the body.

There are three main types of rhabdomyosarcoma:

- **Embryonal.** This type occurs most often in the head and neck area or in the genital or urinary organs, but can occur anywhere in the body. It is the most common type of rhabdomyosarcoma.

- **Alveolar.** This type occurs most often in the arms or legs, chest, abdomen, genital organs, or anal area.

- **Anaplastic.** This is the least common type of rhabdomyosarcoma in children.

Risk Factors For Childhood Rhabdomyosarcoma

Certain genetic conditions increase the risk of childhood rhabdomyosarcoma. Risk factors for rhabdomyosarcoma include having the following inherited diseases:

- Li-Fraumeni syndrome

- Pleuropulmonary blastoma

- Neurofibromatosis type 1 (NF1)

- Costello syndrome

- Beckwith-Wiedemann syndrome (BWS)

- Noonan syndrome

Children who had a high birth weight or were larger than expected at birth may have an increased risk of embryonal rhabdomyosarcoma.

Causes Of Childhood Rhabdomyosarcoma

In most cases, the cause of rhabdomyosarcoma is not known.

Signs And Symptoms Of Childhood Rhabdomyosarcoma

A sign of childhood rhabdomyosarcoma is a lump or swelling that keeps getting bigger.

Signs and symptoms may be caused by childhood rhabdomyosarcoma or by other conditions. The signs and symptoms that occur depend on where the cancer forms. Check with your child's doctor if your child has any of the following:

- A lump or swelling that keeps getting bigger or does not go away. It may be painful.
- Bulging of the eye.
- Headache.
- Trouble urinating or having bowel movements.
- Blood in the urine.
- Bleeding in the nose, throat, vagina, or rectum.

Diagnosis Of Childhood Rhabdomyosarcoma

Diagnostic tests and a biopsy are used to detect (find) and diagnose childhood rhabdomyosarcoma.

The diagnostic tests that are done depend in part on where the cancer forms. The following tests and procedures may be used:

- Physical exam and history
- X-ray
- Computed tomography (CT) scan
- Magnetic resonance imaging (MRI)
- Positron emission tomography (PET) scan
- Bone scan
- Bone marrow aspiration and biopsy
- Lumbar puncture

If these tests show there may be a rhabdomyosarcoma, a biopsy is done. A biopsy is the removal of cells or tissues so they can be viewed under a microscope by a pathologist to check for signs of cancer. Because treatment depends on the type of rhabdomyosarcoma, biopsy samples should be checked by a pathologist who has experience in diagnosing rhabdomyosarcoma.

One of the following types of biopsies may be used:

- Fine-needle aspiration (FNA) biopsy

- Core needle biopsy

- Open biopsy

- Sentinel lymph node biopsy

The following tests may be done on the sample of tissue that is removed:

- Light microscopy

- Immunohistochemistry

- FISH (fluorescence in situ hybridization)

- Reverse transcription–polymerase chain reaction (RT–PCR) test

- Cytogenetic analysis

Prognosis

The prognosis (chance of recovery) and treatment options depend on the following:

- The patient's age.

- Where in the body the tumor started.

- The size of the tumor at the time of diagnosis.

- Whether the tumor has been completely removed by surgery.

- The type of rhabdomyosarcoma (embryonal, alveolar, or anaplastic.)

- Whether there are certain changes in the genes.

- Whether the tumor had spread to other parts of the body at the time of diagnosis.

- Whether the tumor was in the lymph nodes at the time of diagnosis.

- Whether the tumor responds to chemotherapy and/or radiation therapy.

Treatment For Childhood Rhabdomyosarcoma

Three types of standard treatment are used:

Surgery. Surgery (removing the cancer in an operation) is used to treat childhood rhabdomyosarcoma. A type of surgery called wide local excision is often done. A wide local excision is the removal of tumor and some of the tissue around it, including the lymph nodes. A second surgery may be needed to remove all the cancer. Whether surgery is done and the type of surgery done depends on the following:

- Where in the body the tumor started.

- The effect the surgery will have on the way the child will look.

- The effect the surgery will have on the child's important body functions.

- How the tumor responded to chemotherapy or radiation therapy that may have been given first.

In most children with rhabdomyosarcoma, it is not possible to remove all of the tumor by surgery.

Rhabdomyosarcoma can form in many different places in the body and the surgery will be different for each site. Surgery to treat rhabdomyosarcoma of the eye or genital areas is usually a biopsy. Chemotherapy, and sometimes radiation therapy, may be given before surgery to shrink large tumors.

Even if the doctor removes all the cancer that can be seen at the time of the surgery, patients will be given chemotherapy after surgery to kill any cancer cells that are left. Radiation therapy may also be given. Treatment given after the surgery to lower the risk that the cancer will come back, is called adjuvant therapy.

Radiation therapy. Radiation therapy is a cancer treatment that uses high-energy X-rays or other types of radiation to kill cancer cells or stop them from growing. There are two types of radiation therapy:

- External radiation therapy

- Internal radiation therapy

The type and amount of radiation therapy and when it is given depends on the age of the child, the type of rhabdomyosarcoma, where in the body the tumor started, how much tumor remained after surgery, and whether there is tumor in the nearby lymph nodes.

External radiation therapy is usually used to treat childhood rhabdomyosarcoma but in certain cases internal radiation therapy is used.

Chemotherapy. Chemotherapy is a cancer treatment that uses drugs to stop the growth of cancer cells, either by killing the cells or by stopping them from dividing.

Every child treated for rhabdomyosarcoma should receive systemic chemotherapy to decrease the chance the cancer will recur. The type of anticancer drug, dose, and the number of treatments given depends on whether the child has low-risk, intermediate-risk, or high-risk rhabdomyosarcoma.

Childhood Soft Tissue Sarcoma

Soft tissues of the body connect, support, and surround other body parts and organs. The soft tissues include the following:

- Fat

- A mix of bone and cartilage

- Fibrous tissue

- Muscles

- Nerves

- Tendons (bands of tissue that connect muscles to bones)

- Synovial tissues (tissues around joints)

- Blood vessels

- Lymph vessels

Soft tissue sarcoma may be found anywhere in the body. In children, the tumors form most often in the arms, legs, or trunk (chest and abdomen). Childhood soft tissue sarcoma is a disease in which malignant (cancer) cells form in soft tissues of the body.

Types Of Childhood Soft Tissue Sarcoma

There are many different types of soft tissue sarcomas. The soft tissue tumors are grouped based on the type of soft tissue cell where they first formed.

Fat Tissue Tumors

- **Liposarcoma.** This is a rare cancer of the fat cells. Liposarcoma usually forms in the fat layer just under the skin. In children and adolescents, liposarcoma is often low grade (likely to grow and spread slowly).

There are several different types of liposarcoma. Myxoid liposarcoma is usually low grade and responds well to treatment. The cells of myxoid liposarcoma have a certain genetic change called a translocation (part of one chromosome switches places with part of another chromosome). In order to diagnose myxoid liposarcoma, the tumor cells are checked for this genetic change. Pleomorphic liposarcoma is usually high grade (likely to grow and spread quickly) and is less likely to respond well to treatment.

Bone And Cartilage Tumors

Bone and cartilage tumors are a mix of bone cells and cartilage cells. Bone and cartilage tumors include the following types:

- **Extraskeletal mesenchymal chondrosarcoma.** This type of bone and cartilage tumor often affects young adults and occurs in the head and neck.

- **Extraskeletal osteosarcoma.** This type of bone and cartilage tumor is very rare in children and adolescents. It is likely to come back after treatment and may spread to the lungs.

Fibrous (Connective) Tissue Tumors

Fibrous (connective) tissue tumors include the following types:

- **Desmoid-type fibromatosis** (also called desmoid tumor or aggressive fibromatosis). This fibrous tissue tumor is low grade (likely to grow slowly). Desmoid tumors sometimes occur in children with changes in the *adenomatous polyposis coli* (*APC*) gene. Changes in this gene cause familial adenomatous polyposis (FAP). FAP is an inherited condition in which many polyps (growths on mucous membranes) form on the inside walls of the colon and rectum. Genetic counseling (a discussion with a trained professional about inherited diseases and a possible need for gene testing) may be needed.

- **Dermatofibrosarcoma protuberans.** This is a rare tumor of the deep layers of the skin found in children and adults. The cells of this tumor have a certain genetic change called a translocation (part of one chromosome switches places with part of another chromosome). In order to diagnose dermatofibrosarcoma protuberans, the tumor cells are checked for this genetic change.

- **Fibrosarcoma.** There are two types of fibrosarcoma in children and adolescents:

  - **Infantile fibrosarcoma (also called congenital fibrosarcoma).** This type of fibrosarcoma is found in children aged 4 years and younger.

  - **Adult-type fibrosarcoma.** The cells of this tumor do not have the genetic change found in infantile fibrosarcoma. This is the same type of fibrosarcoma found in adults.

- **Inflammatory myofibroblastic tumor.** This is a fibrous tissue tumor that occurs in children and adolescents. It is likely to come back after treatment but rarely spreads to distant parts of the body. A certain genetic change has been found in about half of these tumors.

- **Low-grade fibromyxoid sarcoma.** This is a slow-growing tumor that affects young and middle-aged adults.

- **Myxofibrosarcoma.** This is a rare fibrous tissue tumor that is found less often in children than in adults.

- **Sclerosing epithelioid fibrosarcoma.** This is a rare fibrous tissue tumor that can come back and spread to other places years after treatment. Long-term follow-up is needed.

Skeletal Muscle Tumors

Skeletal muscle is attached to bones and helps the body move.

Rhabdomyosarcoma

Rhabdomyosarcoma is the most common childhood soft tissue sarcoma in children 14 years and younger.

Smooth Muscle Tumors

Smooth muscle lines the inside of blood vessels and hollow internal organs such as the stomach, intestines, bladder, and uterus.

- **Leiomyosarcoma.** This smooth muscle tumor has been linked with *Epstein-Barr* virus in children who also have human immunodeficiency virus (HIV) disease or acquired immune deficiency syndrome (AIDS). Leiomyosarcoma may also form as a second cancer in survivors of inherited retinoblastoma, sometimes many years after the initial treatment for retinoblastoma.

So-Called Fibrohistiocytic Tumors

- **Plexiform fibrohistiocytic tumor.** This is a rare tumor that usually affects children and young adults. The tumor usually starts as a painless growth on or just under the skin on the arm, hand, or wrist. It may rarely spread to nearby lymph nodes or to the lungs.

Peripheral Nervous System Tumors

Peripheral nervous system tumors include the following types:

- **Ectomesenchymoma.** This is a rare, fast-growing tumor of the nerve sheath (protective covering of nerves that are not part of the brain or spinal cord) that occurs mainly in children. Ectomesenchymomas may form in the head and neck, abdomen, perineum, scrotum, arms, or legs.

- **Malignant peripheral nerve sheath tumor.** This is a tumor that forms in the nerve sheath. Some children who have a malignant peripheral nerve sheath tumor have a rare genetic condition called neurofibromatosis type 1 (NF1). This tumor may be low grade or high grade.

- **Malignant triton tumor.** These are very rare, fast-growing tumors that occur most often in children with NF1.

Pericytic (Perivascular) Tumors

Pericytic tumors form in cells that wrap around blood vessels. Pericytic tumors include the following types:

- **Myopericytoma.** Infantile hemangiopericytoma is a type of myopericytoma. Children younger than 1 year at the time of diagnosis may have a better prognosis. In patients older than 1 year, infantile hemangiopericytoma is more likely to spread to other parts of the body, including the lymph nodes and lungs.

- **Infantile myofibromatosis.** Infantile myofibromatosis is another type of myopericytoma. It is a fibrous tumor that often forms in the first 2 years of life. There may be one nodule under the skin, usually in the head and neck area (myofibroma), or nodules in several skin areas, muscle, and bone (myofibromatosis). These tumors may go away without treatment.

Tumors Of Unknown Origin

Tumors of unknown origin (the place where the tumor first formed is not known) include the following types:

- **Alveolar soft part sarcoma.** This is a rare tumor of the soft supporting tissue that connects and surrounds the organs and other tissues. It is most commonly found in the limbs but can occur in the tissues of the mouth, jaws, and face. It may grow slowly and may have spread to other parts of the body at the time of diagnosis. Alveolar soft part sarcoma may have a better prognosis when the tumor is 5 centimeters or smaller or when the tumor is completely removed by surgery. The cells of this tumor usually have a certain genetic change called a translocation (part of one chromosome switches places with part of another chromosome). In order to diagnose alveolar soft part sarcoma, the tumor cells are checked for this genetic change.

- **Clear cell sarcoma of soft tissue.** This is a slow-growing soft tissue tumor that begins in a tendon (tough, fibrous, cord-like tissue that connects muscle to bone or to another part of the body). Clear cell sarcoma most commonly occurs in deep tissue of the foot, heel, and ankle. It may spread to nearby lymph nodes. The cells of this tumor usually have a certain genetic change called a translocation (part of one chromosome switches places with part of another chromosome). In order to diagnose clear cell sarcoma of soft tissue, the tumor cells are checked for this genetic change.

- **Desmoplastic small round cell tumor.** This tumor most often forms in the abdomen, pelvis or tissues around the testes, but it may form in the kidney. Desmoplastic small round cell tumor may also spread to the lungs and other parts of the body. The cells of this tumor usually have a certain genetic change called a translocation (part of one chromosome switches places with part of another chromosome). In order to diagnose desmoplastic small round cell tumor, the tumor cells are checked for this genetic change.

- **Epithelioid sarcoma.** This is a rare sarcoma that usually starts deep in soft tissue as a slow growing, firm lump and may spread to the lymph nodes.

- **Extrarenal (extracranial) rhabdoid tumor.** This is a rare, fast-growing tumor of soft tissues such as the liver and peritoneum. It usually occurs in young children, including newborns, but it can occur in older children and adults. Rhabdoid tumors may be linked to a change in a tumor suppressor gene called *SMARCB1*. This type of gene makes a protein that helps control cell growth. Changes in the *SMARCB1* gene may be inherited (passed on from parents to offspring). Genetic counseling (a discussion with a trained professional about inherited diseases and a possible need for gene testing) may be needed.

- **Extraskeletal myxoid chondrosarcoma.** This is a rare soft tissue sarcoma that may be found in children and adolescents. Over time, it tends to spread to other parts of the body, including the lymph nodes and lungs. The cells of this tumor usually have a genetic change, often a translocation (part of one chromosome switches places with part of another chromosome). In order to diagnose extraskeletal myxoid chondrosarcoma, the tumor cells are checked for this genetic change. The tumor may come back many years after treatment.

- **Perivascular epithelioid cell tumors (PEComas).** Benign (not cancer) PEComas may be found in children with an inherited condition called tuberous sclerosis. They occur in the stomach, intestines, lungs, female reproductive organs, and genitourinary organs.

- **Primitive neuroectodermal tumor (PNET)/extraskeletal Ewing tumor.**

- **Synovial sarcoma.** Synovial sarcoma is a common type of soft tissue sarcoma in children and adolescents. Synovial sarcoma usually forms in the tissues around the joints in the arms or legs, but may also form in the trunk, head, or neck. The cells of this tumor usually have a certain genetic change called a translocation (part of one chromosome switches places with part of another chromosome). Larger tumors have a greater risk of spreading to other parts of the body, including the lungs. Children younger than 10 years and those whose tumor is 5 centimeters or smaller have a better prognosis.

- **Undifferentiated /unclassified sarcoma.** These tumors usually occur in the muscles that are attached to bones and that help the body move.

  - **Undifferentiated pleomorphic sarcoma/malignant fibrous histiocytoma (high-grade).** This type of soft tissue tumor may form in parts of the body where patients have received radiation therapy in the past, or as a second cancer in children with retinoblastoma. The tumor is usually found on the arms or legs and may spread to other parts of the body.

Blood Vessel Tumors

Blood vessel tumors include the following types:

- **Angiosarcoma of the soft tissue.** Angiosarcoma of the soft tissue is a fast-growing tumor that forms in blood vessels or lymph vessels in any part of the body. Most angiosarcomas are in or just under the skin. Those in deeper soft tissue can form in the liver, spleen, and lung. They are very rare in children, who sometimes have more than one tumor in the skin or liver. Rarely, infantile hemangioma may become angiosarcoma of the soft tissue.

- **Epithelioid hemangioendothelioma.** Epithelioid hemangioendotheliomas can occur in children, but are most common in adults between 30 and 50 years of age. They usually occur in the liver, lung, or bone. They may be either fast growing or slow growing. In about a third of cases, the tumor spreads to other parts of the body very quickly.

Risk Factors For Childhood Soft Tissue Sarcoma

Having certain diseases and inherited disorders can increase the risk of childhood soft tissue sarcoma.

Risk factors for childhood soft tissue sarcoma include having the following inherited disorders:

- Li-Fraumeni syndrome.

- Familial adenomatous polyposis (FAP).

- *Retinoblastoma* 1 gene changes.

- *SMARCB1 (INI1)* gene changes.

- Neurofibromatosis type 1 (NF1).

- Werner syndrome.

Other risk factors include the following:

- Past treatment with radiation therapy.

- Having AIDS and *Epstein-Barr* virus infection at the same time.

Signs And Symptoms Of Childhood Soft Tissue Sarcoma

The most common sign of childhood soft tissue sarcoma is a painless lump or swelling in soft tissues of the body. A sarcoma may appear as a painless lump under the skin, often on an arm, a leg, or the trunk. There may be no other signs or symptoms at first. As the sarcoma gets bigger and presses on nearby organs, nerves, muscles, or blood vessels, it may cause signs or symptoms, such as pain or weakness.

Other conditions may cause the same signs and symptoms.

Diagnosis Of Childhood Soft Tissue Sarcoma

The following tests and procedures may be used to detect (find) and diagnose childhood soft tissue sarcoma:

- Physical exam and history

- X-rays

- MRI

- CT scan

- Ultrasound exam

If tests show there may be a soft tissue sarcoma, a biopsy is done.

One of the following types of biopsies is usually used:

- Core needle biopsy

- Incisional biopsy

- Excisional biopsy

Because soft tissue sarcoma can be hard to diagnose, the tissue sample should be checked by a pathologist who has experience in diagnosing soft tissue sarcoma.

One or more of the following laboratory tests may be done to study the tissue samples:

- Molecular test

- Reverse transcription–polymerase chain reaction (RT–PCR) test

- Cytogenetic analysis.

- Immunocytochemistry

Prognosis For Childhood Soft Tissue Sarcoma

The prognosis (chance of recovery) and treatment options depend on the following:

- The part of the body where the tumor first formed.

- The size and grade of the tumor.

- The type of soft tissue sarcoma.

- How deep the tumor is under the skin.

- Whether the tumor has spread to other places in the body.

- The amount of tumor remaining after surgery to remove it.

- Whether radiation therapy was used to treat the tumor.

- The age and sex of the patient.

- Whether the cancer has just been diagnosed or has recurred (come back).

Treatment For Childhood Soft Tissue Sarcoma

Different types of treatments are available for patients with childhood soft tissue sarcoma. Treatment will be overseen by a pediatric oncologist, a doctor who specializes in treating children with cancer. The pediatric oncologist works with other healthcare providers who are experts in treating children with soft tissue sarcoma and who specialize in certain areas of medicine. These may include a pediatric surgeon with special training in the removal of soft tissue sarcomas. The following specialists may also be included:

- Pediatrician

- Radiation oncologist

- Pediatric hematologist

- Pediatric nurse specialist

- Rehabilitation specialist

- Psychologist

- Social worker

- Child-life specialist

Eight types of standard treatment are used:

Surgery. Surgery to completely remove the soft tissue sarcoma is done when possible. If the tumor is very large, radiation therapy or chemotherapy may be given first, to make the tumor smaller and decrease the amount of tissue that needs to be removed during surgery. The following types of surgery may be used:

- Wide local excision

- Amputation

- Lymphadenectomy

- Mohs surgery

- Hepatectomy

A second surgery may be needed to:

- Remove any remaining cancer cells.

- Check the area around where the tumor was removed for cancer cells and then remove more tissue if needed.

If cancer is in the liver, a hepatectomy and liver transplant may be done (the liver is removed and replaced with a healthy one from a donor).

Radiation therapy. Radiation therapy is a cancer treatment that uses high-energy X-rays or other types of radiation to kill cancer cells or keep them from growing. There are two types of radiation therapy:

- External radiation therapy

- Internal radiation therapy

The way the radiation therapy is given depends on the type and stage of the cancer being treated and whether the tumor was completely removed by surgery. External and internal radiation therapy are used to treat childhood soft tissue sarcoma.

Chemotherapy. Chemotherapy is a cancer treatment that uses drugs to stop the growth of cancer cells, either by killing the cells or by stopping them from dividing. The way the chemotherapy is given depends on the type of cancer being treated. Most types of soft tissue sarcoma do not respond to treatment with chemotherapy.

Observation. Observation is closely monitoring a patient's condition without giving any treatment until signs or symptoms appear or change. Observation may be done when:

- Complete removal of the tumor is not possible.

- No other treatments are available.

- The tumor is not likely to damage any vital organs.

Hormone therapy. Hormone therapy is a cancer treatment that removes hormones or blocks their action and stops cancer cells from growing. Hormones are substances made by glands in the body and circulated in the bloodstream. Some hormones can cause certain cancers to grow. If tests show that the cancer cells have places where hormones can attach (receptors), drugs, surgery, or radiation therapy is used to reduce the production of hormones or block them from working. Antiestrogens (drugs that block estrogen), such as tamoxifen, may be used to treat desmoid-type fibromatosis.

Nonsteroidal anti-inflammatory drugs. Nonsteroidal anti-inflammatory drugs (NSAIDs) are drugs (such as aspirin, ibuprofen, and naproxen) that are commonly used to decrease fever, swelling, pain, and redness. In the treatment of desmoid-type fibromatosis, an NSAID called sulindac may be used to help block the growth of cancer cells.

Targeted therapy. Targeted therapy is a type of treatment that uses drugs or other substances to attack cancer cells. Targeted therapies usually cause less harm to normal cells than chemotherapy or radiation do.

Immunotherapy. Immunotherapy is a treatment that uses the patient's immune system to fight disease. Substances made by the body or made in a laboratory are used to boost, direct, or restore the body's natural defenses against disease. Interferon is a type of immunotherapy used to treat epithelioid hemangioendothelioma. It interferes with the division of tumor cells and can slow tumor growth.

Gene therapy. Gene therapy is being studied for childhood synovial sarcoma that has recurred, spread, or cannot be removed by surgery.

Chapter 30

Childhood Vascular Tumors

Childhood vascular tumors form from cells that make blood vessels or lymph vessels.

Vascular tumors can form from abnormal blood vessel or lymph vessel cells anywhere in the body. They may be benign (not cancer) or malignant (cancer). There are many types of vascular tumors. The most common type of childhood vascular tumor is hemangioma, which is a benign tumor that usually goes away on its own.

Because malignant vascular tumors are rare in children, there is not a lot of information about what treatment works best.

Types Of Childhood Vascular Tumors

Childhood vascular tumors may be classified into four groups.

- **Benign tumors.** Benign tumors are not cancer. This summary has information about the following benign vascular tumors:
  - Infantile hemangioma
  - Congenital hemangioma
  - Benign vascular tumors of the liver
  - Spindle cell hemangioma
  - Epithelioid hemangioma

About This Chapter: This chapter includes text excerpted from "Childhood Vascular Tumors Treatment (PDQ®)—Patient Version," National Cancer Institute (NCI), April 7, 2017.

- Pyogenic granuloma (lobular capillary hemangioma)

- Angiofibroma

- Juvenile nasopharyngeal angiofibroma

- **Intermediate (locally aggressive) tumors.** Intermediate tumors that are locally aggressive often spread to the area around the tumor. This summary has information about the following locally aggressive vascular tumors:

  - Kaposiform hemangioendothelioma and tufted angioma

- **Intermediate (rarely metastasizing) tumors.** Intermediate (rarely metastasizing) tumors sometimes spread to other parts of the body. This summary has information about the following vascular tumors that rarely metastasize:

  - Retiform hemangioendothelioma

  - Papillary intralymphatic angioendothelioma

  - Composite hemangioendothelioma

  - Kaposi sarcoma

- **Malignant tumors.** Malignant tumors are cancer. This summary has information about the following malignant vascular tumors:

  - Epithelioid hemangioendothelioma

  - Angiosarcoma of soft tissue

Diagnosis Of Childhood Vascular Tumors

Tests are used to detect (find) and diagnose childhood vascular tumors.

The following tests and procedures may be used:

- Physical exam and history

- Ultrasound exam

- CT scan (CAT scan)

- MRI

- Biopsy

Treatment Of Childhood Vascular Tumors

Eleven types of standard treatment are used:

Beta blocker therapy. Beta blockers are drugs that decrease blood pressure and heart rate. When used in patients with vascular tumors, beta blockers may help shrink the tumors. Beta blocker therapy may be given by vein (IV), by mouth, or placed on the skin (topical). The way the beta blocker therapy is given depends on the type of vascular tumor and where the tumor first formed.

The beta blocker propranolol is usually the first treatment for hemangiomas. Infants treated with IV propranolol may need to have their treatment started in a hospital. Propranolol is also used to treat benign vascular tumor of liver and kaposiform hemangioendothelioma.

Other beta blockers used to treat vascular tumors include atenolol, nadolol, and timolol.

Infantile hemangioma may also be treated with propranolol and steroid therapy or propranolol and topical beta blocker therapy.

Surgery. The following types of surgery may be used to remove many types of vascular tumors:

- Excision

- Laser surgery

- Total hepatectomy and liver transplant

- Curettage

The type of surgery used depends on the type of vascular tumor and where the tumor formed in the body.

For malignant tumors, even if the doctor removes all the cancer that can be seen at the time of the surgery, some patients may be given chemotherapy or radiation therapy after surgery to kill any cancer cells that are left.

Photocoagulation. Photocoagulation is the use of an intense beam of light, such as a laser, to seal off blood vessels or destroy tissue. It is used to treat pyogenic granuloma.

Embolization. Embolization is a procedure that uses particles, such as tiny gelatin sponges or beads, to block blood vessels in the liver. It may be used to treat some benign vascular tumors of the liver and kaposiform hemangioendothelioma.

Chemotherapy. Chemotherapy is a treatment that uses drugs to stop the growth of tumor cells, either by killing the cells or by stopping them from dividing. The way the chemotherapy is given depends on the type of the vascular tumor being treated.

Sclerotherapy. Sclerotherapy is a treatment used to destroy the blood vessel with the tumor. Sclerotherapy is used in the treatment of epithelioid hemangioma.

Radiation therapy. Radiation therapy is a treatment that uses high-energy X-rays or other types of radiation to kill tumor cells or keep them from growing. There are two types of radiation therapy:

- External radiation therapy

- Internal radiation therapy

The way the radiation therapy is given depends on the type of the vascular tumor being treated. External radiation is used to treat some vascular tumors.

Targeted therapy. Targeted therapy is a type of treatment that uses drugs or other substances to attack specific tumor cells.

Immunotherapy. Immunotherapy is a treatment that uses the patient's immune system to fight disease. Interferon is a type of immunotherapy used to treat childhood vascular tumors. It interferes with the division of tumor cells and can slow tumor growth. It is used in the treatment of juvenile nasopharyngeal angiofibroma, kaposiform hemangioendothelioma, and epithelioid hemangioendothelioma.

Other drug therapy. Other drugs used to treat childhood vascular tumors or manage their effects include the following:

- Steroid therapy

- Nonsteroidal anti-inflammatory drugs (NSAIDs)

- Antifibrinolytic therapy

Chapter 31

Testicular Cancer

What Is Testicular Cancer?

Testicular cancer is a disease in which malignant (cancer) cells form in the tissues of one or both testicles.

The testicles are two egg-shaped glands located inside the scrotum (a sac of loose skin that lies directly below the penis). The testicles are held within the scrotum by the spermatic cord, which also contains the vas deferens and vessels and nerves of the testicles.

The testicles are the male sex glands and produce testosterone and sperm. Germ cells within the testicles produce immature sperm that travel through a network of tubules (tiny tubes) and larger tubes into the epididymis (a long coiled tube next to the testicles) where the sperm mature and are stored.

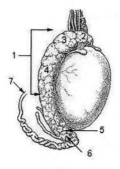

1. Epididymis
2. Head of epididymis
3. Lobules of epididymis
4. Body of epididymis
5. Tail of epididymis
6. Duct of epididymis
7. Deferent duct
   (ductus deferens or vas deferens)

Figure 31.1. Anatomy Of The Testis

(Source: "Testicular Cancer—Anatomy Of The Testis," National Cancer Institute (NCI).)

About This Chapter: This chapter includes text excerpted from "Testicular Cancer Treatment (PDQ®)—Patient Version," National Cancer Institute (NCI), July 7, 2016.

Almost all testicular cancers start in the germ cells. The two main types of testicular germ cell tumors are seminomas and nonseminomas. These two types grow and spread differently and are treated differently. Nonseminomas tend to grow and spread more quickly than seminomas. Seminomas are more sensitive to radiation. A testicular tumor that contains both seminoma and nonseminoma cells is treated as a nonseminoma.

What Are The Risk Factors For Testicular Cancer?

Health history can affect the risk of testicular cancer. Anything that increases the chance of getting a disease is called a risk factor. Having a risk factor does not mean that you will get cancer; not having risk factors doesn't mean that you will not get cancer. Talk with your doctor if you think you may be at risk. Risk factors for testicular cancer include:

- Having had an undescended testicle.
- Having had abnormal development of the testicles.
- Having a personal history of testicular cancer.
- Having a family history of testicular cancer (especially in a father or brother).
- Being white.

What Are The Signs And Symptoms Of Testicular Cancer?

Signs and symptoms of testicular cancer include swelling or discomfort in the scrotum. These and other signs and symptoms may be caused by testicular cancer or by other conditions. Check with your doctor if you have any of the following:

- A painless lump or swelling in either testicle.
- A change in how the testicle feels.
- A dull ache in the lower abdomen or the groin.
- A sudden buildup of fluid in the scrotum.
- Pain or discomfort in a testicle or in the scrotum.

How Is Testicular Cancer Diagnosed?

Tests that examine the testicles and blood are used to detect (find) and diagnose testicular cancer.

The following tests and procedures may be used:

- **Physical exam and history.** An exam of the body to check general signs of health, including checking for signs of disease, such as lumps or anything else that seems unusual. The testicles will be examined to check for lumps, swelling, or pain. A history of the patient's health habits and past illnesses and treatments will also be taken.

- **Ultrasound exam.** A procedure in which high-energy sound waves (ultrasound) are bounced off internal tissues or organs and make echoes. The echoes form a picture of body tissues called a sonogram.

- **Serum tumor marker test.** A procedure in which a sample of blood is examined to measure the amounts of certain substances released into the blood by organs, tissues, or tumor cells in the body. Certain substances are linked to specific types of cancer when found in increased levels in the blood. These are called tumor markers. The following tumor markers are used to detect testicular cancer:

- Alpha-fetoprotein (AFP).

- Beta-human chorionic gonadotropin (β-hCG).

Tumor marker levels are measured before inguinal orchiectomy and biopsy, to help diagnose testicular cancer.

- **Inguinal orchiectomy.** A procedure to remove the entire testicle through an incision in the groin. A tissue sample from the testicle is then viewed under a microscope to check for cancer cells. (The surgeon does not cut through the scrotum into the testicle to remove a sample of tissue for biopsy, because if cancer is present, this procedure could cause it to spread into the scrotum and lymph nodes. It's important to choose a surgeon who has experience with this kind of surgery.) If cancer is found, the cell type (seminoma or nonseminoma) is determined in order to help plan treatment.

What Is The Treatment For Testicular Cancer?

There are different types of treatment for patients with testicular cancer. Different types of treatments are available for patients with testicular cancer. Some treatments are standard (the currently used treatment), and some are being tested in clinical trials. A treatment clinical trial is a research study meant to help improve current treatments or obtain information on new treatments for patients with cancer. When clinical trials show that a new treatment is better than the standard treatment, the new treatment may become the standard treatment. Patients may want to think about taking part in a clinical trial. Some clinical trials are open only to patients who have not started treatment. Treatment for testicular cancer can cause infertility.

Testicular tumors are divided into three groups, based on how well the tumors are expected to respond to treatment.

Good Prognosis

For nonseminoma, all of the following must be true:

- The tumor is found only in the testicle or in the retroperitoneum (area outside or behind the abdominal wall); and
- The tumor has not spread to organs other than the lungs; and
- The levels of all the tumor markers are slightly above normal.

For seminoma, all of the following must be true:

- The tumor has not spread to organs other than the lungs; and
- The level of AFP is normal. β-hCG and lactate dehydrogenase (LDH) may be at any level.

Intermediate Prognosis

For nonseminoma, all of the following must be true:

- The tumor is found in one testicle only or in the retroperitoneum (area outside or behind the abdominal wall); and
- The tumor has not spread to organs other than the lungs; and
- The level of any one of the tumor markers is more than slightly above normal.

For seminoma, all of the following must be true:

- The tumor has spread to organs other than the lungs; and
- The level of AFP is normal. β-hCG and LDH may be at any level.

Poor Prognosis

For nonseminoma, at least one of the following must be true:

- The tumor is in the center of the chest between the lungs; or
- The tumor has spread to organs other than the lungs; or
- The level of any one of the tumor markers is high.

There is no poor prognosis grouping for seminoma testicular tumors.

Standard Treatment

Five types of standard treatment are used:

Surgery. Surgery to remove the testicle (inguinal orchiectomy) and some of the lymph nodes may be done at diagnosis and staging. Tumors that have spread to other places in the body may be partly or entirely removed by surgery.

Even if the doctor removes all the cancer that can be seen at the time of the surgery, some patients may be given chemotherapy or radiation therapy after surgery to kill any cancer cells that are left. Treatment given after the surgery, to lower the risk that the cancer will come back, is called adjuvant therapy.

Radiation therapy. Radiation therapy is a cancer treatment that uses high-energy X-rays or other types of radiation to kill cancer cells or keep them from growing. There are two types of radiation therapy:

- **External radiation therapy** uses a machine outside the body to send radiation toward the cancer.

- **Internal radiation therapy** uses a radioactive substance sealed in needles, seeds, wires, or catheters that are placed directly into or near the cancer.

The way the radiation therapy is given depends on the type and stage of the cancer being treated. External radiation therapy is used to treat testicular cancer.

Chemotherapy. Chemotherapy is a cancer treatment that uses drugs to stop the growth of cancer cells, either by killing the cells or by stopping the cells from dividing. When chemotherapy is taken by mouth or injected into a vein or muscle, the drugs enter the bloodstream and can reach cancer cells throughout the body (systemic chemotherapy). When chemotherapy is placed directly into the cerebrospinal fluid, an organ, or a body cavity such as the abdomen, the drugs mainly affect cancer cells in those areas (regional chemotherapy). The way the chemotherapy is given depends on the type and stage of the cancer being treated.

Surveillance. Surveillance is closely following a patient's condition without giving any treatment unless there are changes in test results. It is used to find early signs that the cancer has recurred (come back). In surveillance, patients are given certain exams and tests on a regular schedule.

High-dose chemotherapy with stem cell transplant. High-dose chemotherapy with stem cell transplant is a method of giving high doses of chemotherapy and replacing blood-forming cells destroyed by the cancer treatment. Stem cells (immature blood cells) are removed from the blood or bone marrow of the patient or a donor and are frozen and stored. After the chemotherapy is completed, the stored stem cells are thawed and given back to the patient through an infusion. These reinfused stem cells grow into (and restore) the body's blood cells.

What Is The Prognosis For Testicular Cancer?

Certain factors affect prognosis (chance of recovery) and treatment options. The prognosis (chance of recovery) and treatment options depend on the following:

- Stage of the cancer (whether it is in or near the testicle or has spread to other places in the body, and blood levels of AFP, β-hCG, and lactate dehydrogenase (LDH)).

- Type of cancer.

- Size of the tumor.

- Number and size of retroperitoneal lymph nodes.

Testicular cancer can usually be cured in patients who receive adjuvant chemotherapy or radiation therapy after their primary treatment.

Chapter 32

Thyroid Cancer

Thyroid tumors form in the tissues of the thyroid gland. The thyroid gland is a butterfly-shaped gland at the base of the throat near the windpipe. The thyroid gland makes important hormones that help control growth, heart rate, body temperature, and how quickly food is changed into energy.

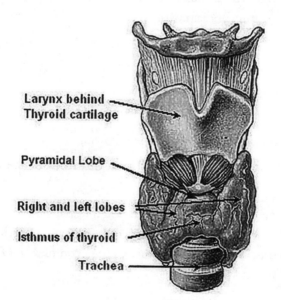

Figure 32.1. Thyroid Gland

(Source: "Thyroid Gland," National Cancer Institute (NCI).)

About This Chapter: This chapter includes text excerpted from "Unusual Cancers Of Childhood Treatment (PDQ®)—Patient Version," National Cancer Institute (NCI), December 8, 2017.

The number of new cases of thyroid cancer in children, adolescents, and young adults has increased in recent years. Childhood thyroid tumors are more common in girls and children aged 15–19 years.

Thyroid tumors may be adenomas (noncancer) or carcinomas (cancer).

- **Adenoma.** Adenomas can grow very large and sometimes make hormones. Adenomas may become malignant (cancer) and spread to the lungs or lymph nodes in the neck.

- **Carcinoma.** There are three types of thyroid cancer:

  - **Papillary.** Papillary thyroid carcinoma is the most common type of thyroid cancer in children. It often spreads to the lymph nodes and may also spread to the lung. The prognosis (chance of recovery) for most patients is very good.

  - **Follicular.** Follicular thyroid carcinoma often spreads to the bone and lung. Sometimes it is inherited (passed from the parent to the child). The prognosis for most patients is very good.

  - **Medullary.** Medullary thyroid carcinoma is often inherited. It may have spread to other parts of the body at the time of diagnosis. The prognosis depends on the size of the tumor at the time of diagnosis.

Papillary and follicular thyroid carcinoma are often referred to as differentiated thyroid carcinoma.

Risk Factors

The risk of thyroid cancer is increased by the following:

- Being exposed to radiation, such as radiation treatment to the neck or atomic bomb radiation.

- Having certain genetic syndromes, such as multiple endocrine neoplasia type 2A (MEN2A) syndrome, multiple endocrine neoplasia type 2B (MEN2B) syndrome, *APC*-associated polyposis, *DICER1* syndrome, Carney complex, *PTEN* hamartoma tumor syndrome, and Werner syndrome.

Signs And Symptoms

Thyroid tumors may cause any of the following signs and symptoms. Check with your child's doctor if your child has any of the following:

- A lump in the neck.

- A lump near the collarbone that does not hurt.

- Trouble breathing.

- Trouble swallowing.

- Hoarseness or a change in the voice.

- Hyperthyroidism (irregular heartbeat, shakiness, weight loss, trouble sleeping, frequent bowel movements, and sweating).

Other conditions that are not thyroid tumors may cause these same signs and symptoms.

Sometimes thyroid tumors do not cause any signs or symptoms.

Diagnostic And Staging Tests

Tests to diagnose and stage thyroid tumors may include the following:

- Physical exam and history.

- Fine-needle aspiration (FNA) biopsy.

- Open biopsy. The biopsy may be done at the same time as surgery to remove all or part of the thyroid.

- X-ray. A chest X-ray may be done if the lymph nodes in the neck are large.

- Computerized tomography (CT) scan.

- Magnetic resonance imaging (MRI).

Other tests used to diagnose and stage thyroid tumors include the following:

- **Ultrasound:** A procedure in which high-energy sound waves (ultrasound) are bounced off internal tissues or organs and make echoes. The echoes form a picture of body tissues called a sonogram. The picture can be printed to be looked at later. This procedure can show the size of a thyroid tumor and whether it is solid or a fluid-filled cyst. Ultrasound may be used to guide a FNA biopsy. A complete ultrasound exam of the neck is done before surgery.

- **Thyroid function test:** The blood is checked for abnormal levels of thyroid-stimulating hormone (TSH). TSH is made by the pituitary gland in the brain. It stimulates the release of thyroid hormone and controls how fast follicular thyroid cells grow. The blood may also be checked for high levels of the hormone calcitonin.

- **Thyroid scan:** If the amount of thyroid stimulating hormone in the child's blood is low, a scan to make images of the thyroid may be done before surgery. A small amount of a radioactive substance is swallowed or injected. The radioactive material collects in the thyroid gland. A special camera linked to a computer detects the radiation given off and makes pictures that show how the thyroid looks and functions.

- **Thyroglobulin test:** The blood is checked for the amount of thyroglobulin, a protein made by the thyroid gland. Thyroglobulin levels are low or absent with normal thyroid function but may be higher with thyroid cancer or other conditions.

Treatment

Treatment of papillary and follicular thyroid carcinoma in children may include the following:

- Surgery to remove the thyroid gland and lymph nodes with cancer, followed by radioactive iodine (RAI) to kill any thyroid cancer cells that are left. Hormone replacement therapy (HRT) is given to make up for the lost thyroid hormone.

- RAI for cancer that has recurred (come back).

Within 12 weeks of surgery, tests are done to find out if thyroid cancer remains in the body. These may include thyroglobulin tests and RAI scans. A radioactive iodine scan (RAI scan) is done to find areas in the body where thyroid cancer cells that were not removed during surgery may be dividing quickly. RAI is used because only thyroid cells take up iodine. A very small amount of RAI is swallowed, travels through the blood, and collects in thyroid tissue and thyroid cancer cells anywhere in the body. Further treatment depends on whether cancer cells remain in the body:

- If no cancer cells are found outside the thyroid, a larger dose of RAI is given to destroy any remaining thyroid tissue.

- If cancer remains in the lymph nodes or has spread to other parts of the body, an even larger dose of RAI is given to destroy any remaining thyroid tissue and thyroid cancer cells.

A whole-body SPECT (single photon emission computed tomography) scan may be done 4–7 days after treatment with RAI, to see if there are areas with cancer cells. A SPECT scan uses a special camera linked to a computer to make 3-dimensional (3-D) pictures of areas inside the body. A very small amount of a radioactive substance is injected into a vein. As the substance travels through the blood, the camera rotates around the body and takes pictures. Areas where thyroid cancer cells are growing will show up brighter in the picture. This procedure may be done just before or after a computerized tomography (CT) scan.

It is common for thyroid cancer to recur (come back), especially in children younger than 10 years and those with cancer in the lymph nodes. Ultrasound and thyroglobulin tests may be done from time to time to check if the cancer has recurred. Lifelong follow-up of thyroid hormone levels in the blood is needed to make sure the right amount of HRT is being given. Talk with your child's doctor to find out how often these tests need to be done.

Treatment of medullary thyroid carcinoma in children may include the following:

- Surgery to remove the tumor.

- Targeted therapy with kinase inhibitors for cancer that has spread to other parts of the body or that has recurred.

Prognosis

The prognosis (chance of recovery) depends on the following:

- The child's gender.

- The size of the tumor.

- Whether the tumor has spread to lymph nodes or other parts of the body at the time of diagnosis.

Part Three
Cancer Awareness, Diagnosis, Treatment, And Prevention

Chapter 33

Common Moles, Dysplastic Nevi, And Risk Of Melanoma

What Is A Common Mole?

A common mole is a growth on the skin that develops when pigment cells (melanocytes) grow in clusters. Most adults have between 10 and 40 common moles. These growths are usually found above the waist on areas exposed to the sun. They are seldom found on the scalp, breast, or buttocks.

Although common moles may be present at birth, they usually appear later in childhood. Most people continue to develop new moles until about age 40. In older people, common moles tend to fade away.

Another name for a mole is a nevus. The plural is nevi.

What Does A Common Mole Look Like?

A common mole is usually smaller than about 5 millimeters wide (about 1/4 inch, the width of a pencil eraser). It is round or oval, has a smooth surface with a distinct edge, and is often dome-shaped. A common mole usually has an even color of pink, tan, or brown. People who have dark skin or hair tend to have darker moles than people with fair skin or blonde hair.

Can A Common Mole Turn Into Melanoma?

Yes, but a common mole rarely turns into melanoma, which is the most serious type of skin cancer.

About This Chapter: This chapter includes text excerpted from "Common Moles, Dysplastic Nevi, And Risk Of Melanoma," National Cancer Institute (NCI), May 3, 2017.

Although common moles are not cancerous, people who have more than 50 common moles have an increased chance of developing melanoma.

People should tell their doctor if they notice any of the following changes in a common mole:

- The color changes

- The mole gets unevenly smaller or bigger (unlike normal moles in children, which get evenly bigger)

- The mole changes in shape, texture, or height

- The skin on the surface becomes dry or scaly

- The mole becomes hard or feels lumpy

- It starts to itch

- It bleeds or oozes

What Is A Dysplastic Nevus?

A dysplastic nevus is a type of mole that looks different from a common mole. (Some doctors use the term "atypical mole" to refer to a dysplastic nevus.) A dysplastic nevus may be bigger than a common mole, and its color, surface, and border may be different. It is usually more than 5 millimeters wide. A dysplastic nevus can have a mixture of several colors, from pink to dark brown. Usually, it is flat with a smooth, slightly scaly, or pebbly surface, and it has an irregular edge that may fade into the surrounding skin.

A dysplastic nevus may occur anywhere on the body, but it is usually seen in areas exposed to the sun, such as on the back. A dysplastic nevus may also appear in areas not exposed to the sun, such as the scalp, breasts, and areas below the waist. Some people have only a couple of dysplastic nevi, but other people have more than 10. People who have dysplastic nevi usually also have an increased number of common moles.

Can A Dysplastic Nevus Turn Into Melanoma?

Yes, but most dysplastic nevi do not turn into melanoma. Most remain stable over time. Researchers estimate that the chance of melanoma is about ten times greater for someone with more than five dysplastic nevi than for someone who has none, and the more dysplastic nevi a person has, the greater the chance of developing melanoma.

What Should People Do If They Have A Dysplastic Nevus?

Everyone should protect their skin from the sun and stay away from sunlamps and tanning booths, but for people who have dysplastic nevi, it is even more important to protect the skin and avoid getting a suntan or sunburn.

In addition, many doctors recommend that people with dysplastic nevi check their skin once a month. People should tell their doctor if they see any of the following changes in a dysplastic nevus:

- The color changes

- It gets smaller or bigger

- It changes in shape, texture, or height

- The skin on the surface becomes dry or scaly

- It becomes hard or feels lumpy

- It starts to itch

- It bleeds or oozes

Another thing that people with dysplastic nevi should do is get their skin examined by a doctor. Sometimes people or their doctors take photographs of dysplastic nevi so changes over time are easier to see. For people with many (more than five) dysplastic nevi, doctors may conduct a skin exam once or twice a year because of the moderately increased chance of melanoma. For people who also have a family history of melanoma, doctors may suggest a more frequent skin exam, such as every 3–6 months.

Should People Have A Doctor Remove A Dysplastic Nevus Or A Common Mole To Prevent It From Changing Into Melanoma?

No. Normally, people do not need to have a dysplastic nevus or common mole removed. One reason is that very few dysplastic nevi or common moles turn into melanoma. Another reason is that even removing all of the moles on the skin would not prevent the development of melanoma because melanoma can develop as a new colored area on the skin. That is why doctors usually remove only a mole that changes or a new colored area on the skin.

What Is Melanoma?

Melanoma is a type of skin cancer that begins in melanocytes. It is potentially dangerous because it can invade nearby tissues and spread to other parts of the body, such as the lung, liver, bone, or brain. The earlier that melanoma is detected and removed, the more likely that treatment will be successful.

Most melanocytes are in the skin, and melanoma can occur on any skin surface. It can develop from a common mole or dysplastic nevus, and it can also develop in an area of apparently normal skin. In addition, melanoma can also develop in the eye, the digestive tract, and other areas of the body.

When melanoma develops in men, it is often found on the head, neck, or back. When melanoma develops in women, it is often found on the back or on the lower legs.

People with dark skin are much less likely than people with fair skin to develop melanoma. When it does develop in people with dark skin, it is often found under the fingernails, under the toenails, on the palms of the hands, or on the soles of the feet.

What Does Melanoma Look Like?

Often the first sign of melanoma is a change in the shape, color, size, or feel of an existing mole. Melanoma may also appear as a new colored area on the skin.

The "ABCDE" rule describes the features of early melanoma:

- **Asymmetry.** The shape of one half does not match the other half.
- **Border that is irregular.** The edges are often ragged, notched, or blurred in outline. The pigment may spread into the surrounding skin.
- **Color that is uneven.** Shades of black, brown, and tan may be present. Areas of white, gray, red, pink, or blue may also be seen.
- **Diameter.** There is a change in size, usually an increase. Melanomas can be tiny, but most are larger than 6 millimeters wide (about 1/4 inch wide).
- **Evolving.** The mole has changed over the past few weeks or months.

Melanomas can vary greatly in how they look. Many show all of the ABCDE features. However, some may show only one or two of the ABCDE features.

In advanced melanoma, the texture of the mole may change. The skin on the surface may break down and look scraped. It may become hard or lumpy. The surface may ooze or bleed. Sometimes the melanoma is itchy, tender, or painful.

How Is Melanoma Diagnosed?

The only way to diagnose melanoma is to remove tissue and check it for cancer cells. The doctor will remove all or part of the skin that looks abnormal. Usually, this procedure takes only a few minutes and can be done in a doctor's office, clinic, or hospital. The sample will be sent to a lab and a pathologist will look at the tissue under a microscope to check for melanoma.

What Are The Differences Between A Common Mole, A Dysplastic Nevus, And A Melanoma?

Common moles, dysplastic nevi, and melanoma vary by size, color, shape, and surface texture. The list below summarizes some differences between moles and cancer. Another important difference is that a common mole or dysplastic nevus will not return after it is removed by a full excisional biopsy from the skin, but melanoma sometimes grows back. Also, melanoma can spread to other parts of the body.

Common Mole (Nevus)

- **Is it cancer?** No. Common moles rarely become cancer.

- **How many people have common moles?** Most American adults—about 300 million people—have common moles.

- **How big are they?** Usually less than 5 millimeters wide, or about 1/4 inch (not as wide as a new pencil eraser).

- **What color are they?** May be pink, tan, brown, black (in people with dark skin), or a color that is very close to a person's normal skin tone. The color is usually even throughout.

- **What shape are they?** Usually round or oval. A common mole has a distinct edge that separates it from the rest of the skin.

- **What is the surface texture?** Begins as a flat, smooth spot on the skin. May become raised and form a smooth bump.

Dysplastic Nevus

- **Is it cancer?** No. A dysplastic nevus is more likely than a common mole to become cancer, but most do not become cancer.

- **How many people have dysplastic nevi?** About 1 in 10 American adults—about 30 million people—have at least one dysplastic nevus.

- **How big are they?** Often wider than 5 millimeters (wider than a new pencil eraser).

- **What color are they?** May be a mixture of tan, brown, and red or pink shades.

- **What shape are they?** Have irregular or notched edges. May fade into the rest of the skin.

- **What is the surface texture?** May have a smooth, slightly scaly, or rough, irregular, and pebbly appearance.

Melanoma

- **Is it cancer?** Yes.

- **How many people have melanoma?** Melanoma is much less common than other kinds of skin cancer. But every year, about 2 in 10,000 Americans—more than 70,000 people—develop melanoma. More than 800,000 Americans alive today have been diagnosed with melanoma.

- **How big are they?** Usually wider than 6 millimeters (wider than a new pencil eraser).

- **What color are they?** Usually uneven in color. May have shades of black, brown, and tan. May also have areas of white, gray, red, pink, or blue.

- **What shape are they?** Often irregular and asymmetrical (the shape of one half does not match the other half). Edges may be ragged, notched, or blurred. May fade into the rest of the skin.

- **What is the surface texture?** May break down and look scraped, become hard or lumpy, or ooze or bleed.

What Should People Do If A Mole Changes, Or They Find A New Mole Or Some Other Change On Their Skin?

People should tell their doctor if they find a new mole or a change in an existing mole. A family doctor may refer people with an unusual mole or other concerns about their skin to a dermatologist. A dermatologist is a doctor who specializes in diseases of the skin. Also, some plastic surgeons, general surgeons, internists, cancer specialists, and family doctors have special training in moles and melanoma.

What Factors Increase The Chance Of Melanoma?

People with the following risk factors have an increased chance of melanoma:

- **Having a dysplastic nevus**

- **Having more than 50 common moles**

- **Sunlight:** Sunlight is a source of UV radiation, which causes skin damage that can lead to melanoma and other skin cancers.

  - **Severe, blistering sunburns:** People who have had at least one severe, blistering sunburn have an increased chance of melanoma. Although people who burn easily are more likely to have had sunburns as a child, sunburns during adulthood also increase the chance of melanoma.

  - **Lifetime sun exposure:** The greater the total amount of sun exposure over a lifetime, the greater the chance of melanoma.

  - **Tanning:** Although having skin that tans well lowers the risk of sunburn, even people who tan well without sunburning increase their chance of melanoma by spending time in the sun without protection.

  Sunlight can be reflected by sand, water, snow, ice, and pavement. The sun's rays can get through clouds, windshields, windows, and light clothing.

  In the United States, skin cancer is more common where the sun is strong. For example, a larger proportion of people in Texas than Minnesota get skin cancer. Also, the sun is strong at higher elevations, such as in the mountains.

- **Sunlamps and tanning booths:** UV radiation from artificial sources, such as sunlamps and tanning booths, can cause skin damage and melanoma. Healthcare providers strongly encourage people, especially young people, to avoid using sunlamps and tanning booths. The risk of skin cancer is greatly increased by using sunlamps and tanning booths before age 30.

- **Personal history:** People who have had melanoma have an increased risk of developing other melanomas.

- **Family history:** Melanoma sometimes runs in families. People who have two or more close relatives (mother, father, sister, brother, or child) with melanoma have an increased chance of melanoma. In rare cases, members of a family will have an inherited disorder, such as xeroderma pigmentosum, that makes the skin extremely sensitive to the sun and greatly increases the chance of melanoma.

- **Skin that burns easily:** People who have fair (pale) skin that burns easily in the sun, blue or gray eyes, red or blond hair, or many freckles have an increased chance of melanoma.

- **Certain medical conditions or medicines:** Medical conditions or medicines (such as some antibiotics, hormones, or antidepressants) that make skin more sensitive to the sun or that suppress the immune system increase the chance of melanoma.

How Can People Protect Their Skin From The Sun?

The best way to prevent melanoma is to limit exposure to sunlight. Having a suntan or sunburn means that the skin has been damaged by the sun, and continued tanning or burning increases the chance of developing melanoma.

Chapter 34

Specialized Children's Cancer Centers

Although cancer in children is rare, it is the leading cause of death by disease past infancy among children in the United States. In 2017, it is estimated that 15,270 children and adolescents ages 0–19 years will be diagnosed with cancer and 1,790 will die of the disease in the United States. Among children ages 0–14 years, it is estimated that 10,270 will be diagnosed with cancer.

The most common types of cancer diagnosed in children ages 0–14 years in the United States are leukemias, followed by brain and other central nervous system tumors, lymphomas, soft tissue sarcomas (of which half are rhabdomyosarcoma), neuroblastoma, and kidney tumors. The most common types of cancer diagnosed in 15–19-year-olds are lymphomas, followed by brain and other central nervous system tumors, leukemias, gonadal (testicular and ovarian) germ cell tumors, thyroid cancer, and melanoma.

As of January 1, 2014 (the most recent date for which data exists), approximately 419,000 survivors of childhood and adolescent cancer (diagnosed at ages 0–19 years) were alive in the United States. The number of survivors will continue to increase, given that the incidence of childhood cancer has been rising slightly in recent decades and that survival rates overall are improving.

Where Do Children With Cancer Get Treated?

Children who have cancer are often treated at a children's cancer center, which is a hospital or a unit within a hospital that specializes in diagnosing and treating children and adolescents

About This Chapter: This chapter includes text excerpted from "Cancer In Children And Adolescents," National Cancer Institute (NCI), August 24, 2017.

who have cancer. Most children's cancer centers treat patients up to 20 years of age. The health professionals at these centers have specific training and expertise to provide comprehensive care for children, adolescents, and their families.

Children's cancer centers also participate in clinical trials. The improvements in survival for children with cancer that have occurred over the past half century have been achieved because of treatment advances that were studied and proven to be effective in clinical trials.

More than 90 percent of children and adolescents who are diagnosed with cancer each year in the United States are cared for at a children's cancer center that is affiliated with the National Cancer Institute (NCI)-supported Children's Oncology Group (COG). COG is the world's largest organization that performs clinical research to improve the care and treatment of children and adolescents with cancer. Each year, approximately 4,000 children who are diagnosed with cancer enroll in a COG-sponsored clinical trial. Every children's cancer center that participates in COG has met strict standards of excellence for childhood cancer care. Families can ask their pediatrician or family doctor for a referral to a children's cancer center. Families and health professionals can call NCI's Contact Center at 800-4-CANCER (800-422-6237) to learn more about children's cancer centers that belong to COG.

Children's Oncology Group (COG) member institutions:

- treat more than 90 percent of the children and adolescents who are diagnosed with cancer each year in the United States

- have more than 8,000 physicians, nurses, and other experts in childhood cancer who work at more than 200 children's hospitals, university medical centers, and cancer centers throughout the United States and Canada, and at a growing number of international sites

- participate in clinical trials, which are research studies that help doctors to develop better treatments for children with cancer

(Source: "Children With Cancer—A Guide For Parents," National Cancer Institute (NCI).)

Can Children Who Have Cancer Be Treated At The National Institutes Of Health (NIH) Clinical Center?

Children with cancer may be eligible to be treated in clinical trials at the National Institutes of Health (NIH) Clinical Center in Bethesda, Maryland. Because the NIH Clinical Center is a research hospital, only patients who have a specific type or stage of cancer that is under study can be accepted for treatment. In some cases, patients with conditions that are rare or difficult to diagnose may also be accepted for treatment at the Clinical Center. All patients who are treated at the Clinical Center must be referred by a physician.

NCI's Pediatric Oncology Branch (POB) conducts clinical trials for children, adolescents, and young adults with a wide variety of cancers. Patients with newly diagnosed cancer, as well as patients whose cancers have come back after treatment, may be eligible to participate in a clinical trial. Physicians at the POB can also provide a second opinion on a patient's diagnosis or treatment plan. Parents can call 301-496-4256 (local) or 877-624-4878 (toll-free) weekdays between 8:30 a.m. and 5:00 p.m. ET to learn if their child is eligible to participate in a clinical trial.

Chapter 35

Cancer Staging

Stage refers to the extent of your cancer, such as how large the tumor is, and if it has spread. Knowing the stage of your cancer helps your doctor:

- Understand how serious your cancer is and your chances of survival

- Plan the best treatment for you

- Identify clinical trials that may be treatment options for you

A cancer is always referred to by the stage it was given at diagnosis, even if it gets worse or spreads. Information about how a cancer has changed over time gets added onto the original stage. So, the stage doesn't change, even though the cancer might.

How Stage Is Determined

To learn the stage of your disease, your doctor may order X-rays, lab tests, and other tests or procedures.

Systems That Describe Stage

There are many staging systems. Some, such as the tumor, node, metastasis (TNM) staging system, are used for many types of cancer. Others are specific to a particular type of cancer. Most staging systems include information about:

- Where the tumor is located in the body

About This Chapter: This chapter includes text excerpted from "Cancer Staging," National Cancer Institute (NCI), March 9, 2015.

- The cell type (such as, adenocarcinoma or squamous cell carcinoma (SCC))

- The size of the tumor

- Whether the cancer has spread to nearby lymph nodes

- Whether the cancer has spread to a different part of the body

- Tumor grade, which refers to how abnormal the cancer cells look and how likely the tumor is to grow and spread

---

What Is Tumor Grade?

Tumor grade is the description of a tumor based on how abnormal the tumor cells and the tumor tissue look under a microscope. It is an indicator of how quickly a tumor is likely to grow and spread. If the cells of the tumor and the organization of the tumors' tissue are close to those of normal cells and tissue, the tumor is called "well-differentiated." These tumors tend to grow and spread at a slower rate than tumors that are "undifferentiated" or "poorly differentiated," which have abnormal-looking cells and may lack normal tissue structures. Based on these and other differences in microscopic appearance, doctors assign a numerical "grade" to most cancers. The factors used to determine tumor grade can vary between different types of cancer.

Tumor grade is not the same as the stage of a cancer. Cancer stage refers to the size and/or extent (reach) of the original (primary) tumor and whether or not cancer cells have spread in the body. Cancer stage is based on factors such as the location of the primary tumor, tumor size, regional lymph node involvement (the spread of cancer to nearby lymph nodes), and the number of tumors present.

(Source: "Tumor Grade," National Cancer Institute (NCI).)

The TNM Staging System

The TNM system is the most widely used cancer staging system. Most hospitals and medical centers use the TNM system as their main method for cancer reporting. You are likely to see your cancer described by this staging system in your pathology report, unless you have a cancer for which a different staging system is used. Examples of cancers with different staging systems include brain and spinal cord tumors and blood cancers.

In the TNM system:

- The T refers to the size and extent of the main tumor. The main tumor is usually called the primary tumor.

- The N refers to the number of nearby lymph nodes that have cancer.

- The M refers to whether the cancer has metastasized. This means that the cancer has spread from the primary tumor to other parts of the body.

When your cancer is described by the TNM system, there will be numbers after each letter that give more details about the cancer—for example, T1N0MX or T3N1M0. The following explains what the letters and numbers mean:

Primary tumor (T)

- TX: Main tumor cannot be measured.

- T0: Main tumor cannot be found.

- T1, T2, T3, T4: Refers to the size and/or extent of the main tumor. The higher the number after the T, the larger the tumor or the more it has grown into nearby tissues. T's may be further divided to provide more detail, such as T3a and T3b.

Regional lymph nodes (N)

- NX: Cancer in nearby lymph nodes cannot be measured.

- N0: There is no cancer in nearby lymph nodes.

- N1, N2, N3: Refers to the number and location of lymph nodes that contain cancer. The higher the number after the N, the more lymph nodes that contain cancer.

Distant metastasis (M)

- MX: Metastasis cannot be measured.

- M0: Cancer has not spread to other parts of the body.

- M1: Cancer has spread to other parts of the body.

Other Ways To Describe Stage

The TNM system helps describe cancer in great detail. But, for many cancers, the TNM combinations are grouped into five less detailed stages. When talking about your cancer, your doctor or nurse may describe it as one of these stages:

Another staging system that is used for all types of cancer groups the cancer into one of five main categories. This staging system is more often used by cancer registries than by

Table 35.1. Different Categories Of Staging

Stage	What It Means
Stage 0	Abnormal cells are present but have not spread to nearby tissue. Also called carcinoma in situ, or CIS. CIS is not cancer, but it may become cancer.
Stage I, Stage II, and Stage III	Cancer is present. The higher the number, the larger the cancer tumor and the more it has spread into nearby tissues.
Stage IV	The cancer has spread to distant parts of the body.

doctors. But, you may still hear your doctor or nurse describe your cancer in one of the following ways:

- **In situ**—Abnormal cells are present but have not spread to nearby tissue.

- **Localized**—Cancer is limited to the place where it started, with no sign that it has spread.

- **Regional**—Cancer has spread to nearby lymph nodes, tissues, or organs.

- **Distant**—Cancer has spread to distant parts of the body.

- **Unknown**—There is not enough information to figure out the stage.

Chapter 36

Chemotherapy

Chemotherapy (also called chemo) is a type of cancer treatment that uses drugs to kill cancer cells.

How Chemotherapy Works Against Cancer

Chemotherapy works by stopping or slowing the growth of cancer cells, which grow and divide quickly. Chemotherapy is used to:

- **Treat cancer.** Chemotherapy can be used to cure cancer, lessen the chance it will return, or stop or slow its growth.

- **Ease cancer symptoms.** Chemotherapy can be used to shrink tumors that are causing pain and other problems.

Who Receives Chemotherapy?

Chemotherapy is used to treat many types of cancer. For some people, chemotherapy may be the only treatment you receive. But most often, you will have chemotherapy and other cancer treatments. The types of treatment that you need depends on the type of cancer you have, if it has spread and where, and if you have other health problems.

About This Chapter: This chapter includes text excerpted from "Chemotherapy To Treat Cancer," National Cancer Institute (NCI), April 29, 2015.

How Chemotherapy Is Used With Other Cancer Treatments

When used with other treatments, chemotherapy can:

- Make a tumor smaller before surgery or radiation therapy. This is called neoadjuvant chemotherapy (NAC).

- Destroy cancer cells that may remain after treatment with surgery or radiation therapy. This is called adjuvant chemotherapy.

- Help other treatments work better.

- Kill cancer cells that have returned or spread to other parts of your body.

Chemotherapy Can Cause Side Effects

Chemotherapy not only kills fast-growing cancer cells, but also kills or slows the growth of healthy cells that grow and divide quickly. Examples are cells that line your mouth and intestines and those that cause your hair to grow. Damage to healthy cells may cause side effects, such as mouth sores, nausea, and hair loss. Side effects often get better or go away after you have finished chemotherapy.

The most common side effect is fatigue, which is feeling exhausted and worn out. You can prepare for fatigue by:

- Asking someone to drive you to and from chemotherapy

- Planning time to rest on the day of and day after chemotherapy

- Asking for help with meals and child care on the day of and at least one day after chemotherapy

There are many ways you can help manage chemotherapy side effects.

How Much Does Chemotherapy Cost?

The cost of chemotherapy depends on:

- The types and doses of chemotherapy used
- How long and how often chemotherapy is given
- Whether you get chemotherapy at home, in a clinic or office, or during a hospital stay
- The part of the country where you live

What To Expect When Receiving Chemotherapy

Chemotherapy may be given in many ways. Some common ways include:

- **Oral.** The chemotherapy comes in pills, capsules, or liquids that you swallow

- **Intravenous (IV).** The chemotherapy goes directly into a vein

- **Injection.** The chemotherapy is given by a shot in a muscle in your arm, thigh, or hip, or right under the skin in the fatty part of your arm, leg, or belly

- **Intrathecal.** The chemotherapy is injected into the space between the layers of tissue that cover the brain and spinal cord

- **Intraperitoneal (IP).** The chemotherapy goes directly into the peritoneal cavity, which is the area in your body that contains organs such as your intestines, stomach, and liver

- **Intra arterial (IA).** The chemotherapy is injected directly into the artery that leads to the cancer

- **Topical.** The chemotherapy comes in a cream that you rub onto your skin

Chemotherapy is often given through a thin needle that is placed in a vein on your hand or lower arm. Your nurse will put the needle in at the start of each treatment and remove it when treatment is over. Intravenous (IV) chemotherapy may also be given through catheters or ports, sometimes with the help of a pump.

- **Catheter.** A catheter is a thin, soft tube. A doctor or nurse places one end of the catheter in a large vein, often in your chest area. The other end of the catheter stays outside your body. Most catheters stay in place until you have finished your chemotherapy treatments. Catheters can also be used to give you other drugs and to draw blood. Be sure to watch for signs of infection around your catheter.

- **Port.** A port is a small, round disc that is placed under your skin during minor surgery. A surgeon puts it in place before you begin your course of treatment, and it remains there until you have finished. A catheter connects the port to a large vein, most often in your chest. Your nurse can insert a needle into your port to give you chemotherapy or draw blood. This needle can be left in place for chemotherapy treatments that are given for longer than one day. Be sure to watch for signs of infection around your port.

- **Pump.** Pumps are often attached to catheters or ports. They control how much and how fast chemotherapy goes into a catheter or port, allowing you to receive your chemotherapy outside of the hospital. Pumps can be internal or external. External pumps remain outside your body. Internal pumps are placed under your skin during surgery.

How Your Doctor Decides Which Chemotherapy Drugs To Give You

There are many different chemotherapy drugs. Which ones are included in your treatment plan depends mostly on:

- The type of cancer you have and how advanced it is

- Whether you have had chemotherapy before

- Whether you have other health problems, such as diabetes or heart disease

Where You Go For Chemotherapy

You may receive chemotherapy during a hospital stay, at home, or as an outpatient at a doctor's office, clinic, or hospital. Outpatient (OP) means you do not stay overnight. No matter where you go for chemotherapy, your doctor and nurse will watch for side effects and help you manage them.

How Often You Receive Chemotherapy

Treatment schedules for chemotherapy vary widely. How often and how long you get chemotherapy depends on:

- Your type of cancer and how advanced it is

- Whether chemotherapy is used to:

  - Cure your cancer

  - Control its growth

  - Ease symptoms

- The type of chemotherapy you are getting

- How your body responds to the chemotherapy

You may receive chemotherapy in cycles. A cycle is a period of chemotherapy treatment followed by a period of rest. For instance, you might receive chemotherapy every day for one week followed by three weeks with no chemotherapy. These four weeks make up one cycle. The rest period gives your body a chance to recover and build new healthy cells.

Missing A Chemotherapy Treatment

It is best not to skip a chemotherapy treatment. But, sometimes your doctor may change your chemotherapy schedule if you are having certain side effects. If this happens, your doctor or nurse will explain what to do and when to start treatment again.

How Chemotherapy May Affect You

Chemotherapy affects people in different ways. How you feel depends on:

- The type of chemotherapy you are getting
- The dose of chemotherapy you are getting
- Your type of cancer
- How advanced your cancer is
- How healthy you are before treatment

Since everyone is different and people respond to chemotherapy in different ways, your doctor and nurses cannot know for sure how you will feel during chemotherapy.

How Will I Know If My Chemotherapy Is Working?

You will see your doctor often. During these visits, they will ask you how you feel, do a physical exam, and order medical tests and scans. Tests might include blood tests. Scans might include magnetic resonance imaging (MRI), computed tomography (CT), or positron emission tomography (PET) scans.

You cannot tell if chemotherapy is working based on its side effects. Some people think that severe side effects mean that chemotherapy is working well, or that no side effects mean that chemotherapy is not working. The truth is that side effects have nothing to do with how well chemotherapy is fighting your cancer.

Special Diet Needs

Chemotherapy can damage the healthy cells that line your mouth and intestines and cause eating problems. Tell your doctor or nurse if you have trouble eating while you are receiving chemotherapy. You might also find it helpful to speak with a dietitian.

Chapter 37

Hormone Therapy

Hormone therapy is a cancer treatment that slows or stops the growth of cancer that uses hormones to grow. Hormone therapy is also called hormonal therapy, hormone treatment, or endocrine therapy.

How Hormone Therapy Works Against Cancer

Hormone therapy is used to treat cancer. Hormone therapy can lessen the chance that cancer will return or stop or slow its growth.

Types Of Hormone Therapy

Hormone therapy falls into two broad groups, those that block the body's ability to produce hormones and those that interfere with how hormones behave in the body.

Who Receives Hormone Therapy

Hormone therapy is most often used along with other cancer treatments. The types of treatment that you need depend on the type of cancer, if it has spread and how far, if it uses hormones to grow, and if you have other health problems.

About This Chapter: This chapter includes text excerpted from "Hormone Therapy To Treat Cancer," National Cancer Institute (NCI), April 29, 2015.

How Hormone Therapy Is Used With Other Cancer Treatments

When used with other treatments, hormone therapy can:

- Make a tumor smaller before surgery or radiation therapy. This is called neo-adjuvant therapy.

- Lower the risk that cancer will come back after the main treatment. This is called adjuvant therapy.

- Destroy cancer cells that have returned or spread to other parts of your body.

Hormone Therapy Can Cause Side Effects

Because hormone therapy blocks your body's ability to produce hormones or interferes with how hormones behave, it can cause unwanted side effects. The side effects you have will depend on the type of hormone therapy you receive and how your body responds to it. People respond differently to the same treatment, so not everyone gets the same side effects. Some side effects also differ if you are a boy or a girl.

Some common side effects for boys who receive hormone therapy include:

- Weakened bones

- Diarrhea

- Nausea

- Fatigue

Some common side effects for women who receive hormone therapy for breast cancer include:

- Hot flashes

- Vaginal dryness

- Changes in your periods

- Nausea

- Mood changes

- Fatigue

How Much Hormone Therapy Costs

The cost of hormone therapy depends on:

- The types of hormone therapy you receive
- How long and how often you receive hormone therapy
- The part of the country where you live

Talk with your health insurance company about what services it will pay for. Most insurance plans pay for hormone therapy for their members.

What To Expect When Receiving Hormone Therapy

How Hormone Therapy Is Given

Hormone therapy may be given in many ways. Some common ways include:

- **Oral.** Hormone therapy comes in pills that you swallow.
- **Injection.** The hormone therapy is given by a shot in a muscle in your arm, thigh, or hip, or right under the skin in the fatty part of your arm, leg, or belly.
- **Surgery.** You may have surgery to remove organs that produce hormones. In women, the ovaries are removed. In men, the testicles are removed.

Where You Receive Hormone Therapy

Where you receive treatment depends on which hormone therapy you are getting and how it is given. You may take hormone therapy at home. Or, you may receive hormone therapy in a doctor's office, clinic, or hospital.

How Hormone Therapy May Affect You

Hormone therapy affects people in different ways. How you feel depends on the type of cancer you have, how advanced it is, the type of hormone therapy you are getting, and the dose. Your doctors and nurses cannot know for certain how you will feel during hormone therapy.

Special Diet Needs

Hormone therapy may cause weight gain. Talk with your doctor, nurse, or dietitian if weight gain becomes a problem for you.

Chapter 38

Immunotherapy

Immunotherapy is a type of cancer treatment that helps your immune system fight cancer. The immune system helps your body fight infections and other diseases. It is made up of white blood cells and organs and tissues of the lymph system.

Immunotherapy is a type of biological therapy.

What Is Biological Therapy?

Biological therapy involves the use of living organisms, substances derived from living organisms, or laboratory-produced versions of such substances to treat disease. For patients with cancer, biological therapies may be used to treat the cancer itself or the side effects of other cancer treatments.

(Source: "Biological Therapies For Cancer," National Cancer Institute (NCI).)

Types Of Immunotherapy

Many different types of immunotherapy are used to treat cancer. They include:

- **Monoclonal antibodies,** which are drugs that are designed to bind to specific targets in the body. They can cause an immune response that destroys cancer cells.

  Other types of monoclonal antibodies can "mark" cancer cells so it is easier for the immune system to find and destroy them. These types of monoclonal antibodies may also be referred to as targeted therapy.

About This Chapter: This chapter includes text excerpted from "Cancer Treatment—Immunotherapy To Treat Cancer," National Cancer Institute (NCI), May 4, 2017.

- **Adoptive cell transfer,** which is a treatment that attempts to boost the natural ability of your T cells to fight cancer. T cells are a type of white blood cell and part of the immune system. Researchers take T cells from the tumor. They then isolate the T cells that are most active against your cancer or modify the genes in them to make them better able to find and destroy your cancer cells. Researchers then grow large batches of these T cells in the lab.

You may have treatments to reduce your immune cells. After these treatments, the T cells that were grown in the lab will be given back to you via a needle in your vein. The process of growing your T cells in the lab can take 2–8 weeks, depending on how fast they grow.

- **Cytokines,** which are proteins that are made by your body's cells. They play important roles in the body's normal immune responses and also in the immune system's ability to respond to cancer. The two main types of cytokines used to treat cancer are called interferons and interleukins.

- **Treatment vaccines,** which work against cancer by boosting your immune system's response to cancer cells. Treatment vaccines are different from the ones that help prevent disease.

- **BCG,** which stands for Bacillus Calmette-Guérin, is an immunotherapy that is used to treat bladder cancer. It is a weakened form of the bacteria that causes tuberculosis. When inserted directly into the bladder with a catheter, BCG causes an immune response against cancer cells. It is also being studied in other types of cancer.

Who Receives Immunotherapy

Immunotherapy is not yet as widely used as surgery, chemotherapy, and radiation therapy. However, immunotherapies have been approved to treat people with many types of cancer.

Many other immunotherapies are being studied in clinical trials, which are research studies involving people.

How Immunotherapy Works Against Cancer

One reason that cancer cells thrive is because they are able to hide from your immune system. Certain immunotherapies can mark cancer cells so it is easier for the immune system to find and destroy them. Other immunotherapies boost your immune system to work better against cancer.

Immunotherapy Can Cause Side Effects

Immunotherapy can cause side effects, which affect people in different ways. The side effects you may have and how they make you feel will depend on how healthy you are before treatment, your type of cancer, how advanced it is, the type of therapy you are getting, and the dose. Doctors and nurses cannot know for certain how you will feel during treatment.

The most common side effects are skin reactions at the needle site. These side effects include:

- Pain

- Swelling

- Soreness

- Redness

- Itchiness

- Rash

You may have flu-like symptoms, which include:

- Fever

- Chills

- Weakness

- Dizziness

- Nausea or vomiting

- Muscle or joint aches

- Fatigue

- Headache

- Trouble breathing

- Low or high blood pressure

Other side effects might include:

- Swelling and weight gain from retaining fluid

- Heart palpitations

- Sinus congestion

- Diarrhea
- Risk of infection

Immunotherapies may also cause severe or even fatal allergic reactions. However, these reactions are rare.

How Immunotherapy Is Given

Different forms of immunotherapy may be given in different ways. These include:

- **Intravenous (IV).** The immunotherapy goes directly into a vein.
- **Oral.** The immunotherapy comes in pills or capsules that you swallow.
- **Topical.** The immunotherapy comes in a cream that you rub onto your skin. This type of immunotherapy can be used for very early skin cancer.
- **Intravesical.** The immunotherapy goes directly into the bladder.

Where You Go For Your Immunotherapy Treatment

You may receive immunotherapy in a doctor's office, clinic, or outpatient unit in a hospital. Outpatient means you do not spend the night in the hospital.

How Often You Will Receive Immunotherapy Treatment

How often and how long you receive immunotherapy depends on:

- Your type of cancer and how advanced it is
- The type of immunotherapy you get
- How your body reacts to treatment

You may have treatment every day, week, or month. Some immunotherapies are given in cycles. A cycle is a period of treatment followed by a period of rest. The rest period gives your body a chance to recover, respond to the immunotherapy, and build new healthy cells.

How To Tell Whether Immunotherapy Is Working

You will see your doctor often. He or she will give you physical exams and ask you how you feel. You will have medical tests, such as blood tests and different types of scans. These tests will measure the size of your tumor and look for changes in your blood work.

Chapter 39

Precision Medicine

Precision medicine is an approach to patient care that allows doctors to select treatments that are most likely to help patients based on a genetic understanding of their disease. This may also be called personalized medicine. The idea of precision medicine is not new, but recent advances in science and technology have helped speed up the pace of this area of research.

When you are diagnosed with cancer, you usually receive the same treatment as others who have same type and stage of cancer. Even so, different people may respond differently, and doctors didn't know why. After decades of research, scientists now understand that patients' tumors have genetic changes that cause cancer to grow and spread. They have also learned that the changes that occur in one person's cancer may not occur in others who have the same type of cancer. And, the same cancer-causing changes may be found in different types of cancer.

The Promise Of Precision Medicine

The hope of precision medicine is that treatments will one day be tailored to the genetic changes in each person's cancer. Scientists see a future when genetic tests will help decide which treatments a patient's tumor is most likely to respond to, sparing the patient from receiving treatments that are not likely to help. Research studies are going on now to test whether treating patients with treatments that target the cancer-causing genetic changes in their tumors, no matter where the cancer develops in the body, will help them. Many of these treatments are drugs known as targeted therapies.

About This Chapter: This chapter includes text excerpted from "Precision Medicine In Cancer Treatment," National Cancer Institute (NCI), October 3, 2017.

> ## What Are Targeted Cancer Therapies?
>
> Targeted cancer therapies are drugs or other substances that block the growth and spread of cancer by interfering with specific molecules ("molecular targets") that are involved in the growth, progression, and spread of cancer. Targeted cancer therapies are sometimes called "molecularly targeted drugs," "molecularly targeted therapies," "precision medicines," or similar names.
>
> *(Source: "Targeted Cancer Therapies," National Cancer Institute (NCI).)*

If you need treatment for cancer, you may receive a combination of treatments, including surgery, chemotherapy, radiation therapy, and immunotherapy. Which treatments you receive usually will depend on the type of cancer, its size, and whether it has spread. With precision medicine, information about genetic changes in your tumor can help decide which treatment will work best for you.

There are drugs that have been proven effective against cancers with specific genetic changes and are approved by the U.S. Food and Drug Administration (FDA). Approved treatments should be available wherever you have cancer treatment.

Precision Medicine As A Treatment Approach

Even though researchers are making progress every day, the precision medicine approach to cancer treatment is not yet part of routine care for most patients. Many new treatments designed to target a specific change are being tested right now in precision medicine clinical trials. Some clinical trials are accepting patients with specific types and stages of cancer. Others accept patients with a variety of cancer types and stages. To be eligible for precision medicine trials, your tumor must have a genetic change that can be targeted by a treatment being tested.

Precision Medicine Does Not Yet Apply To Everyone

If there is a targeted drug or other treatment approved for your type of cancer, you will likely be tested to see if the genetic change targeted by the treatment is present in your cancer. For instance, people with melanoma, some leukemias, and breast, lung, colon, and rectal cancers usually have their cancers tested for certain genetic changes when they are diagnosed. Since additional genetic changes that can drive cancer may occur over time, you might also have your cancer tested if it comes back or gets worse.

If there is not an approved targeted treatment for your type of cancer, you still may be tested for genetic changes. For instance, your cancer may be tested to see if you can join a precision medicine clinical trial.

How Genetic Changes In Your Cancer Are Identified

To figure out which genetic changes are in your cancer, you may need to have a biopsy. A biopsy is a procedure in which your doctor removes a sample of the cancer. This sample will be sent to a special lab, where a machine called a deoxyribonucleic acid (DNA) sequencer looks for genetic changes that may be causing the cancer to grow. The process of looking for genetic changes in cancer may be called DNA sequencing, genomic testing, molecular profiling, or tumor profiling.

Paying For Precision Medicine

Testing for genetic changes in your cancer may be covered by your insurance.

If you join a precision medicine clinical trial, the cost of testing for genetic changes may be covered by the organization sponsoring the trial. To be sure, check with the trial staff and make sure that you understand your consent form.

Treatment using precision medicine can be expensive. It takes many years, sometimes decades, of research to develop treatments that target the changes that cause cancer to develop, grow, and spread. So, by the time these treatments are available on the market, they are often very expensive.

Chapter 40

Radiation Therapy

Radiation therapy (also called radiotherapy) is a cancer treatment that uses high doses of radiation to kill cancer cells and shrink tumors. At low doses, radiation is used in X-rays to see inside your body, as with X-rays of your teeth or broken bones.

How Radiation Therapy Works Against Cancer

At high doses, radiation therapy kills cancer cells or slows their growth by damaging their deoxyribonucleic acid (DNA). Cancer cells whose DNA is damaged beyond repair stop dividing or die. When the damaged cells die, they are broken down and removed by the body. Radiation therapy does not kill cancer cells right away. It takes days or weeks of treatment before DNA is damaged enough for cancer cells to die. Then, cancer cells keep dying for weeks or months after radiation therapy ends.

Types Of Radiation Therapy

There are two main types of radiation therapy, external beam and internal.

External Beam Radiation Therapy

External beam radiation therapy comes from a machine that aims radiation at your cancer. The machine is large and may be noisy. It does not touch you, but can move around you, sending radiation to a part of your body from many directions. External beam radiation

About This Chapter: This chapter includes text excerpted from "Cancer Treatment—Radiation Therapy To Treat Cancer," National Cancer Institute (NCI), July 19, 2017.

therapy is a local treatment, which means it treats a specific part of your body. For example, if you have cancer in your lung, you will have radiation only to your chest, not to your whole body.

Internal Radiation Therapy

Internal radiation therapy is a treatment in which a source of radiation is put inside your body. The radiation source can be solid or liquid. Internal radiation therapy with a solid source is called brachytherapy. In this type of treatment, seeds, ribbons, or capsules that contain a radiation source are placed in your body in or near the tumor. Like external beam radiation therapy, brachytherapy is a local treatment and treats only a specific part of your body.

Internal radiation therapy with a liquid source is called systemic therapy. Systemic means that the treatment travels in the blood to tissues throughout your body, seeking out and killing cancer cells. You receive systemic radiation therapy by swallowing or through a vein, via an intravenous (IV) line.

The type of radiation therapy that you may have depends on many factors, including:

- The type of cancer

- The size of the tumor

- The tumor's location in the body

- How close the tumor is to normal tissues that are sensitive to radiation

- Your general health and medical history

- Whether you will have other types of cancer treatment

- Other factors, such as your age and other medical conditions

Why People With Cancer Receive Radiation Therapy

Radiation therapy is used to treat cancer and ease cancer symptoms. When treatments are used to ease symptoms, they are known as palliative treatments. External beam radiation may shrink tumors to treat pain and other problems caused by the tumor, such as trouble breathing or loss of bowel and bladder control. Pain from cancer that has spread to the bone can be treated with systemic radiation therapy drugs called radiopharmaceuticals. When used to treat cancer, radiation therapy can cure cancer, prevent it from returning, or stop or slow its growth.

Types Of Cancer That Are Treated With Radiation Therapy

External beam radiation therapy is used to treat many types of cancer. Brachytherapy is often used to treat cancers of the head and neck, breast, cervix, and eye. Systemic radiation therapy is most often used to treat certain types of thyroid cancer. This treatment uses radioactive iodine, which is also known as I-131.

How Radiation Is Used With Other Cancer Treatments

For some people, radiation may be the only treatment you need. But, most often, you will have radiation therapy with other cancer treatments, such as surgery, chemotherapy, and immunotherapy. Radiation therapy may be given before, during, or after these other treatments to improve the chances that treatment will work. The timing of when radiation therapy is given depends on the type of cancer being treated and whether the goal of radiation therapy is to treat the cancer or ease symptoms.

When radiation is combined with surgery, it can be given:

- Before surgery, to shrink the size of the cancer so it can be removed by surgery and be less likely to return.

- During surgery, so that it goes straight to the cancer without passing through the skin. Radiation therapy used this way is called intraoperative radiation. With this technique, doctors can more easily protect nearby normal tissues from radiation.

- After surgery to kill any cancer cells that remain.

Lifetime Dose Limits

There is a limit to the amount of radiation an area of your body can safely receive over the course of your lifetime. Depending on how much radiation an area has already been treated with, you may not be able to have radiation therapy to that area a second time. But, if one area of the body has already received the safe lifetime dose of radiation, another area might still be treated if the distance between the two areas is large enough.

Radiation Therapy Can Cause Side Effects

Radiation not only kills or slows the growth of cancer cells, it can also affect nearby healthy cells. Damage to healthy cells can cause side effects. Many people who get radiation therapy have fatigue. Fatigue is feeling exhausted and worn out. It can happen all at once or come on slowly. People feel fatigue in different ways and you may feel more or less fatigue than someone else who is getting the same amount of radiation therapy to the same part of the body.

Other radiation therapy side effects you may have depend on the part of the body that is treated. To see which side effects you might expect, find the part of your body being treated in the following table 40.1. Discuss this with your doctor or nurse. Ask them about your chances of getting each side effect.

Table 40.1. Treatment Areas And Possible Side Effects

Part Of The Body Being Treated	Possible Side Effects
Brain	Fatigue Hair loss Nausea and vomiting Skin changes Headache Blurry vision
Breast	Fatigue Hair loss Skin changes Swelling (Edema) Tenderness
Chest	Fatigue Hair loss Skin changes Throat changes, such as trouble swallowing Cough Shortness of breath
Head and Neck	Fatigue Hair loss Mouth changes Skin changes Taste changes Throat changes, such as trouble swallowing Less active thyroid gland

Table 40.1. Continued

Part Of The Body Being Treated	Possible Side Effects
Pelvis	Diarrhea Fatigue Hair loss Nausea and vomiting Sexual problems (men) Fertility problems (men) Sexual problems (women) Fertility problems (women) Skin changes Urinary and bladder changes
Rectum	Diarrhea Fatigue Hair loss Sexual problems (men) Fertility problems (men) Sexual problems (women) Fertility problems (women) Skin changes Urinary and bladder changes
Stomach and Abdomen	Diarrhea Fatigue Hair loss Nausea and vomiting Skin changes Urinary and bladder change

Healthy cells that are damaged during radiation treatment usually recover within a few months after treatment is over. But sometimes people may have side effects that do not improve. Other side effects may show up months or years after radiation therapy is over. These are called late effects. Whether you might have late effects, and what they might be, depends on the part of your body that was treated, other cancer treatments you've had, genetics, and other factors, such as smoking. Ask your doctor or nurse which late effects you should watch for.

How Much Radiation Therapy Costs

Radiation therapy can be expensive. It uses complex machines and involves the services of many healthcare providers. The exact cost of your radiation therapy depends on the cost of healthcare where you live, what type of radiation therapy you get, and how many treatments you need.

Talk with your health insurance company about what services it will pay for. Most insurance plans pay for radiation therapy.

What To Expect When Having External Beam Radiation Therapy

How Often You Will Have External Beam Radiation Therapy

Most people have external beam radiation therapy once a day, five days a week, Monday through Friday. Radiation is given in a series of treatments to allow healthy cells to recover and to make radiation more effective. How many weeks you have treatment depends on the type of cancer you have, the goal of your treatment, the radiation dose, and the radiation schedule.

The span of time from your first radiation treatment to the last is called a course of treatment.

Researchers are looking at different ways to adjust the radiation dose or schedule in order to reach the total dose of radiation more quickly or to limit damage to healthy cells. Different ways of delivering the total radiation dose include:

- Accelerated fractionation, which is treatment given in larger daily or weekly doses to reduce the number of weeks of treatment.

- Hyperfractionation, which is a smaller dose than the usual daily dose of radiation given more than once a day.

- Hypofractionation, which is larger doses given once a day or less often to reduce the number of treatments.

Researchers hope these different schedules for delivering radiation may be more effective and cause fewer side effects than the usual way of doing it or be as effective but more convenient.

Where You Go For External Beam Radiation Therapy

Most of the time, you will get external beam radiation therapy as an outpatient. This means that you will have treatment at a clinic or radiation therapy center and will not stay the night in the hospital.

What Happens Before Your First External Beam Radiation Therapy Treatment

You will have a 1–2-hour meeting with your doctor or nurse before you begin radiation therapy. At this time, you will have a physical exam, talk about your medical history, and maybe have imaging tests. Your doctor or nurse will discuss external beam radiation therapy, its benefits and side effects, and ways you can care for yourself during and after treatment. You can then choose whether to have external beam radiation therapy.

If you decide to have external beam radiation therapy, you will be scheduled for a treatment planning session called a simulation. At this time:

- A radiation oncologist (a doctor who specializes in using radiation to treat cancer) and radiation therapist will figure out your treatment area. You may also hear the treatment area referred to as the treatment port or treatment field. These terms refer to the places in your body that will get radiation. You will be asked to lie very still while X-rays or scans are taken.

- The radiation therapist will tattoo or draw small dots of colored ink on your skin to mark the treatment area. These dots will be needed throughout your course of radiation therapy. The radiation therapist will use them to make sure you are in exactly the same position for every treatment. The dots are about the size of a freckle. If the dots are tattooed, they will remain on your skin for the rest of your life. Ink markings will fade over time. Be careful not to remove them and tell the radiation therapist if they have faded or lost color.

- A body mold may be made of the part of the body that is being treated. This is a plastic or plaster form that keeps you from moving during treatment. It also helps make sure that you are in exactly the same position for each treatment

- If you are getting radiation to the head and neck area you may be fitted for a mask. The mask has many air holes. It attaches to the table where you will lie for your treatments. The mask helps keep your head from moving so that you are in exactly the same position for each treatment.

What To Wear For Your Treatments

Wear clothes that are comfortable and made of soft fabric, such as fleece or cotton. Choose clothes that are easy to take off, since you may need to expose the treatment area or change into a hospital gown. Do not wear clothes that are tight, such as close-fitting collars or waistbands, near your treatment area. Also, do not wear jewelry, adhesive bandages, or powder in the treatment area.

What Happens During A Treatment Session

- You may be asked to change into a hospital gown or robe.

- You will go to the treatment room where you will receive radiation. The temperature in this room will be very cool.

- Depending on where your cancer is, you will either lie down on a treatment table or sit in a special chair. The radiation therapist will use the dots on your skin and body mold or face mask, if you have one, to help you get into the right position.

- You may see colored lights pointed at your skin marks. These lights are harmless and help the therapist position you for treatment.

- You will need to stay very still so the radiation goes to the exact same place each time. You will get radiation for 1–5 minutes. During this time, you can breathe normally.

The radiation therapist will leave the room just before your treatment begins. He or she will go to a nearby room to control the radiation machine. The therapist watches you on a TV screen or through a window and talks with you through a speaker in the treatment room. Make sure to tell the therapist if you feel sick or are uncomfortable. He or she can stop the radiation machine at any time. You will hear the radiation machine and see it moving around, but you won't be able to feel, hear, see, or smell the radiation. Most visits last from 30 minutes to an hour, with most of that time spent helping you get into the correct position.

How To Relax For Treatment Sessions

Keep yourself busy while you wait:

- Read a book or magazine.

- Work on crossword puzzles or needlework.

- Use headphones to listen to music or recorded books.

- Meditate, breathe deeply, pray, use imagery, or find other ways to relax.

External Beam Radiation Therapy Will Not Make You Radioactive

People often wonder if they will be radioactive when they are having treatment with radiation. External beam radiation therapy will not make you radioactive. You may safely be around other people, even pregnant women, babies, and young children.

What To Expect When Having Internal Radiation Therapy

What Happens Before Your First Internal Radiation Therapy Treatment

You will have a 1–2-hour meeting with your doctor or nurse to plan your treatment before you begin internal radiation therapy. At this time, you will have a physical exam, talk about your medical history, and maybe have imaging tests. Your doctor will discuss the type of internal radiation therapy that is best for you, its benefits and side effects, and ways you can care for yourself during and after treatment. You can then decide whether to have internal radiation therapy.

How Brachytherapy Is Put In Place

Most brachytherapy is put in place through a catheter, which is a small, stretchy tube. Sometimes, brachytherapy is put in place through a larger device called an applicator. The way the brachytherapy is put in place depends on your type of cancer. Your doctor will place the catheter or applicator into your body before you begin treatment.

Techniques for placing brachytherapy include:

- **Interstital brachytherapy**, in which the radiation source is placed within the tumor. This technique is used for prostate cancer, for instance.

- **Intracavity brachytherapy**, in which the radiation source is placed within a body cavity or a cavity created by surgery. For example, radiation can be placed in the vagina to treat cervical or endometrial cancer.

- **Episcleral brachytherapy**, in which the radiation source is attached to the eye. This technique is used to treat melanoma of the eye.

Once the catheter or applicator is in place, the radiation source is placed inside it. The radiation source may be kept in place for a few minutes, for many days, or for the rest of your life. How long it remains in place depends on the type of radiation source, your type of cancer, where the cancer is in your body, your health, and other cancer treatments you have had.

Types Of Brachytherapy

There are three types of brachytherapy:

1. **Low-dose rate (LDR) implants.** In this type of brachytherapy, the radiation source stays in place for 1–7 days. You are likely to be in the hospital during this time. Once

your treatment is finished, your doctor will remove the radiation source and the catheter or applicator.

2. **High-dose rate (HDR) implants.** In this type of brachytherapy, the radiation source is left in place for just 10–20 minutes at a time and then taken out. You may have treatment twice a day for 2–5 days or once a week for 2–5 weeks. The schedule depends on your type of cancer. During the course of treatment, your catheter or applicator may stay in place, or it may be put in place before each treatment. You may be in the hospital during this time, or you may make daily trips to the hospital to have the radiation source put in place. As with LDR implants, your doctor will remove the catheter or applicator once you have finished treatment.

3. **Permanent implants.** After the radiation source is put in place, the catheter is removed. The implants remain in your body for the rest of your life, but the radiation gets weaker each day. As time goes on, almost all the radiation will go away. When the radiation is first put in place, you may need to limit your time around other people and take other safety measures. Be extra careful not to spend time with children or pregnant women.

Internal Radiation Therapy Makes You Give Off Radiation

With systemic radiation, your body fluids (urine, sweat, and saliva) will give off radiation for a while. With brachytherapy, your body fluids will not give off radiation, but the radiation source in your body will. If the radiation you receive is a very high dose, you may need to follow some safety measures. These measures may include:

- Staying in a private hospital room to protect others from radiation coming from your body

- Being treated quickly by nurses and other hospital staff. They will provide all the care you need, but may stand at a distance, talk with you from the doorway of your room, and wear protective clothing.

Your visitors will also need to follow safety measures, which may include:

- Not being allowed to visit when the radiation is first put in

- Needing to check with the hospital staff before they go to your room

- Standing by the doorway rather than going into your hospital room

- Keeping visits short (30 minutes or less each day). The length of visits depends on the type of radiation being used and the part of your body being treated.

- Not having visits from pregnant women and children younger than a year old

You may also need to follow safety measures once you leave the hospital, such as not spending much time with other people. Your doctor or nurse will talk with you about any safety measures you should follow when you go home.

What To Expect When The Catheter Is Removed

Once you finish treatment with light dependent resistor (LDR) or HDR implants, the catheter will be removed. Here are some things to expect:

- You will get medicine for pain before the catheter or applicator is removed.

- The area where the catheter or applicator was might be tender for a few months.

- There is no radiation in your body after the catheter or applicator is removed. It is safe for people to be near you—even young children and pregnant women.

For a week or two, you may need to limit activities that take a lot of effort. Ask your doctor what kinds of activities are safe for you and which ones you should avoid.

Special Diet Needs

Radiation can cause side effects that make it hard to eat, such as nausea, mouth sores, and throat problems called esophagitis. Since your body uses a lot of energy to heal during radiation therapy, it is important that you eat enough calories and protein to maintain your weight during treatment. If you are having trouble eating and maintaining your weight, talk to your doctor or nurse. You might also find it helpful to speak with a dietitian.

Chapter 41

Stem Cell Transplant

Stem cell transplants are procedures that restore blood-forming stem cells in people who have had theirs destroyed by the very high doses of chemotherapy or radiation therapy that are used to treat certain cancers.

Blood-forming stem cells are important because they grow into different types of blood cells. The main types of blood cells are:

1. White blood cells, which are part of your immune system and help your body fight infection

2. Red blood cells, which carry oxygen throughout your body

3. Platelets, which help the blood clot

You need all three types of blood cells to be healthy.

Types Of Stem Cell Transplants

In a stem cell transplant, you receive healthy blood-forming stem cells through a needle in your vein. Once they enter your bloodstream, the stem cells travel to the bone marrow, where they take the place of the cells that were destroyed by treatment. The blood-forming stem cells that are used in transplants can come from the bone marrow, bloodstream, or umbilical cord. Transplants can be:

• Autologous, which means the stem cells come from you, the patient.

About This Chapter: This chapter includes text excerpted from "Stem Cell Transplants In Cancer Treatment," National Cancer Institute (NCI), April 29, 2015.

- Allogeneic, which means the stem cells come from someone else. The donor may be a blood relative but can also be someone who is not related.

- Syngeneic, which means the stem cells come from your identical twin, if you have one.

To reduce possible side effects and improve the chances that an allogeneic transplant will work, the donor's blood-forming stem cells must match yours in certain ways.

How Stem Cell Transplants Work Against Cancer

Stem cell transplants do not usually work against cancer directly. Instead, they help you recover your ability to produce stem cells after treatment with very high doses of radiation therapy, chemotherapy, or both.

However, in multiple myeloma and some types of leukemia, the stem cell transplant may work against cancer directly. This happens because of an effect called graft-versus-tumor that can occur after allogeneic transplants. Graft-versus-tumor occurs when white blood cells from your donor (the graft) attack any cancer cells that remain in your body (the tumor) after high-dose treatments. This effect improves the success of the treatments.

Who Receives Stem Cell Transplants

Stem cell transplants are most often used to help people with leukemia and lymphoma. They may also be used for neuroblastoma and multiple myeloma. Stem cell transplants for other types of cancer are being studied in clinical trials, which are research studies involving people.

Stem Cell Transplants Can Cause Side Effects

The high doses of cancer treatment that you have before a stem cell transplant can cause problems such as bleeding and an increased risk of infection. Talk with your doctor or nurse about other side effects that you might have and how serious they might be.

If you have an allogeneic transplant, you might develop a serious problem called graft-versus-host disease. Graft-versus-host disease can occur when white blood cells from your donor (the graft) recognize cells in your body (the host) as foreign and attack them. This problem can cause damage to your skin, liver, intestines, and many other organs. It can occur a few weeks after the transplant or much later. Graft-versus-host disease can be treated with steroids or other drugs that suppress your immune system.

The closer your donor's blood-forming stem cells match yours, the less likely you are to have graft-versus-host disease. Your doctor may also try to prevent it by giving you drugs to suppress your immune system.

How Much Stem Cell Transplants Cost

Stem cells transplants are complicated procedures that are very expensive. Most insurance plans cover some of the costs of transplants for certain types of cancer. Talk with your health plan about which services it will pay for. Talking with the business office where you go for treatment may help you understand all the costs involved.

What To Expect When Receiving A Stem Cell Transplant

Where You Go For A Stem Cell Transplant

When you need an allogeneic stem cell transplant, you will need to go to a hospital that has a specialized transplant center. The National Marrow Donor Program® maintains a list of transplant centers in the United States that can help you find a transplant center.

Unless you live near a transplant center, you may need to travel from home for your treatment. You might need to stay in the hospital during your transplant, you may be able to have it as an outpatient, or you may need to be in the hospital only part of the time. When you are not in the hospital, you will need to stay in a hotel or apartment nearby. Many transplant centers can assist with finding nearby housing.

How Long It Takes To Have A Stem Cell Transplant

A stem cell transplant can take a few months to complete. The process begins with treatment of high doses of chemotherapy, radiation therapy, or a combination of the two. This treatment goes on for a week or two. Once you have finished, you will have a few days to rest.

Next, you will receive the blood-forming stem cells. The stem cells will be given to you through an IV catheter. This process is like receiving a blood transfusion. It takes 1–5 hours to receive all the stem cells.

After receiving the stem cells, you begin the recovery phase. During this time, you wait for the blood cells you received to start making new blood cells.

291

Even after your blood counts return to normal, it takes much longer for your immune system to fully recover—several months for autologous transplants and 1–2 years for allogeneic or syngeneic transplants.

How Stem Cell Transplants May Affect You

Stem cell transplants affect people in different ways. How you feel depends on:

- The type of transplant that you have

- The doses of treatment you had before the transplant

- How you respond to the high-dose treatments

- Your type of cancer

- How advanced your cancer is

- How healthy you were before the transplant

Since people respond to stem cell transplants in different ways, your doctor or nurses cannot know for sure how the procedure will make you feel.

How To Tell If Your Stem Cell Transplant Worked

Doctors will follow the progress of the new blood cells by checking your blood counts often. As the newly transplanted stem cells produce blood cells, your blood counts will go up.

Special Diet Needs

The high-dose treatments that you have before a stem cell transplant can cause side effects that make it hard to eat, such as mouth sores and nausea. Tell your doctor or nurse if you have trouble eating while you are receiving treatment. You might also find it helpful to speak with a dietitian.

Chapter 42

Surgery

Surgery, when used to treat cancer, is a procedure in which a surgeon removes cancer from your body. Surgeons are medical doctors with special training in surgery.

How Surgery Is Performed

Surgeons often use small, thin knives, called scalpels, and other sharp tools to cut your body during surgery. Surgery often requires cuts through skin, muscles, and sometimes bone. After surgery, these cuts can be painful and take some time to recover from.

Anesthesia keeps you from feeling pain during surgery. Anesthesia refers to drugs or other substances that cause you to lose feeling or awareness. There are three types of anesthesia:

1. Local anesthesia causes loss of feeling in one small area of the body.

2. Regional anesthesia causes loss of feeling in a part of the body, such as an arm or leg.

3. General anesthesia causes loss of feeling and a complete loss of awareness that seems like a very deep sleep.

There are other ways of performing surgery that do not involve cuts with scalpels. Some of these include:

- **Cryosurgery**

 Cryosurgery is a type of treatment in which extreme cold produced by liquid nitrogen or argon gas is used to destroy abnormal tissue. Cryosurgery may be used to treat

About This Chapter: Text in this chapter begins with excerpts from "Cancer Treatment—Surgery To Treat Cancer," National Cancer Institute (NCI), April 29, 2015; Text under the heading "Technologies Enhance Tumor Surgery" is excerpted from "Technologies Enhance Tumor Surgery," *NIH News in Health*, National Institutes of Health (NIH), February 2016.

early-stage skin cancer, retinoblastoma, and precancerous growths on the skin and cervix. Cryosurgery is also called cryotherapy.

- **Lasers**

  This is a type of treatment in which powerful beams of light are used to cut through tissue. Lasers can focus very accurately on tiny areas, so they can be used for precise surgeries. Lasers can also be used to shrink or destroy tumors or growths that might turn into cancer.

  Lasers are most often used to treat tumors on the surface of the body or on the inside lining of internal organs. Examples include basal cell carcinoma, cervical changes that might turn into cancer, and cervical, vaginal, esophageal, and nonsmall cell lung cancer.

- **Hyperthermia**

  Hyperthermia is a type of treatment in which small areas of body tissue are exposed to high temperatures. The high heat can damage and kill cancer cells or make them more sensitive to radiation and certain chemotherapy drugs. Radiofrequency ablation is one type of hyperthermia that uses high-energy radio waves to generate heat. Hyperthermia is not widely available and is being studied in clinical trials.

- **Photodynamic therapy**

  Photodynamic therapy is a type of treatment that uses drugs which react to a certain type of light. When the tumor is exposed to this light, these drugs become active and kill nearby cancer cells. Photodynamic therapy is used most often to treat or relieve symptoms caused by skin cancer, mycosis fungoides, and nonsmall cell lung cancer.

Types Of Surgery

There are many types of surgery. The types differ based on the purpose of the surgery, the part of the body that requires surgery, the amount of tissue to be removed, and, in some cases, what the patient prefers.

Surgery may be open or minimally invasive.

- In open surgery, the surgeon makes one large cut to remove the tumor, some healthy tissue, and maybe some nearby lymph nodes.

- In minimally invasive surgery, the surgeon makes a few small cuts instead of one large one. She inserts a long, thin tube with a tiny camera into one of the small cuts. This tube is called a laparoscope. The camera projects images from the inside of the body onto a monitor, which allows the surgeon to see what she is doing. They use special surgery tools that are inserted through the other small cuts to remove the tumor and some healthy tissue.

Because minimally invasive surgery requires smaller cuts, it takes less time to recover from than open surgery.

Who Has Surgery

Many people with cancer are treated with surgery. Surgery works best for solid tumors that are contained in one area. It is a local treatment, meaning that it treats only the part of your body with the cancer. It is not used for leukemia (a type of blood cancer) or for cancers that have spread. Sometimes surgery will be the only treatment you need. But most often, you will also have other cancer treatments.

How Surgery Works Against Cancer

Depending on your type of cancer and how advanced it is, surgery can be used to:

- **Remove the entire tumor**

  Surgery removes cancer that is contained in one area.

- **Debulk a tumor**

  Surgery removes some, but not all, of a cancer tumor. Debulking is used when removing an entire tumor might damage an organ or the body. Removing part of a tumor can help other treatments work better.

- **Ease cancer symptoms**

  Surgery is used to remove tumors that are causing pain or pressure.

Risks Of Surgery

Surgeons are highly trained and will do everything they can to prevent problems during surgery. Even so, sometimes problems do occur. Common problems are:

- **Pain**

  After surgery, most people will have pain in the part of the body that was operated on. How much pain you feel will depend on the extent of the surgery, the part of your body where you had surgery, and how you feel pain.

Your doctor or nurse can help you manage pain after surgery. Talk with your doctor or nurse before surgery about ways to control pain. After surgery, tell them if your pain is not controlled.

- **Infection**

    Infection is another problem that can happen after surgery. To help prevent infection, follow your nurse's instructions about caring for the area where you had surgery. If you do develop an infection, your doctor can prescribe a medicine (called an antibiotic) to treat it.

Other risks of surgery include bleeding, damage to nearby tissues, and reactions to the anesthesia. Talk to your doctor about possible risks for the type of surgery you will have.

How Much Surgery Costs

The cost of surgery depends on many factors, including:

- The type of surgery you have
- How many specialists are involved in your surgery
- If you need local, regional, or general anesthesia
- Where you have surgery—at an outpatient clinic, a doctor's office, or the hospital
- If you need to stay in the hospital, and for how long
- The part of the country where you live

Talk with your health insurance company about what services it will pay for. Most insurance plans pay for surgery to treat cancer. To learn more, talk with the business office of the clinic or hospital where you go for treatment. If you need financial assistance, there are organizations that may be able to help. Call toll-free 800-4-CANCER (800-422-6237) to ask for information on organizations that may help.

Where You Have Surgery

Where you have surgery depends on

- The type of surgery
- How extensive it is
- Where the surgeon practices
- The type of facility your insurance will cover

You can have outpatient surgery in a doctor's office, surgery center, or hospital. Outpatient means that you do not spend the night. Or, you may have surgery in the hospital and stay the night. How many nights you stay will depend on the type of surgery you have and how quickly you recover.

What To Expect Before, During, And After Surgery

Before Surgery

Before surgery, a nurse may call you to tell you how to prepare. He or she may tell you about tests and exams you need to have before the surgery. Common tests that you may need, if you have not had them lately, are:

- Blood tests
- Chest X-ray
- Electrocardiogram (ECG)

You may not be able to eat or drink for a certain period of time before the surgery. It is important to follow the instructions about eating and drinking. If you don't, your surgery may need to be rescheduled. You may also be asked to have supplies on hand for taking care of your wounds after surgery. Supplies might include antiseptic ointment and bandages.

During Surgery

Once you are under anesthesia, the surgeon removes the cancer, usually along with some healthy tissue around it. Removing this healthy tissue helps improve the chances that all the cancer has been removed.

Sometimes, the surgeon might also remove lymph nodes or other tissues near the tumor. These tissues will be checked under a microscope to see if the cancer has spread. Knowing if the nearby tissue contains cancer will help your doctors suggest the best treatment plan for you after surgery.

After Surgery

Once you are ready to go home after surgery, the nurse will tell you how to take care of yourself. He or she will explain:

- How to control pain
- Activities you should and should not do

- How to take care of your wound
- How to spot signs of infection and steps to take if you do
- When you can return to work

You will have at least one more visit with the surgeon a week or two after you go home. For more complex surgeries, you may need to see the surgeon more often. You may have stitches removed, and the surgeon will check to make sure you are healing as you should.

Special Diet Needs Before And After Surgery

Surgery increases your need for good nutrition. If you are weak or underweight, you may need to eat a high-protein, high-calorie diet before surgery. Some types of surgery may change how your body uses food. Surgery can also affect eating if you have surgery of the mouth, stomach, intestines, or throat. If you have trouble eating after surgery, you may be given nutrients through a feeding tube or IV (through a needle directly into a vein). Talk with a dietitian for help with eating problems caused by surgery.

Technologies Enhance Tumor Surgery

For surgeons, removing a tumor is a balancing act. Cut out too much and you risk removing healthy tissues that have important functions. Remove too little and you may leave behind cancer cells that could grow back into a tumor over time.

National Institutes of Health (NIH)-funded researchers are developing new technologies to help surgeons determine exactly where tumors end and healthy tissue begins. Their ultimate goal is to make surgery for cancer patients safer and more effective.

Surgeons go through many years of training to understand the subtle cues that can distinguish tumor from normal surroundings. Sometimes the tumor is a slightly different color than healthy tissue, or it feels different. It might also bleed more readily or could contain calcium deposits. Even with these cues, however, surgeons don't always get it right.

In today's operating rooms, pathologists can often help surgeons determine if all of a tumor has been taken out. A pathologist may view the edges of the tissue under a microscope and look for cancer cells. If they're found, the surgeon will remove more tissue from the patient and send these again to the pathologist for review. This process can occur repeatedly while the patient remains on the operating table and continue until no cancer cells are detected.

In the days following an operation, the pathologist conducts a more thorough review of the tissue. If cancer cells are found at the margins, the patient may undergo a second surgery to remove cancer that was left behind.

Orringer is part of a research team that's testing a new technology that could help surgeons tell the difference between a tumor and healthy brain tissue during surgery. The team developed a special microscope with NIH support that shoots a pair of low-energy lasers at the tissue. That causes the chemical bonds in the tissue's molecules to vibrate. The vibrations are then analyzed by a computer and used to create detailed images of the tissue.

From a molecular point of view, the components of a tumor differ from those in healthy tissue. This specialized microscope can reveal differences between the tissues that can't be seen with the naked eye.

Orringer and colleagues developed a computer program that can quickly analyze the images and assess whether or not cancer cells are present. This type of analysis could help surgeons decide whether all of a tumor has been cut out. To date, Orringer has used the specialized microscope to help remove cancer tissue in nearly 100 patients with brain tumors.

Other researchers are taking different approaches. For example, Dr. Quyen Nguyen—a head and neck surgeon at the University of California, San Diego—has developed a fluorescent molecule that's currently being tested in clinical trials. The patient receives an injection of the molecules before surgery. When exposed to certain types of light, these molecules cause cancer cells to glow, making them easier to spot and remove. The surgeon then uses a near-infrared camera to visualize the glowing tumor cells while operating.

Nguyen is also developing a fluorescent molecule to light up nerves. Accidental nerve injury during surgery can leave patients with loss of movement or feeling. In some cases, sexual function may be impaired.

The fluorescent molecule could help surgeons detect hard-to-spot nerves, so they can be protected. The nerve-tagging molecule is now being tested in animal studies.

Other NIH-funded researchers are focusing on ways to speed up cancer surgeries. Dr. Milind Rajadhyaksha, a researcher at Memorial Sloan Kettering Cancer Center, has developed a microscope technique to reduce the amount of time it takes to perform a common surgery for removing non-melanoma skin cancers.

Each year about 2 million people in the United States undergo Mohs surgery, in which a doctor successively removes suspicious areas until the surrounding skin tissue is free of cancer. The procedure can take several hours, because each time more tissue is removed, it has to be prepared and reviewed under a microscope to determine if cancer cells remain. This step can take up to 30 minutes.

The technique developed by Rajadhyaksha shortens the time for assessing removed tissue to less than 5 minutes, which greatly reduces the overall length of the procedure. Tissue is mounted in a specialized microscope that uses a focused laser line to do multiple scans of the tissue. The resulting image "strips" are then combined, like a mosaic, into a complete microscopic image of the tissue.

About 1,000 specialized skin surgeries have already been performed guided by this technique. Rajadhyaksha is currently developing an approach that would allow doctors to use the technology directly on a patient's skin, before any tissue has been removed. This would allow doctors to identify the edges of tumors before the start of surgery and reduce the need for several pre-surgical "margin-mapping" biopsies.

Chapter 43

Cancer And Complementary Health Therapies

Complementary and alternative medicine (CAM) is the term for medical products and practices that are not part of standard medical care.

- **Standard medical care** is medicine that is practiced by health professionals who hold an M.D. (medical doctor) or D.O. (doctor of osteopathy) degree. It is also practiced by other health professionals, such as physical therapists, physician assistants, psychologists, and registered nurses. Standard medicine may also be called biomedicine or allopathic, Western, mainstream, orthodox, or regular medicine. Some standard medical care practitioners are also practitioners of CAM.

- **Complementary medicine** is treatments that are used along with standard medical treatments but are not considered to be standard treatments. One example is using acupuncture to help lessen some side effects of cancer treatment.

- **Alternative medicine** is treatments that are used instead of standard medical treatments. One example is using a special diet to treat cancer instead of anticancer drugs that are prescribed by an oncologist.

- **Integrative medicine** is a total approach to medical care that combines standard medicine with the CAM practices that have been shown to be safe and effective. They treat the patient's mind, body, and spirit.

About This Chapter: This chapter includes text excerpted from "Complementary And Alternative Medicine," National Cancer Institute (NCI), April 10, 2015.

Are CAM Approaches Safe?

Some CAM therapies have undergone careful evaluation and have been found to be safe and effective. However there are others that have been found to be ineffective or possibly harmful. Less is known about many CAM therapies, and research has been slower for a number of reasons:

- Time and funding issues

- Problems finding institutions and cancer researchers to work with on the studies

- Regulatory issues

CAM therapies need to be evaluated with the same long and careful research process used to evaluate standard treatments. Standard cancer treatments have generally been studied for safety and effectiveness through an intense scientific process that includes clinical trials with large numbers of patients.

Natural Does Not Mean Safe

CAM therapies include a wide variety of botanicals and nutritional products, such as dietary supplements, herbal supplements, and vitamins. Many of these "natural" products are considered to be safe because they are present in, or produced by, nature. However, that is not true in all cases. In addition, some may affect how well other medicines work in your body. For example, the herb St. John's wort, which some people use for depression, may cause certain anticancer drugs not to work as well as they should.

Herbal supplements may be harmful when taken by themselves, with other substances, or in large doses. For example, some studies have shown that kava kava, an herb that has been used to help with stress and anxiety, may cause liver damage.

Vitamins can also have unwanted effects in your body. For example, some studies show that high doses of vitamins, even vitamin C, may affect how chemotherapy and radiation work. Too much of any vitamin is not safe, even in a healthy person.

Tell your doctor if you're taking any dietary supplements, no matter how safe you think they are. This is very important. Even though there may be ads or claims that something has been used for years, they do not prove that it's safe or effective.

Supplements do not have to be approved by the federal government before being sold to the public. Also, a prescription is not needed to buy them. Therefore, it's up to consumers to decide what is best for them.

National Cancer Institute (NCI) and the National Center for Complementary and Integrative Health (NCCIH) are currently sponsoring or cosponsoring various clinical trials that test CAM treatments and therapies in people. Some study the effects of complementary approaches used in addition to conventional treatments, and some compare alternative therapies with conventional treatments.

What Should Patients Do When Using Or Considering CAM Therapies?

Cancer patients who are using or considering using complementary or alternative therapy should talk with their doctor or nurse. Some therapies may interfere with standard treatment or even be harmful. It is also a good idea to learn whether the therapy has been proven to do what it claims to do.

To find a CAM practitioner, ask your doctor or nurse to suggest someone. Or ask if someone at your cancer center, such as a social worker or physical therapist can help you. Choosing a CAM practitioner should be done with as much care as choosing a primary care provider.

Patients, their families, and their healthcare providers can learn about CAM therapies and practitioners from the following government agencies:

- National Center for Complementary and Integrative Health (NCCIH)
- NCI Office of Cancer Complementary and Alternative Medicine (OCCAM)
- Office of Dietary Supplements (ODS)

Chapter 44

Cancer Prevention

What Is Cancer Prevention?

Cancer prevention is action taken to lower the chance of getting cancer. In 2017, more than 1.6 million people will be diagnosed with cancer in the United States. In addition to the physical problems and emotional distress caused by cancer, the high costs of care are also a burden to patients, their families, and to the public. By preventing cancer, the number of new cases of cancer is lowered. Hopefully, this will reduce the burden of cancer and lower the number of deaths caused by cancer.

Cancer is not a single disease but a group of related diseases. Many things in our genes, our lifestyle, and the environment around us may increase or decrease our risk of getting cancer.

Scientists are studying many different ways to help prevent cancer, including the following:

- Ways to avoid or control things known to cause cancer.

- Changes in diet and lifestyle.

- Finding precancerous conditions early. Precancerous conditions are conditions that may become cancer.

- Chemoprevention (medicines to treat a precancerous condition or to keep cancer from starting).

- Risk-reducing surgery.

About This Chapter: This chapter includes text excerpted from "Cancer Prevention Overview (PDQ®)—Patient Version," National Cancer Institute (NCI), August 11, 2017.

What Is Carcinogenesis?

Carcinogenesis is the series of steps that take place as a normal cell becomes a cancer cell. Cells are the smallest units of the body and they make up the body's tissues. Each cell contains genes that guide the way the body grows, develops, and repairs itself. There are many genes that control whether a cell lives or dies, divides (multiplies), or takes on special functions, such as becoming a nerve cell or a muscle cell.

Mutations In Genes Occur During Carcinogenesis

Changes (mutations) in genes can cause normal controls in cells to break down. When this happens, cells do not die when they should and new cells are produced when the body does not need them. The buildup of extra cells may cause a mass (tumor) to form.

Tumors can be benign or malignant (cancerous). Malignant tumor cells invade nearby tissues and spread to other parts of the body. Benign tumor cells do not invade nearby tissues or spread.

What Are The Risk Factors For Cancer?

Scientists study risk factors and protective factors to find ways to prevent new cancers from starting. Anything that increases your chance of developing cancer is called a cancer risk factor; anything that decreases your chance of developing cancer is called a cancer protective factor.

Some risk factors for cancer can be avoided, but many cannot. For example, both smoking and inheriting certain genes are risk factors for some types of cancer, but only smoking can be avoided. Risk factors that a person can control are called modifiable risk factors.

Many other factors in our environment, diet, and lifestyle may cause or prevent cancer. This chapter reviews only the major cancer risk factors and protective factors that can be controlled or changed to reduce the risk of cancer.

Factors That Are Known To Increase The Risk Of Cancer

Cigarette Smoking And Tobacco Use

Tobacco use is strongly linked to an increased risk for many kinds of cancer. Smoking cigarettes is the leading cause of the following types of cancer:

- Acute myelogenous leukemia (AML)

- Bladder cancer

- Esophageal cancer

- Kidney cancer

- Lung cancer

- Oral cavity cancer

- Pancreatic cancer

- Stomach cancer

Not smoking or quitting smoking lowers the risk of getting cancer and dying from cancer. Scientists believe that cigarette smoking causes about 30 percent of all cancer deaths in the United States.

Infections

Certain viruses and bacteria are able to cause cancer. Viruses and other infection-causing agents cause more cases of cancer in the developing world (about 1 in 4 cases of cancer) than in developed nations (less than 1 in 10 cases of cancer). Examples of cancer-causing viruses and bacteria include:

- Human papillomavirus (HPV) increases the risk for cancers of the cervix, penis, vagina, anus, and oropharynx.

- Hepatitis B and hepatitis C viruses increase the risk for liver cancer.

- *Epstein-Barr* virus increases the risk for Burkitt lymphoma.

- *Helicobacter pylori* increases the risk for gastric cancer.

Two vaccines to prevent infection by cancer-causing agents have already been developed and approved by the U.S. Food and Drug Administration (FDA). One is a vaccine to prevent infection with hepatitis B virus. The other protects against infection with strains of HPV that cause cervical cancer. Scientists continue to work on vaccines against infections that cause cancer.

Radiation

Being exposed to radiation is a known cause of cancer. There are two main types of radiation linked with an increased risk for cancer:

- Ultraviolet radiation from sunlight: This is the main cause of nonmelanoma skin cancers.

- Ionizing radiation including:

  - Medical radiation from tests to diagnose cancer such as X-rays, computerized tomography (CT) scans, fluoroscopy, and nuclear medicine scans.

  - Radon gas in our homes.

Scientists believe that ionizing radiation causes leukemia, thyroid cancer, and breast cancer in women. Ionizing radiation may also be linked to myeloma and cancers of the lung, stomach, colon, esophagus, bladder, and ovary. Being exposed to radiation from diagnostic X-rays increases the risk of cancer in patients and X-ray technicians.

The growing use of CT scans over the last 20 years has increased exposure to ionizing radiation. The risk of cancer also increases with the number of CT scans a patient has and the radiation dose used each time.

Immunosuppressive Medicines After Organ Transplant

Immunosuppressive medicines are used after an organ has been transplanted from one person to another. These medicines stop an organ that has been transplanted from being rejected. These medicines decrease the body's immune response to help keep the organ from being rejected. Immunosuppressive medicines are linked to an increased risk of cancer because they lower the body's ability to keep cancer from forming.

Factors That May Affect The Risk Of Cancer

Diet

The foods that you eat on a regular basis make up your diet. Diet is being studied as a risk factor for cancer. It is hard to study the effects of diet on cancer because a person's diet includes foods that may protect against cancer and foods that may increase the risk of cancer.

It is also hard for people who take part in the studies to keep track of what they eat over a long period of time. This may explain why studies have different results about how diet affects the risk of cancer.

Some studies show that fruits and nonstarchy vegetables may protect against cancers of the mouth, esophagus, and stomach. Fruits may also protect against lung cancer.

Some studies have shown that a diet high in fat, proteins, calories, and red meat increases the risk of colorectal cancer, but other studies have not shown this.

It is not known if a diet low in fat and high in fiber, fruits, and vegetables lowers the risk of colorectal cancer.

Alcohol

Studies have shown that drinking alcohol is linked to an increased risk of the following types of cancers:

- Breast cancer
- Colorectal cancer (in men)
- Esophageal cancer
- Oral cancer

Drinking alcohol may also increase the risk of liver cancer and female colorectal cancer.

Physical Activity

Studies show that people who are physically active have a lower risk of certain cancers than those who are not. It is not known if physical activity itself is the reason for this.

Studies show a strong link between physical activity and a lower risk of colorectal cancer. Some studies show that physical activity protects against postmenopausal breast cancer and endometrial cancer.

Obesity

Studies show that obesity is linked to a higher risk of the following types of cancer:

- Colorectal cancer
- Endometrial cancer
- Esophageal cancer
- Kidney cancer
- Pancreatic cancer
- Postmenopausal breast cancer

Some studies show that obesity is also a risk factor for cancer of the gallbladder and liver cancer.

It is not known if losing weight lowers the risk of cancers that have been linked to obesity.

Diabetes

Some studies show that having diabetes may slightly increase the risk of having the following types of cancer:

- Bladder cancer
- Breast cancer in women
- Colorectal cancer
- Endometrial cancer
- Liver cancer
- Lung cancer
- Oral cancer
- Oropharyngeal cancer
- Ovarian cancer
- Pancreatic cancer

Diabetes and cancer share some of the same risk factors. These risk factors include the following:

- Being older
- Being obese
- Smoking
- Not eating a healthy diet
- Not exercising

Because diabetes and cancer share these risk factors, it is hard to know whether the risk of cancer is increased more by diabetes or by these risk factors.

Studies are being done to see how medicine that is used to treat diabetes affects cancer risk.

Environmental Risk Factors

Being exposed to chemicals and other substances in the environment has been linked to some cancers:

- Links between air pollution and cancer risk have been found. These include links between lung cancer and secondhand tobacco smoke, outdoor air pollution, and asbestos.

- Drinking water that contains a large amount of arsenic has been linked to skin, bladder, and lung cancers.

Studies have been done to see if pesticides and other pollutants increase the risk of cancer. The results of those studies have been unclear because other factors can change the results of the studies.

Interventions That Are Known To Lower Cancer Risk

An intervention is a treatment or action taken to prevent or treat disease, or improve health in other ways. Many studies are being done to find ways to keep cancer from starting or recurring (coming back).

Chemoprevention

Chemoprevention is the use of substances to lower the risk of cancer, or keep it from recurring. The substances may be natural or made in the laboratory. Some chemopreventive agents are tested in people who are at high risk for a certain type of cancer. The risk may be because of a precancerous condition, family history, or lifestyle factors.

Taking one of the following agents may lower the risk of cancer:

- Selective estrogen receptor modulators (SERMS) such as tamoxifen or raloxifene have been shown to reduce the risk of breast cancer in women at high risk. SERMS may cause side effects, such as hot flashes, so they are not often used for prevention of cancer.

- Finasteride has been shown to lower the risk of prostate cancer.

- COX-2 inhibitors may prevent colon and breast cancer. COX-2 inhibitors may cause heart problems. Because COX-2 inhibitors may cause heart problems there have not been many studies on their use to prevent cancer.

- Aspirin may prevent colorectal cancer. Bleeding in the gastrointestinal tract or brain is a side effect of aspirin. Because aspirin may cause bleeding problems there have not been many studies on their use to prevent cancer. Clinical trials are taking place in many parts of the country.

How Can Cancer Be Prevented?

Screening for cervical and colorectal cancers as recommended helps prevent these diseases by finding precancerous lesions so they can be treated before they become cancerous. Screening for cervical, colorectal, and breast cancers also helps find these diseases at an early stage, when treatment works best. Centers for Disease Control and Prevention (CDC) offers free or low-cost mammograms and Pap tests nationwide, and free or low-cost colorectal cancer screening in six states.

Vaccines (shots) also help lower cancer risk. The human papillomavirus (HPV) vaccine helps prevent most cervical cancers and several other kinds of cancer. The hepatitis B vaccine can help lower liver cancer risk.

You can reduce your risk of getting cancer by making healthy choices like keeping a healthy weight, avoiding tobacco, limiting the amount of alcohol you drink, and protecting your skin.

(Source: "Cancer Prevention And Control—How To Prevent Cancer Or Find It Early," Centers for Disease Control and Prevention (CDC).)

Chapter 45

Talking With Your Healthcare Team

There is a lot to learn about cancer and your treatment. There are many things to remember. And if you're scared or confused, it can be even harder to take it all in. But, there are things you can do to make it easier to learn.

Express Yourself Clearly

Describe your problem or concern briefly.

> You can play an active role in your healthcare by talking to your doctor. Clear and honest communication between you and your physician can help you both make smart choices about your health. It's important to be honest and upfront about your symptoms even if you feel embarrassed or shy. Have an open dialogue with your doctor—ask questions to make sure you understand your diagnosis, treatment, and recovery.
>
> Here are a few tips that can help you talk to your doctor and make the most of your appointment:
>
> • Write down a list of questions and concerns before your appointment.
>
> • Consider bringing a close friend or family member with you.
>
> • Take notes about what the doctor says, or ask a friend or family member to take notes for you.

About This Chapter: Text in this chapter begins with excerpts from "Coping—Talking With Your Health Care Team," National Cancer Institute (NCI), September 8, 2017; Text beginning with the heading "Questions To Ask About Your Diagnosis" is excerpted from "Questions To Ask Your Doctor About Your Diagnosis," National Cancer Institute (NCI), September 14, 2016.

- Learn how to access your medical records, so you can keep track of test results, diagnoses, treatments plans, and medications and prepare for your next appointment.
- Ask for the doctor's contact information and their preferred method of communication.
- Remember that nurses and pharmacists are also good sources of information.

(Source: "Clear Communication—Talking To Your Doctor," National Institutes of Health (NIH).)

Ask Your Doctor Or Nurse To Write Down The Name And Stage Of Your Cancer

There are many different types of cancer. "Stage" refers to the size of the cancer tumor and how far it has spread in your body. Knowing the name and stage of your cancer will help you find out more about your cancer and help your doctor decide which treatment choices you have.

Systems That Describe Stage

There are many staging systems. Some, such as the tumor, nodes, and metastasis (TNM) staging system, are used for many types of cancer. Others are specific to a particular type of cancer. Most staging systems include information about:

- Where the tumor is located in the body
- The cell type (such as, adenocarcinoma or squamous cell carcinoma)
- The size of the tumor
- Whether the cancer has spread to nearby lymph nodes
- Whether the cancer has spread to a different part of the body
- Tumor grade, which refers to how abnormal the cancer cells look and how likely the tumor is to grow and spread

(Source: "Cancer Staging," National Cancer Institute (NCI).)

Learn About Your Treatment Choices

Ask your doctor to tell you about your treatment options. Ask how each treatment can help and which side effects you might have. Try to learn all you can about each choice. Let your doctor know if you need more time to think about these issues before you choose one.

Ask As Many Questions As You Need To

Your doctor needs to know your questions and concerns. Write down your questions and bring them with you to your visit. Ask your most important questions first, in case the doctor runs out of time. If you have a lot of questions, you may want to plan extra time to talk.

Let Your Doctor Know Your Concerns About Costs

Your healthcare team wants to know if you're worried about finances for your cancer treatment so they can help you find ways to manage them.

Don't Worry If Your Questions Seem Silly Or Don't Make Sense

All your questions are important and deserve an answer. It's okay to ask the same question more than once. It's also okay to ask your doctor to use simpler words and explain terms that are new to you. To make sure you understand, use your own words to repeat back what you heard the doctor say.

Take Someone With You When You See The Doctor

Ask a family member or friend to go with you when you see your doctor. This person can help by listening, taking notes, and asking questions. If you can't find someone to go with you, ask your doctor if he or she will talk with a friend or family member over the phone.

Take Notes Or Ask To Record Your Conversation With Your Doctor

Many patients have trouble remembering what they talk about with their doctor. Take notes or ask if you can record the conversation.

Know That You Have A Right To Privacy

Your medical information is protected under the Health Insurance Portability and Accountability Act (HIPAA). This law gives you the right to receive and review your medical records. It also gives you the right to choose who your information is shared with, including friends or family members. This may be face-to-face, over the phone, or in writing. Your healthcare provider should let you know about your privacy rights, but make sure to ask any questions you may have about this topic.

What Does The HIPAA Privacy Rule Do?

The HIPAA Privacy Rule has set national standards to protect individuals' medical records and other personal health information.

- It gives patients more control over their health information.
- It sets boundaries on the use and release of health records.
- It establishes appropriate safeguards that healthcare providers and others must achieve to protect the privacy of health information.
- It holds violators accountable, with civil and criminal penalties that can be imposed if they violate patients' privacy rights.
- And it strikes a balance when public responsibility supports disclosure of some forms of data—for example, to protect public health.

For patients—it means being able to make informed choices when seeking care and reimbursement for care based on how personal health information may be used.

(Source: "HIPAA For Individuals—What Does The HIPAA Privacy Rule Do?" U.S. Department of Health and Human Services (HHS).)

Questions To Ask About Your Diagnosis

Learning that you have cancer can be a shock and you may feel overwhelmed at first. When you meet with your doctor, you will hear a lot of information. These questions may help you learn more about your cancer and what you can expect next.

- What type of cancer do I have?
- What is the stage of my cancer?
- Has it spread to other areas of my body?
- Will I need more tests before treatment begins? Which ones?
- Will I need a specialist(s) for my cancer treatment?
- Will you help me find a doctor to give me another opinion on the best treatment plan for me?

- How serious is my cancer?

- What are my chances of survival?

Questions To Ask About Your Treatment

You may want to ask your doctor some of the following questions before you decide on your cancer treatment.

Questions About Cancer Treatment

- What are the ways to treat my type and stage of cancer?

- What are the benefits and risks of each of these treatments?

- What treatment do you recommend? Why do you think it is best for me?

- When will I need to start treatment?

- Will I need to be in the hospital for treatment? If so, for how long?

- What is my chance of recovery with this treatment?

- How will we know if the treatment is working?

- Would a clinical trial (research study) be right for me?

- How do I find out about studies for my type and stage of cancer?

Questions About Finding A Specialist And Getting A Second Opinion

- Will I need a specialist(s) for my cancer treatment?

- Will you help me find a doctor to give me another opinion on the best treatment plan for me?

Questions About Surgery

- Is surgery an option for me? If so, what kind of surgery do you suggest?

- How long will I stay in the hospital?

- If I have pain, how will it be controlled?

Questions About Other Types Of Treatment

- Where will I go for treatment?

- How is the treatment given?

- How long will each treatment session take?

- How many treatment sessions will I have?

- Should a family member or friend come with me to my treatment sessions?

Questions About Side Effects

- What are the possible side effects of the treatment?

- What side effects may happen during or between my treatment sessions?

- Are there any side effects that I should call you about right away?

- Are there any lasting effects of the treatment?

- Will this treatment affect my ability to have children?

- How can I prevent or treat side effects?

Questions About Medicines And Other Products You Might Be Taking

- Do I need to tell you about the medicines I am taking now?

- Should I tell you about dietary supplements (such as vitamins, minerals, herbs, or fish oil) that I am taking?

- Could any drugs or supplements change the way that cancer treatment works?

Questions To Ask Your Doctor About Treatment Clinical Trials

If you are thinking about taking part in a clinical trial, be sure to ask your doctor, "Is there a clinical trial that I can join?" If your doctor offers you a trial, here are some questions you may want to ask.

Questions About The Trial

- What is the purpose of the trial?

- Why do the researchers believe that the treatment being studied may be better than the one being used now? Why may it not be better?

- How long will I be in the trial?

- What kinds of tests and treatments are involved?

- How will the doctor know if the treatment is working?

- How will I be told about the trial's results?

- How long do I have to make up my mind about joining this trial?

- Who can I speak with about questions I have during and after the trial?

- Who will be in charge of my care?

- Is there someone I can talk to who has been in the trial?

Questions About Risks And Benefits

- What are the possible side effects or risks of the new treatment?

- What are the possible benefits?

- How do the possible risks and benefits of this trial compared to those of the standard treatment?

Questions About Your Rights

- How will my health information be kept private?

- What happens if I decide to leave the trial?

Questions About Costs

- Will I have to pay for any of the treatments or tests?

- What costs will my health insurance cover?

- Who pays if I'm injured in the trial?

- Who can help answer any questions from my insurance company?

Questions About Daily Life

- How could the trial affect my daily life?

- How often will I have to come to the hospital or clinic?

- Will I have to stay in the hospital during the clinical trial? If so, how often and for how long?

- Will I have to travel long distances?

- Will I have check-ups after the trial?

Questions About Comparing Choices

- What are my other treatment choices, including standard treatments?

- How does the treatment I would receive in this trial compare with the other treatment choices?

- What will happen to my cancer without treatment?

Questions To Ask Your Doctor When You Have Finished Treatment

When you have finished your cancer treatment, you will talk with your doctor about next steps and follow-up care. You may want to ask your doctor some of the following questions:

- How long will it take for me to get better and feel more like myself?

- What kind of care should I expect after my treatment?

- What long-term health issues can I expect as a result of my cancer and its treatment?

- What is the chance that my cancer will return?

- What symptoms should I tell you about?

- What can I do to be as healthy as possible?

- Which doctor should I see for my follow-up care? How often?

- What tests do I need after treatment is over? How often will I have the tests?

- What records do I need to keep about my treatment?

- Can you suggest a support group that might help me?

Questions To Ask Your Doctor About Advanced Cancer

Communication is important throughout cancer care. If you learn that you have advanced cancer, you will have choices to make about your care and what steps you need to take. For many, it's hard to ask questions about what these steps should be. Some patients with advanced cancer benefit from active treatment, while others do not.

Whether you've just been diagnosed, or the standard treatment isn't working, it's important to ask your healthcare team what to expect in the future. Studies show that patients who have these discussions with their doctor have a better quality of life than those who don't.

You can hope for the best while still being informed about your choices. The more information you have, the better decisions you and your loved ones can make about how you want to move forward with your care. When you meet with your doctor, consider asking some of the following questions:

Questions About Your Cancer

- What does "advanced cancer" mean for me?

- How long can I live with my advanced cancer?

- Are there tests I should have now to better understand the extent of my cancer?

Questions About Treatment Choices

- What's the best we can hope for by trying another treatment? What's the goal?

- What are my treatment choices? Which do you recommend for me and why?

- Is this treatment plan meant to help side effects, slow the growth of my cancer, or both?

- Is there a chance that a new treatment will be found while we try the old one?

- Would a clinical trial be right for me?

- What kind of care will I receive to keep me comfortable if I decide not to have active treatment for my cancer?

Questions About Symptoms And Side Effects

- What are the possible side effects and other downsides of this treatment? How likely are they?

- How can I manage the symptoms of my advanced cancer or the side effects of its treatment?

- Can you refer me to a palliative care specialist to help me cope with my side effects?

Questions About Making The Transition From Cancer Treatment To Hospice Care

- How do I decide whether to continue or stop cancer treatment?

- When should I consider having hospice care?

- How can I make sure I have the best quality of life possible—that I am comfortable and free of pain?

- Can I have hospice care in my home, or do I have to go to a special facility?

- How can I get help with financial and legal issues (for example, paying for hospice care or preparing a will or an advance directive)?

- How can I get help with my spiritual needs?

Talking about these questions may help you decide whether to continue or to begin active treatment. Tell your healthcare team exactly what you want to know, and how much you can take in. If possible, it's best to involve your loved ones in this process. It will help you figure out your needs and the needs of others close to you.

Part Four
Cancer Survivorship

Chapter 46

Cancer Survivors: After Cancer Treatment Ends

While cancer survivors are living longer after their diagnosis, at least one-third of the more than 15 million survivors in the United States face physical, mental, social, job, or financial problems related to their cancer experience. These psychosocial and physical concerns may affect family members, friends, and others who provide comfort and care to survivors.

Through data, translation, and partnership, the Centers for Disease Control and Prevention (CDC) works to address these and other challenges faced by cancer survivors and improve survivors' health and quality of life.

Physical Health Concerns

Some behaviors, experiences, or other factors increase some survivors' risk of having their first cancer come back, getting a new cancer, and having other health problems. Factors that increase such risks for cancer survivors include:

- The side effects of treatment.

- Genetic factors, such as those that can cause hereditary breast and ovarian cancer and Lynch syndrome.

- Unhealthy behaviors like smoking, obesity, and lack of physical activity.

- Other risk factors that contributed to the first cancer.

About This Chapter: Text in this chapter begins with excerpts from "Cancer Prevention And Control—Improving Health And Quality Of Life After Cancer," Centers for Disease Control and Prevention (CDC), June 1, 2017; Text under the heading "After Treatment" is excerpted from "Adolescents And Young Adults With Cancer," National Cancer Institute (NCI), May 15, 2015.

What Can Be Done?

After treatment ends, cancer survivors should get follow-up care—routine checkups and other cancer screenings. Follow-up care can help find new or returning cancers early and look for side effects of cancer treatment.

Survivors also can lower their risk of getting a new or second cancer by healthy choices like:

- Avoiding tobacco

- Limiting alcohol use

- Avoiding too much exposure to ultraviolet rays from the sun and tanning beds

- Eating a diet rich in fruits and vegetables

- Keeping a healthy weight

- Being physically active

Mental Health Concerns

Cancer survivors may experience mental health concerns that affect their emotions, behavior, memory, and ability to concentrate. For example, cancer survivors may feel emotional distress like depression or anxiety about their cancer returning. Cancer survivors who have other chronic illnesses are more likely to have mental health problems and poorer quality of life. Fewer than one-third of survivors who have mental health concerns talk to their doctor about them, and many survivors don't use services like professional counseling or support groups.

What Can Be Done?

- Survivors should talk to their healthcare providers about their mental health before, during, and after cancer treatment.

- Survivors should talk to their healthcare providers about mental health screening to check for and monitor changes in anxiety, depression, and other mental health concerns.

- Psychologists, social workers, and patient navigators can help survivors find appropriate and affordable mental health and social support services in both hospital and community settings.

- Physical activity has been linked to lower rates of depression among cancer survivors.

After Treatment

For many young people, the completion of treatment is something to celebrate. However, this time may also bring new challenges. You may worry that cancer will return or struggle to get used to new routines. Some young people enter this new phase feeling stronger, whereas others are more fragile. Most young people say the transition after treatment took longer and was more challenging than they anticipated. While most of the side effects that you had during treatment will go away, long-term side effects, such as fatigue, may take time to go away. Other side effects, called late effects, may not occur until months or even years after treatment.

Although follow-up care is important for all survivors, it is especially important for young adults. These check-ups can both reassure you and help to prevent and/or treat medical and psychological problems. Some young adults receive follow-up care at the hospital where they were treated, and others see specialists at late effect clinics. Talk with your healthcare team to learn what follow-up care you should receive and about possible places to receive it.

Chapter 47

Follow-Up Care After Cancer Treatment

While the completion of your cancer treatment is something to celebrate, it may also bring new challenges. You may worry that the cancer will return. You may struggle to get used to new routines. Some families enter this new phase feeling stronger, whereas others are more fragile. Many families are surprised by anxious feelings that arise during this long-awaited time, when they expected to feel only relief. Instead of this being a time to go back to life as it used to be, it may be a time of continued adjustment, as you leave the security of the people on your healthcare team. Some said the transition to life after treatment took longer and was more challenging than they thought it would be.

Get a written copy of your treatment summary and survivorship care plan. Ask for recommendations to hospitals that offer the type of follow-up or survivorship care that you need.

Treatment Summary

The treatment summary includes both diagnostic and treatment information, such as:

- Type of cancer, severity (stage, grade, or risk group), date of diagnosis, and pathology report

- Type(s) of treatment received, including the names and doses of all medications, as well as the total amounts and sites of any radiation therapy received

- Treatment dates

About This Chapter: This chapter includes text excerpted from "Coping With Cancer—Care For Childhood Cancer Survivors," National Cancer Institute (NCI), May 4, 2016.

- Key reports and scans, such as computerized tomography (CT) scans and magnetic resonance imaging (MRI)

- Side effects and/or complications experienced during treatment

- Supportive care received (also called palliative care)—such as counseling or physical therapy

- Identifying number and title of the clinical trial, if you were in a clinical trial

- Names and contact information of key people on your healthcare team

Survivorship Care Plan

A survivorship care plan (also called a follow-up care plan) is developed for each teen. Survivorship care plans are based on the type of cancer and treatment you received. For example, some teens may need to return for visits each month for the first year after they have completed treatment. Others may not need to return as often. Here is the type of information that's included in follow-up care plans for teens who have been treated for cancer:

- Exams and tests/procedures to check for the recurrence or metastasis of cancer, and a schedule of when they are needed

- Care and support to manage any long-term side effects and check for late effects

- Psychosocial support or counseling, and referrals as needed

- Referrals for legal aid or financial support, as needed

- Referrals to, and coordination with, specialists such as cardiologists, education specialist, endocrinologists, physical therapists, and psychologists and to appropriate treatments, clinical studies, and rehabilitation specialists

- Recommendations for healthy behaviors, such as advice regarding nutrition and physical exercise

- Family-based care, education, and outreach to you and your family

Follow-Up Care Clinics/Survivorship Clinics

Places that specialize in follow-up care for teens who have been treated for cancer are called follow-up care clinics or survivorship clinics. At these clinics, you will see specialists (in cardiology, endocrinology, fertility, nutrition, psychology, and/or pulmonology, for example) who will monitor your health. These clinics are usually found within hospitals.

If the hospital where you were treated does not have such a clinic, ask your doctor to recommend one.

Long-Term And Late Effects

Although many side effects go away once treatment has ended, long-term side effects, such as fatigue, may take some time to go away. Other side effects, called late effects, may not occur until months or years after treatment.

Whether or not you may have late effects of treatment depends on the type of cancer you had and how it was treated, as well as personal factors, such as:

- **Cancer-related factors** such as the type of cancer, where it was in the body, and how it affected tissues and organs

- **Treatment-related factors** such as the type and dose of treatment(s) or the type of surgery

- **Patient-related factors** such as your gender, age at diagnosis, length of time since diagnosis/treatment, personal and family health history, and health habits

Types Of Late Effects

Late effects may be physical, emotional, or cognitive. Knowing what symptoms to be aware of and when they may occur can help you plan for your needs. Not knowing what to expect can cause anxiety. However, knowing about late effects that may or may not happen to them in the future can be overwhelming. Many teens find it helpful to ask their doctor what to focus on at each step of their recovery.

Physical Late Effects

Physical late effects involve changes to organs, tissues, and/or body functions. They may affect your growth and development. Some teens who have been treated for cancer have many physical late effects, whereas others have relatively few.

Emotional Late Effects

Emotional late effects include changes to your mood, feelings, and actions. Many teens are very resilient after cancer treatment. Others experience social and/or emotional problems. If you are not sleeping well and no longer enjoy activities that you once did, it is important to talk with your doctor about having you evaluated for depression.

Some teens develop posttraumatic stress disorder (PTSD). This anxiety disorder arises in reaction to physical injury or severe mental or emotional distress. Symptoms of PTSD may include having flashbacks about diagnosis or treatment, avoiding places that are reminders of the experience, and being fearful, irritable, unable to sleep, or having difficulty concentrating. Ask your healthcare team to suggest resources for mental health support in your area.

Cognitive Late Effects

Cognitive late effects include changes in your ability to memorize, learn, and think. These types of late effects are more likely to occur in teens who've had certain cancers such as brain and spinal cord tumors, head and neck cancers, and some types of leukemia, such as acute lymphocytic leukemia (ALL). Treatments such as radiation therapy to the head and certain types of chemotherapy also increase the risk of cognitive late effects. These late effects are also more likely in children who were very young during treatment, who received very high doses of treatment, and whose treatment lasted for a long time.

Teens with cognitive late effects may have a more difficult time:

- Memorizing or remembering

- Learning (handwriting, spelling, reading, vocabulary, and/or math may be particularly challenging)

- Thinking (including concentrating, completing work on time, doing work that involves multiple steps, problem solving, and planning)

Chapter 48

Cancer Fatigue

Fatigue is the most common side effect of cancer treatment.

Cancer treatments such as chemotherapy, radiation therapy, and biologic therapy can cause fatigue in cancer patients. Fatigue is also a common symptom of some types of cancer. Patients describe fatigue as feeling tired, weak, worn-out, heavy, slow, or that they have no energy or get-up-and-go. Fatigue in cancer patients may be called cancer fatigue, cancer-related fatigue, and cancer treatment-related fatigue.

Fatigue related to cancer is different from fatigue that healthy people feel.

When a healthy person is tired by day-to-day activities, their fatigue can be relieved by sleep and rest. Cancer-related fatigue is different. Cancer patients get tired after less activity than people who do not have cancer. Also, cancer-related fatigue is not completely relieved by sleep and rest and may last for a long time. Fatigue usually decreases after cancer treatment ends, but patients may still feel some fatigue for months or years.

Fatigue can decrease a patient's quality of life.

Fatigue can affect all areas of life by making the patient too tired to take part in daily activities, relationships, social events, and community activities. Patients may miss work or school, spend less time with friends and family, or spend more time sleeping. In some cases, physical fatigue leads to mental fatigue and mood changes. This can make it hard for the patient to pay attention, remember things, and think clearly. Money may become a problem if the patient needs to take leave from a job or stop working completely. Job loss can lead to the loss of health

About This Chapter: This chapter includes text excerpted from "Fatigue (PDQ®)—Patient Version," National Cancer Institute (NCI), June 30, 2017.

insurance. All these things can lessen the patient's quality of life and self-esteem. Getting help with fatigue may prevent some of these problems and improve quality of life.

Causes Of Fatigue In Cancer Patients

Fatigue in cancer patients may have more than one cause. Doctors do not know all the reasons cancer patients have fatigue. Many conditions may cause fatigue at the same time. Fatigue in cancer patients may be caused by the following:

- Cancer treatment with chemotherapy, radiation therapy, and some biologic therapies.

- Anemia (a lower than normal number of red blood cells (RBCs)).

- Hormone levels that are too low or too high.

- Trouble breathing or getting enough oxygen.

- Heart trouble.

- Infection.

- Pain.

- Stress.

- Loss of appetite or not getting enough calories and nutrients.

- Dehydration (loss of too much water from the body, such as from severe diarrhea or vomiting).

- Changes in how well the body uses food for energy.

- Loss of weight, muscle, and/or strength.

- Medicines that cause drowsiness.

- Problems getting enough sleep.

- Being less active.

- Other medical conditions.

Fatigue is common in people with advanced cancer who are not receiving cancer treatment.

How Cancer Treatments Cause Fatigue Is Not Known

Doctors are trying to better understand how cancer treatments such as surgery, chemotherapy, and radiation therapy cause fatigue. Some studies show that fatigue is caused by:

- The need for extra energy to repair and heal body tissue damaged by treatment.

- The buildup of toxic substances that are left in the body after cells are killed by cancer treatment.

- The effect of biologic therapy on the immune system.

- Changes in the body's sleep-wake cycle.

When they begin cancer treatment, many patients are already tired from medical tests, surgery, and the emotional stress of coping with the cancer diagnosis. After treatment begins, fatigue may get worse. Patients who are older, have advanced cancer, or receive more than one type of treatment (for example, both chemotherapy and radiation therapy) are more likely to have long-term fatigue.

Different cancer treatments have different effects on a patient's energy level. The type and schedule of treatments can affect the amount of fatigue caused by cancer therapy.

Fatigue Caused By Chemotherapy

Patients treated with chemotherapy usually feel the most fatigue in the days right after each treatment. Then the fatigue decreases until the next treatment. Fatigue usually increases with each cycle. Some studies have shown that patients have the most severe fatigue about midway through all the cycles of chemotherapy. Fatigue decreases after chemotherapy is finished, but patients may not feel back to normal until a month or more after the last treatment. Many patients feel fatigued for months or years after treatment ends.

Fatigue during chemotherapy may be increased by the following:

- Pain.

- Depression.

- Anxiety.

- Anemia. Some types of chemotherapy stop the bone marrow from making enough new red blood cells, causing anemia (too few red blood cells to carry oxygen to the body).

- Lack of sleep caused by some anticancer drugs.

Fatigue Caused By Radiation Therapy

Many patients receiving radiation therapy have fatigue that keeps them from being as active as they want to be. After radiation therapy begins, fatigue usually increases until midway through the course of treatments and then stays about the same until treatment ends. For many patients, fatigue improves after radiation therapy stops. However, in some patients, fatigue will last months or years after treatment ends. Some patients never have the same amount of energy they had before treatment.

Cancer-related fatigue has been studied in patients with breast cancer and prostate cancer. The amount of fatigue they felt and the time of day the fatigue was worst was different in different patients.

In men with prostate cancer, fatigue was increased by having the following symptoms before radiation therapy started:

- Poor sleep.

- Depression.

In women with breast cancer, fatigue was increased by the following:

- Working while receiving radiation therapy.

- Having children at home.

- Depression.

- Anxiety.

- Trouble sleeping.

- Younger age.

- Being underweight.

- Having advanced cancer or other medical conditions.

Fatigue Caused By Biologic Therapy

Biologic therapy often causes flu-like symptoms. These symptoms include being tired physically and mentally, fever, chills, muscle pain, headache, and not feeling well in general. Some patients may also have problems thinking clearly. Fatigue symptoms depend on the type of biologic therapy used.

Fatigue Caused By Surgery

Fatigue is often a side effect of surgery, but patients usually feel better with time. However, fatigue caused by surgery can be worse when the surgery is combined with other cancer treatments.

Anemia Is A Common Cause Of Fatigue

Anemia affects the patient's energy level and quality of life. Anemia may be caused by the following:

- The cancer.

- Cancer treatments.

- A medical condition not related to the cancer.

The effects of anemia on a patient depend on the following:

- How quickly the anemia occurs.

- The patient's age.

- The amount of plasma (fluid part of the blood) in the patient's blood.

- Other medical conditions the patient has.

Side Effects Related To Nutrition May Cause Or Increase Fatigue

The body's energy comes from food. Fatigue may occur if the body does not take in enough food to give the body the energy it needs. For many patients, the effects of cancer and cancer treatments make it hard to eat well. In people with cancer, three major factors may affect nutrition:

- A change in the way the body is able to use food. A patient may eat the same amount as before having cancer, but the body may not be able to absorb and use all the nutrients from the food. This is caused by the cancer or its treatment.

- A decrease in the amount of food eaten because of low appetite, nausea, vomiting, diarrhea, or a blocked bowel.

- An increase in the amount of energy needed by the body because of a growing tumor, infection, fever, or shortness of breath.

Anxiety And Depression Are The Most Common Psychological Causes Of Fatigue In Cancer Patients

The emotional stress of cancer can cause physical problems, including fatigue. It's common for cancer patients to have changes in moods and attitudes. Patients may feel anxiety and fear before and after a cancer diagnosis. These feelings may cause fatigue. The effect of the disease on the patient's physical, mental, social, and financial well-being can increase emotional distress.

About 15–25 percent of patients who have cancer get depressed, which may increase fatigue caused by physical factors. The following are signs of depression:

- Feeling tired mentally and physically.

- Loss of interest in life.

- Problems thinking.

- Loss of sleep.

- Feeling a loss of hope.

Some patients have more fatigue after cancer treatments than others do.

Fatigue May Be Increased When It Is Hard For Patients To Learn And Remember

During and after cancer treatment, patients may find they cannot pay attention for very long and have a hard time thinking, remembering, and understanding. This is called attention fatigue. Sleep helps to relieve attention fatigue, but sleep may not be enough when the fatigue is related to cancer. Taking part in restful activities and spending time outdoors may help relieve attention fatigue.

Not Sleeping Well May Cause Fatigue

Some people with cancer are not able to get enough sleep. The following problems related to sleep may cause fatigue:

- Waking up during the night.

- Not going to sleep at the same time every night.

- Sleeping during the day and less at night.

- Not being active during the day.

Poor sleep affects people in different ways. For example, the time of day that fatigue is worse may be different. Some patients who have trouble sleeping may feel more fatigue in the morning. Others may have severe fatigue in both the morning and the evening.

Even in patients who have poor sleep, fixing sleep problems does not always improve fatigue. A lack of sleep may not be the cause of the fatigue.

Medicines Other Than Chemotherapy May Add To Fatigue

Patients may take medicines for cancer symptoms, such as pain, or conditions other than the cancer. These medicines may cause the patient to feel sleepy. Opioids, antidepressants, and antihistamines have this side effect. If many of these medicines are taken at the same time, fatigue may be worse.

Taking opioids over time may lower the amount of sex hormones made in the testicles and ovaries. This can lead to fatigue as well as sexual problems and depression.

Assessment Of Fatigue

An assessment is done to find out the level of fatigue and how it affects the patient's daily life.

There is no test to diagnose fatigue, so it is important for the patient to tell family members and the healthcare team if fatigue is a problem. To assess fatigue, the patient is asked to describe how bad the fatigue is, how it affects daily activities, and what makes the fatigue better or worse. The doctor will look for causes of fatigue that can be treated.

An assessment of fatigue includes a physical exam and blood tests.

The assessment process may include the following:

- Physical exam:

    This is an exam of the body to check general signs of health or anything that seems unusual. The doctor will check for problems such as trouble breathing or loss of muscle strength. The patient's walking, posture, and joint movements will be checked.

- Rating the level of fatigue:

    The patient is asked to rate the level of fatigue (how bad the fatigue is). There is no standard way to rate fatigue. The doctor may ask the patient to rate the fatigue on a scale from 0–10. Other ways to rate fatigue check for how much the fatigue affects the patient's quality of life.

- A series of questions about the following:

    - When the fatigue started, how long it lasts, and what makes it better or worse.

    - Symptoms or side effects, such as pain, the patient is having from the cancer or the treatments.

- Medicines being taken.

- Sleeping and resting habits.

- Eating habits and changes in appetite or weight.

- How the fatigue affects daily activities and lifestyle.

- How the fatigue affects being able to work.

- Whether the patient has depression, anxiety, or pain.

- Health habits and past illnesses and treatments.

- Blood tests to check for anemia:

The most common blood tests to check if the number of red blood cells is normal are:

- Complete blood count (CBC) with differential: A procedure in which a sample of blood is taken and checked for the following:

  - The number of red blood cells and platelets.

  - The number and type of white blood cells.

  - The amount of hemoglobin (the protein that carries oxygen) in the red blood cells.

  - The portion of the blood sample made up of red blood cells.

- Peripheral blood smear: A procedure in which a sample of blood is checked for the number and kinds of white blood cells, the number of platelets, and changes in the shape of blood cells.

- Other blood tests may be done to check for other conditions that affect red blood cells. These include a bone marrow aspiration and biopsy or a Coombs' test. Blood tests to check the levels of vitamin B12, iron, and erythropoietin may also be done.

- Checking for other causes of fatigue that can be treated.

A fatigue assessment is repeated at different times to see if there are patterns of fatigue.

A fatigue assessment is repeated to see if there is a pattern for when fatigue starts or becomes worse. Fatigue may be worse right after a chemotherapy treatment, for example. The same method of measuring fatigue is used at each assessment. This helps show changes in fatigue over time.

Treatments For Fatigue

Fatigue in cancer patients is often treated by relieving related conditions such as anemia and depression.

Treatment of fatigue depends on the symptoms and whether the cause of fatigue is known. When the cause of fatigue is not known, treatment is usually given to relieve symptoms and teach the patient ways to cope with fatigue.

Treatment Of Anemia

Treating anemia may help decrease fatigue. When known, the cause of the anemia is treated. When the cause is not known, treatment for anemia is supportive care and may include the following:

- Change in diet

- Transfusions of red blood cells

- Medicine

  - Epoetin alfa

  - Darbepoetin alfa

Treatment Of Pain

If pain is making fatigue worse, the patient's pain medicine may be changed or the dose may be increased. If too much pain medicine is making fatigue worse, the patient's pain medicine may be changed or the dose may be decreased.

Treatment Of Depression

Fatigue in patients who have depression may be treated with antidepressant drugs. Psychostimulant drugs may help some patients have more energy and a better mood, and help them think and concentrate.

Psychostimulants have side effects, especially with long-term use. Some of the possible side effects include the following:

- Trouble sleeping.

- Euphoria (feelings of extreme happiness).

- Headache.

- Nausea.

- Anxiety.

- Mood changes.

- Loss of appetite.

- Nightmares.

- Paranoia (feelings of fear and distrust of other people).

- Serious heart problems.

The doctor may prescribe low doses of a psychostimulant to be used for a short time in patients with advanced cancer who have severe fatigue. Talk to your doctor about the risks and benefits of these drugs.

Drugs For Fatigue Related To Cancer

The following drugs are being studied for fatigue related to cancer:

- Bupropion

- Dexamethasone

Dietary Supplements For Fatigue Related To Cancer

The following dietary supplements are being studied for fatigue related to cancer:

- L-carnitine

- Ginseng is an herb used to treat fatigue which may be taken in capsules of ground ginseng root.

Treatment Of Fatigue May Include Teaching The Patient Ways To Increase Energy And Cope With Fatigue In Daily Life

- Exercise

  - Qigong

  - Tai chi

  - Yoga

- A schedule of activity and rest
  - Lie in bed for sleep only.
  - Take naps for no longer than one hour.
  - Avoid noise (like television and radio) during sleep.
- Talk therapy

Self-Care For Fatigue

Learning about the risk of cancer-related fatigue and how to reduce fatigue may help you cope with it better and improve quality of life. For example, some patients in treatment worry that having fatigue means the treatment is not working. Anxiety over this can make fatigue even worse. Some patients may feel that reporting fatigue is complaining. Knowing that fatigue is a normal side effect that should be reported and treated may make it easier to manage.

Working with the healthcare team to learn about the following may help patients cope with fatigue:

- How to cope with fatigue as a normal side effect of treatment.
- The possible medical causes of fatigue such as not enough fluids, electrolyte imbalance, breathing problems, or anemia.
- How patterns of rest and activity affect fatigue.
- How to schedule important daily activities during times of less fatigue, and give up less important activities.
- The kinds of activities that may help you feel more alert (walking, gardening, bird watching).
- The difference between fatigue and depression.
- How to avoid or change situations that cause stress.
- How to avoid or change activities that cause fatigue.
- How to change your surroundings to help decrease fatigue.
- Exercise programs that are right for you and decrease fatigue.
- The importance of eating enough food and drinking enough fluids.
- Physical therapy for patients who have nerve problems or muscle weakness.

- Respiratory therapy for patients who have trouble breathing.

- How to tell if treatments for fatigue are working.

Fatigue After Cancer Treatment Ends

Fatigue continues to be a problem for many cancer survivors long after treatment ends and the cancer is gone. Studies show that some patients continue to have moderate-to-severe fatigue years after treatment. Long-term therapies such as tamoxifen can also cause fatigue. In children who were treated for brain tumors and cured, fatigue may continue after treatment.

The causes of fatigue after treatment ends are different than the causes of fatigue during treatment. Treating fatigue after treatment ends also may be different from treating it during cancer therapy.

Since fatigue may greatly affect the quality of life for cancer survivors, long-term follow-up care is important.

Chapter 49

Cancer Pain

Cancer, treatment for cancer, or diagnostic tests may cause you to feel pain.

Pain is one of the most common symptoms in cancer patients. Pain can be caused by cancer, treatment for cancer, or a combination of factors. Tumors, surgery, intravenous chemotherapy, radiation therapy, targeted therapy, supportive care therapies such as bisphosphonates, and diagnostic procedures may cause you pain.

Younger patients are more likely to have cancer pain and pain flares than older patients. Patients with advanced cancer have more severe pain, and many cancer survivors have pain that continues after cancer treatment ends.

Pain control can improve your quality of life.

Pain can be controlled in most patients who have cancer. Although cancer pain cannot always be relieved completely, there are ways to lessen pain in most patients. Pain control can improve your quality of life all through your cancer treatment and after it ends.

Pain can be managed before, during, and after diagnostic and treatment procedures.

Many diagnostic and treatment procedures are painful. It helps to start pain control before the procedure begins. Some drugs may be used to help you feel calm or fall asleep. Treatments such as imagery or relaxation can also help control pain and anxiety related to treatment. Knowing what will happen during the procedure and having a relative or friend stay with you may also help lower anxiety.

About This Chapter: This chapter includes text excerpted from "Cancer Pain (PDQ®)—Patient Version," National Cancer Institute (NCI), August 31, 2017.

Different cancer treatments may cause specific types of pain.

Patients may have different types of pain depending on the treatments they receive, including:

- Spasms, stinging, and itching caused by intravenous chemotherapy.

- Mucositis (sores or inflammation in the mouth or other parts of the digestive system) caused by chemotherapy or targeted therapy.

- Skin pain, rash, or hand-foot syndrome (redness, tingling, or burning in the palms of the hands and/or the soles of feet) caused by chemotherapy or targeted therapy.

- Pain in joints and muscles throughout the body caused by paclitaxel or aromatase inhibitor therapy.

- Osteonecrosis of the jaw caused by bisphosphonates given for cancer that has spread to the bone.

- Pain syndromes caused by radiation, including:

  - Pain from brachytherapy.

  - Pain from the position the patient stays in during radiation therapy.

  - Mucositis.

  - Inflammation of the mucous membranes in areas that were treated with radiation.

  - Dermatitis (inflammation of the skin in areas that were treated with radiation).

  - Pain flares (a temporary worsening of pain in the treated area).

Cancer pain may affect quality of life and ability to function even after treatment ends.

Pain that is severe or continues after cancer treatment ends increases the risk of anxiety and depression. Patients may be disabled by their pain or feel that they are losing support once their care moves from their oncology team back to their primary care team. Feelings of anxiety and depression can worsen cancer pain and make it harder to control.

Each patient needs a personal plan to control cancer pain.

Each person's diagnosis, cancer stage, response to pain, and personal likes and dislikes are different. For this reason, each patient needs a personal plan to control cancer pain. You, your family, and your healthcare team can work together to manage your pain. As part of your pain control plan, your healthcare provider can give you and your family members written instructions to control your pain at home.

Assessment Of Cancer Pain

You and your healthcare team work together to assess cancer pain. It's important that the cause of the pain is found early and treated quickly. Your healthcare team will help you measure pain levels often, including at the following times:

- After starting cancer treatment.

- When there is new pain.

- After starting any type of pain treatment.

To learn about your pain, the healthcare team will ask you to describe the pain with the following questions:

- When did the pain start?

- How long does the pain last?

- Where is the pain? You will be asked to show exactly where the pain is on your body or on a drawing of a body.

- How strong is the pain?

- Have there been changes in where or when the pain occurs?

- What makes the pain better or worse?

- Is the pain worse during certain times of the day or night?

- Is there breakthrough pain (intense pain that flares up quickly even when pain control medicine is being used)?

- Do you have symptoms, such as trouble sleeping, fatigue, depression, or anxiety?

- Does pain get in the way of activities of daily life, such as eating, bathing, or moving around?

Your healthcare team will also take into account:

- Past and current pain treatments.

- Prognosis (chance of recovery).

- Other conditions you may have, such as kidney, liver, or heart disease.

- Past and current use of nicotine, alcohol, or sleeping pills.

- Personal or family history of substance abuse.

- Personal history of childhood sexual abuse.

- Your own choices.

This information will be used to decide how to help relieve your pain. This may include drugs or other treatments. In some cases, patients are referred to pain specialists or palliative care specialists. Your healthcare team will work with you to decide whether the benefits of treatment outweigh any risks and how much improvement you should expect. After pain control is started, the doctor will continue to assess how well it is working for you and make changes if needed. A family member or caregiver may be asked to give answers for a patient who has a problem with speech, language, or understanding.

Physical and neurological exams will be done to help plan pain control.

Your healthcare team will also assess your psychological, social, and spiritual needs.

Using Drugs To Control Cancer Pain

Your doctor will prescribe drugs to help relieve your pain. These drugs need to be taken at scheduled times to keep a constant level of the drug in the body to help keep the pain from coming back. Drugs may be taken by mouth or given in other ways, such as by infusion or injection.

Your doctor may prescribe extra doses of a drug that can be taken as needed for pain that occurs between scheduled doses of the drug. The doctor will adjust the drug dose for your needs.

A scale from 0–10 is used to measure how severe the pain is and decide which pain medicine to use. On this scale:

- 0 means no pain.

- 1–3 means mild pain.

- 4–6 means moderate pain.

- 7–10 means severe pain.

Acetaminophen and Nonsteroidal anti-inflammatory drugs (NSAIDs) help relieve mild pain. They may be given with opioids for moderate to severe pain.

Pain relievers of this type include:

- Acetaminophen

- Celecoxib

- Diclofenac

- Ibuprofen

- Ketoprofen

- Ketorolac

Patients, who are taking acetaminophen or NSAIDs need to be closely watched for side effects.

Opioids work very well to relieve moderate to severe pain. Some patients with cancer pain stop getting pain relief from opioids if they take them for a long time. This is called tolerance. Larger doses or a different opioid may be needed if your body stops responding to the same dose. Tolerance of an opioid is a physical dependence on it. This is not the same as addiction (psychological dependence).

Since 1999, there have been four times the number of prescriptions written for opioids and four times the number of deaths caused by drug overdose in the United States. Although most patients who are prescribed opioids for cancer pain use them safely, a small percentage of patients may become addicted to opioids. Your doctor will carefully prescribe and monitor your opioid doses so that you are treated for pain safely.

There are several types of opioids:

- Buprenorphine

- Codeine

- Diamorphine

- Fentanyl

- Hydrocodone

- Hydromorphone

- Methadone

- Morphine (the most commonly used opioid for cancer pain)

- Oxycodone

- Oxymorphone

- Tapentadol

- Tramadol

The doctor will prescribe drugs and the times they should be taken in order to best control your pain. Also, it is important that patients and family caregivers know how to safely use, store, and dispose of opioids.

Receiving opioids on a regular schedule helps relieve the pain and keeps it from getting worse. The amount of time between doses depends on which opioid you are using. The correct dose is the amount of opioid that controls your pain with the fewest side effects. The dose will be slowly adjusted until there is a good balance between pain relief and side effects. If opioid tolerance does occur, the dose may be increased or a different opioid may be needed.

Opioids may be given by the following ways:

- Mouth
- Rectum
- Skin patches
- Nose spray
- Intravenous (IV) line
- Subcutaneous injection
- Intraspinal injection

Your doctor will discuss the side effects with you before opioid treatment begins and will watch you for side effects. The following are the most common side effects:

- Constipation
- Nausea
- Drowsiness
- Dry mouth

Nausea and drowsiness most often occur when opioid treatment is first started and usually get better within a few days.

Opioids slow down the muscle contractions and movement in the stomach and intestines, which can cause hard stools. To keep the stool soft and prevent constipation, it's important to drink plenty of fluids. Unless there are problems such as a blocked bowel or diarrhea, you will be given a treatment plan to follow to prevent constipation and information on how to avoid problems with your intestines while taking opioids.

Other side effects of opioid treatment include the following:

- Vomiting.

- Low blood pressure.

- Dizziness.

- Trouble sleeping.

- Trouble thinking clearly.

- Delirium or hallucinations.

- Trouble urinating.

- Problems with breathing.

- Severe itching.

- Problems with sexual function.

- Hot flashes.

- Depression.

- Hypoglycemia.

Talk with your doctor about side effects that bother you or become severe. Your doctor may decrease the dose of the opioid, change to a different opioid, or change the way the opioid is given to help decrease the side effects.

Other drugs may be given while you are taking opioids for pain relief. These are drugs that help the opioids work better, treat symptoms, and relieve certain types of pain. The following types of drugs may be used:

- Antidepressants

- Anticonvulsants

- Local anesthetics

- Corticosteroids

- Stimulants

- Bisphosphonates and denosumab

There are big differences in how patients respond to these drugs. Side effects are common and should be reported to your doctor.

Bisphosphonates (pamidronate, zoledronic acid, and ibandronate) are drugs that are sometimes used when cancer has spread to the bones. They are given as an intravenous infusion and combined with other treatments to decrease pain and reduce risk of broken bones. However, bisphosphonates sometimes cause severe side effects. Talk to your doctor if you have severe muscle or bone pain. Bisphosphonate therapy may need to be stopped.

The use of bisphosphonates is also linked to the risk of bisphosphonate-associated osteonecrosis (BON). Denosumab is another drug that may be used when cancer has spread to the bones. It is given as a subcutaneous injection and may help prevent and relieve pain.

Other Treatments For Cancer Pain

Most cancer pain can be controlled with drug treatments, but some patients have too many side effects from drugs or have pain in a certain part of the body that needs to be treated in a different way. You can talk to your doctor to help decide which methods work best to relieve your pain. These other treatments include:

Nerve Blocks

A nerve block is the injection of either a local anesthetic or a drug into or around a nerve to block pain. Nerve blocks help control pain that can't be controlled in other ways. Nerve blocks may also be used to find where the pain is coming from, to predict how the pain will respond to long-term treatments, and to prevent pain after certain procedures.

Neurological Treatments

Surgery can be done to insert a device that delivers drugs or stimulates the nerves with mild electric current. In rare cases, surgery may be done to destroy a nerve or nerves that are part of the pain pathway.

Cordotomy

Cordotomy is a less common surgical procedure that is used to relieve pain by cutting certain nerves in the spinal cord. This blocks pain and also hot/cold feelings. This procedure may be chosen for patients who are near the end of life and have severe pain that cannot be relieved in other ways.

Palliative Care

Certain patients are helped by palliative care services. Palliative care providers may also be called supportive care providers. They work in teams that include doctors, nurses, mental health specialists, social workers, chaplains, pharmacists, and dietitians. Some of the goals of palliative care are to:

- Improve quality of life for patients and their families.

- Manage pain and nonpain symptoms.

- Support patients who need higher doses of opioids, have a history of substance abuse, or are coping with emotional and social problems.

Radiation Therapy

Radiation therapy is used to relieve pain in patients with skin lesions, tumors, or cancer that has spread to the bone. This is called palliative radiation therapy. It may be given as local therapy directly to the tumor or to larger areas of the body. Radiation therapy helps drugs and other treatments work better by shrinking tumors that are causing pain. Radiation therapy may help patients with bone pain move more freely and with less pain.

The following types of radiation therapy may be used:

External Radiation Therapy

External radiation therapy uses a machine outside the body to send high-energy X-rays or other types of radiation toward the cancer. External radiation therapy relieves pain from cancer that has spread to the bone. Radiation therapy may be given in a single dose or divided into several smaller doses given over a period of time. The decision whether to have a single or divided dose may depend on how easy it is to get the treatments and how much they cost. Patients may have a pain flare (a temporary worsening of pain in the treated area) after receiving palliative radiation therapy for cancer that has spread to the bone, but this side effect is only temporary.

Radiopharmaceuticals

Radiopharmaceuticals are drugs that have a radioactive substance that may be used to diagnose or treat disease, including cancer. Radiopharmaceuticals may also be used to relieve pain from cancer that has spread to the bone. A single dose of a radioactive agent injected into a vein may relieve pain when cancer has spread to several areas of bone and/or when there are too many areas to treat with external radiation therapy.

Physical Medicine And Rehabilitation

Patients with cancer and pain may lose their strength, freedom of movement, and ability to manage their daily activities. Physical therapy or occupational therapy may help these patients.

353

Physical medicine uses physical methods, such as exercise and machines to prevent and treat disease or injury.

Physical methods to treat weakness, muscle wasting, and muscle and bone pain include the following:

- Exercise to strengthen and stretch weak muscles, loosen stiff joints, help coordination and balance, and strengthen the heart.

- Changing position (for patients who are not able to move on their own).

- Limiting the movement of painful areas or broken bones.

Some patients may be referred to a physiatrist (a doctor who specializes in physical medicine) who can develop a personal plan for them. Some physiatrists are also trained in procedures to treat and manage pain.

Complementary Therapies

Complementary and alternative therapies combined with standard treatment may be used to treat pain. They may also be called integrative therapies. Acupuncture, support groups, and hypnosis are a few integrative therapies that have been used to relieve pain.

Acupuncture

Acupuncture is an integrative therapy that applies needles, heat, pressure, and other treatments to one or more places on the skin called acupuncture points. Acupuncture may be used to control pain, including pain related to cancer.

Hypnosis

Hypnosis may help you relax and may be combined with other thinking and behavior methods. Hypnosis to relieve pain works best in people who are able to concentrate and use imagery and who are willing to practice the technique.

Support Groups

Support groups help many patients. Religious counseling may also help by offering spiritual care and social support.

Chapter 50

Late Effects: Chronic Problems That Can Result After Cancer And Treatment

Nervous System Changes (Neuropathy)

Sometimes cancer treatment can cause damage to your nervous system. This is called neuropathy or problems with nerve function. Sometimes these symptoms can be made worse by other conditions, such as diabetes, kidney failure, alcoholism, and malnutrition. Most people first notice symptoms in their hands or feet, usually starting with their fingertips and toes. Sometimes, the tingling and pain move up the fingers to the hands or from the toes to the feet.

Common symptoms include tingling, burning, weakness, or numbness in your hands or feet; sudden, sharp, stabbing, or electric shock pain sensations; loss of sensation of touch; loss of balance or difficulty walking; clumsiness; trouble picking up objects or buttoning clothes; hearing loss; jaw pain; constipation; and being more—or less—sensitive to heat and cold. Symptoms can start when you begin chemotherapy or after treatment. If they do, tell your healthcare team right away. Symptoms can improve over time, but it may take up to a year or more.

Getting Help

- Treatments include medications, topical creams, and pain patches.

- Other approaches include acupuncture, physical therapy, and exercise.

About This Chapter: This chapter includes text excerpted from "Facing Forward—Life After Cancer Treatment," National Cancer Institute (NCI), May 2014. Reviewed December 2017.

Managing Nervous System Changes

- **Be careful** when handling knives, scissors, and other sharp objects.
- **Avoid falling.** Walk slowly, hold onto handrails, and put no-slip bath mats in your tub or shower. Remove area rugs or cords you could trip over. Steady yourself when you walk by using a cane or other device.
- **Wear tennis shoes or other footwear with rubber soles.**
- **Use a thermometer and gloves instead of your bare hand.** These can help you avoid being burned when checking water temperature. If possible, lower the temperature setting on your hot water heater.
- **Allow yourself time to rest.**

Lymphedema Or Swelling

Lymphedema is a swelling of a part of the body caused by the buildup of lymph fluids. It often happens in the arm, leg, face, or neck. It can be caused by cancer or its treatment. There are many different types of lymphedema. Some types happen right after surgery, are mild, and don't last long. Other types can occur months or years after cancer treatment and can be quite painful. These types can also develop after an insect bite, minor injury, or burn.

People who are at risk for lymphedema are those who have had:

- **Breast cancer.** If you had radiation therapy, or had your underarm lymph nodes removed, or had radiation in the underarm area after your lymph nodes were removed

- **Melanoma of the arms or legs.** If you had lymph nodes removed and/or had radiation therapy

- **Prostate cancer.** If you had surgery or radiation therapy to the whole pelvis

- **Cancer of the female or male reproductive organs.** If you had surgery to remove lymph nodes or had radiation therapy

- **Other cancers that have spread to the lower abdominal area.** The pressure from the growing tumor can make it hard for your body to drain fluid.

Getting Help

Your doctor or nurse may be able to help you find ways to prevent and relieve lymphedema. Ask about:

- **Skin care.** It's important to keep your skin clean. You should also use lotion to keep it moist.

- **Exercise.** Find out about exercises to help the body drain lymph fluid and what types of exercise you should not do.

- **Ways to treat lymphedema.** Your doctor may suggest:

  - Keeping the arm or leg raised above your chest for periods of time

  - Having special types of massage that can help by moving the lymph fluid from where it has settled

  - Wearing special elastic sleeves and clothing that can help lymph fluid drain

  - Losing weight

  - Finding sources of emotional support to help you cope

  - Avoiding procedures done in the area with lymphedema, such as shots or blood tests

---

Preventing Or Relieving Lymphedema

Other cancer survivors have found these tips helpful:

- Watch for signs of swelling or infection (redness, pain, heat, fever). Tell your doctor or nurse if your arm or leg is painful or swollen.
- Keep your arm or leg free of cuts, insect bites, and sunburn. Try not to have shots or blood tests done in that area.
- Eat a well-balanced, protein-rich, low-salt diet.
- Keep regular follow-up appointments with your doctor.
- Wear loose-fitting clothing on your arm or leg.
- Protect the area. Try not to use that arm or leg to figure out how hot or cold something is, such as bath water or cooked food. You may be less able to feel hot and cold now.

Mouth Or Teeth Problems

Many people who have been treated for cancer develop problems with their mouth or teeth. Some problems go away after treatment. Others last a long time, while some may never go away. Some problems may develop months or years after your treatment has ended.

Radiation or surgery to the head and neck can cause problems with your teeth and gums; the soft, moist lining of your mouth; glands that make saliva (spit); and jawbones. If you were treated with certain types of chemotherapy, you may also have these problems. This can cause:

- Dry mouth

- Cavities and other kinds of tooth problems

- Loss of or change in sense of taste

- Painful mouth and gums

- Infections in your mouth

- Jaw stiffness or jawbone changes

Who Has These Problems?

- Almost all people who have had radiation therapy to the head and neck

- Most people who have had bone marrow transplants

- About 2 out of every 5 people treated with chemotherapy

Getting Help

If you find that problems persist after cancer treatment ends, talk with your doctor about possible causes and ways to control mouth pain.

Try to see your dentist soon after you are done with treatment. Ask how often you should have checkups and ways to take care of your mouth and teeth.

Preventing Or Relieving Mouth Or Teeth Problems

- **Keep your mouth moist.**
  - Drink a lot of water.
  - Suck on ice chips.
  - Chew sugarless gum or suck on sugar-free hard candy.
  - Use a saliva substitute to help moisten your mouth.
- **Keep your mouth clean.**
  - Brush your teeth, gums, and tongue with an extra-soft toothbrush after every meal and at bedtime. If it hurts, soften the bristles in warm water.

- Ask your dentist for tooth sponges, such as Toothettes® or Dentips®, that you can use in place of a toothbrush.
- Use a mild fluoride toothpaste (like children's toothpaste) and a mouthwash without alcohol.
- Floss your teeth gently every day. If your gums bleed or hurt, stay away from the areas that are bleeding or sore, but keep flossing your other teeth.
- Rinse your mouth several times a day with a solution of 1/4 teaspoon baking soda and 1/8 teaspoon salt in 1 cup of warm water. Follow with a plain water rinse.
- If you have dentures, clean, brush, and rinse them after meals. Have your dentist check them to make sure they still fit you well.
- **If your mouth is sore, remember to stay away from:**
- Sharp, crunchy foods, like chips, that can scrape or cut your mouth
- Foods that are hot, spicy, or high in acid, like citrus fruits and juices, which can irritate your mouth
- Sugary foods, like candy or soda, that can cause cavities
- Toothpicks (they can cut your mouth)
- All tobacco products
- Alcoholic drinks

Changes In Weight And Eating Habits

Some survivors who have had certain kinds of chemotherapy or medicines have problems with weight gain. Sometimes the added pounds stay on even when treatment ends. Breast cancer survivors who have had certain types of chemotherapy gain weight in a different way—they may lose muscle and gain fat tissue. Unfortunately, the usual ways people try to lose weight may not work for them. Try to be patient with yourself. Look for the positive things that you can control, such as eating a healthy diet. Try to focus on the fact that treatment is over, and you are trying to get stronger with time. Some cancer survivors have the opposite problem: they have no desire to eat, and they lose weight. Some men say that weight loss or loss of muscle tone is a bigger concern for them than weight gain. It makes them feel less strong and like less of a man.

Managing A Healthy Weight

For weight issues, ask your doctor or nurse about:

- Doing strength-building exercises, if you have lost muscle or gained fat tissue

- Talking to a dietitian or nutritionist who can help you plan a healthy diet that won't add extra pounds

---

Regaining A Lost Appetite

Here are some tips that have helped others improve their appetites:

- **Start with small meals.** Five small meals a day may be easier to manage than three larger ones.
- **Focus on your favorite foods.** If the thought of eating still lacks appeal, try the foods you really liked before treatment to jump-start your appetite. Try adding some fresh fruit, juice, or other flavoring to improve the taste.
- **Stay active.** A short walk before a meal can help you feel hungry.

Trouble Swallowing

Some people who have had radiation therapy or chemotherapy may find it hard to eat because they have trouble swallowing. People who have had radiation therapy to the head, neck, breast, or chest or those who have had surgery involving the larynx may also have this problem.

Getting Help

- Eat soft, bland foods moistened with sauces or gravies. Puddings, ice cream, soups, applesauce, and bananas and other soft fruits are nourishing and usually easy to swallow.

- Use a blender to process solid foods.

- Ask for advice from your healthcare team, including your doctor, nurse, nutritionist, and/or speech pathologist.

- Tilt your head back or move it forward while you are eating.

- Have a sip of water every few minutes to help you swallow and talk more easily. Carry a water bottle with you so you always have some handy.

Bladder Or Bowel Control Problems

Bladder and bowel problems are among the most upsetting issues people face after cancer treatment. People often feel ashamed or fearful to go out in public. This loss of control can happen after treatment for bladder, prostate, colon, rectal, ovarian, or other cancers. Your surgery may have left you with no bladder or bowel control at all. Or perhaps you still have some control, but you make lots of sudden trips to the bathroom. The opposite problem can happen when a medicine you are taking for pain causes constipation.

Getting Help

It is very important to tell your doctor about any changes in your bladder or bowel habits. Ask your doctor or nurse about:

- Problems with constipation

- Kegel exercises

- Medicines that may help

- Help in coping with ostomies. If you have an ostomy, an opening from inside the body to the outside to pass urine or waste material, there are services and support groups to help you cope with changes.

Chapter 51

Fertility Issues In Girls And Boys After Cancer Treatment

Many cancer treatments can affect a girl's fertility. Most likely, your doctor will talk with you about whether or not cancer treatment may increase the risk of, or cause, infertility. However, not all doctors bring up this topic. Sometimes you or a family member being treated for cancer may need to initiate this conversation.

Whether or not fertility is affected depends on factors such as:

- your baseline fertility

- your age at the time of treatment

- the type of cancer and treatment(s)

- the amount (dose) of treatment

- the length (duration) of treatment

- the amount of time that has passed since cancer treatment

- other personal health factors

It's important to learn how the recommended cancer treatment may affect fertility before starting treatment, whenever possible. Consider asking questions such as:

- Could treatment increase the risk of, or cause, infertility? Could treatment make it difficult to become pregnant or carry a pregnancy in the future?

About This Chapter: Text in this chapter begins with excerpts from "Fertility Issues In Girls And Women With Cancer," National Cancer Institute (NCI), September 22, 2017; Text beginning with the heading "Cancer Treatments May Affect Boys Fertility" is excerpted from "Fertility Issues In Boys And Men With Cancer," National Cancer Institute (NCI), September 22, 2017.

- Are there other recommended cancer treatments that might not cause fertility problems?

- Which fertility option(s) would you advise for me?

- What fertility preservation options are available at this hospital? At a fertility clinic?

- Would you recommend a fertility specialist (such as a reproductive endocrinologist) who I could talk with to learn more?

- Is condom use advised, based on the treatment I'm receiving?

- Is birth control recommended?

- After treatment, what are the chances that my fertility will return? How long might it take for my fertility to return?

Cancer Treatments May Affect Girls' Fertility

Cancer treatments are important for your future health, but they may harm reproductive organs and glands that control fertility. Changes to your fertility may be temporary or permanent. Talk with your healthcare team to learn what to expect, based on your treatment(s):

- Chemotherapy (especially alkylating agents) can affect the ovaries, causing them to stop releasing eggs and estrogen. This is called primary ovarian insufficiency (POI). Sometimes POI is temporary and your menstrual periods and fertility return after treatment. Other times, damage to your ovaries is permanent and fertility doesn't return. You may have hot flashes, night sweats, irritability, vaginal dryness, and irregular or no menstrual periods. Chemotherapy can also lower the number of healthy eggs in the ovaries.

- Radiation therapy to or near the abdomen, pelvis, or spine can harm nearby reproductive organs. Some organs, such as the ovaries, can often be protected by ovarian shielding or by oophoropexy—a procedure that surgically moves the ovaries away from the radiation area. Radiation therapy to the brain can also harm the pituitary gland. This gland is important because it sends signals to the ovaries to make hormones such as estrogen that are needed for ovulation. The amount of radiation given and the part of your body being treated both play a role in whether or not fertility is affected.

- Surgery for cancers of the reproductive system and for cancers in the pelvis region can harm nearby reproductive tissues and cause scarring, which can affect your fertility. The size and location of the tumor are important factors in whether or not fertility is affected.

- Hormone therapy (also called endocrine therapy) used to treat cancer can disrupt the menstrual cycle, which may affect your fertility. Side effects depend on the specific hormones used and may include hot flashes, night sweats, and vaginal dryness.

- Bone marrow transplants, peripheral blood stem cell transplants, and other stem cell transplants involve receiving high doses of chemotherapy and/or radiation. These treatments can damage the ovaries and may cause infertility.

- Other treatments: Talk with your doctor to learn whether or not other types of treatment such as immunotherapy and targeted cancer therapy may affect your fertility.

Fertility Preservation Options For Girls

Girls with cancer have options to preserve their fertility. These procedures may be available at the hospital where you are receiving cancer treatment or at a fertility preservation clinic.

Talk with your doctor about the best option(s) for you based on your age, the type of cancer you have, and the specific treatment(s) you will be receiving. The success rate, financial cost, and availability of these procedures varies.

- Egg freezing (also called egg or oocyte cryopreservation) is a procedure in which eggs are removed from the ovary and frozen. Later the eggs can be thawed, fertilized with sperm in the lab to form embryos, and placed in a woman's uterus. Egg freezing is a newer procedure than embryo freezing.

- Embryo freezing (also called embryo banking or embryo cryopreservation) is a procedure in which eggs are removed from the ovary. They are then fertilized with sperm in the lab to form embryos and frozen for future use.

- Ovarian shielding (also called gonadal shielding) is a procedure in which a protective cover is placed on the outside of the body, over the ovaries and other parts of the reproductive system, to shield them from scatter radiation.

- Ovarian tissue freezing (also called ovarian tissue cryopreservation) is still considered an experimental procedure, for young girls who haven't gone through puberty and don't have mature eggs. It involves surgically removing part or all of an ovary and then freezing the ovarian tissue, which contains eggs. Later, the tissue is thawed and placed back in a woman. Although pregnancies have occurred as a result of this procedure, it's only an option for some types of cancer.

- Ovarian transposition (also called oophoropexy) is an operation to move the ovaries away from the part of the body receiving radiation. This procedure may be done during surgery to remove the cancer or through laparoscopic surgery.

- Radical trachelectomy (also called radical cervicectomy) is surgery used to treat women with early-stage cervical cancer who would like to have children. This operation removes the cervix, nearby lymph nodes, and the upper part of the vagina. The uterus is then attached to the remaining part of the vagina, with a special band that serves as the cervix.

- Treatment with gonadotropin-releasing hormone agonist (also called GnRHa), a substance that causes the ovaries to stop making estrogen and progesterone. Research is ongoing to assess the effectiveness of giving GnRHa to protect the ovaries.

If you choose to take steps to preserve your fertility, your doctor and a fertility specialist will work together to develop a treatment plan that includes fertility preservation, whenever possible.

Cancer Treatments May Affect Boys' Fertility

Cancer treatments are important for your future health, but they may harm reproductive organs and glands that control fertility. Changes to your fertility may be temporary or permanent. Talk with your healthcare team to learn what to expect based on your treatment(s):

- Chemotherapy (especially alkylating drugs) can damage sperm in men and sperm-forming cells (germ cells) in young boys.

- Hormone therapy (also called endocrine therapy) can decrease the production of sperm.

- Radiation therapy to the reproductive organs as well as radiation near the abdomen, pelvis, or spine may lower sperm counts and testosterone levels, causing infertility. Radiation may also destroy sperm cells and the stem cells that make sperm. Radiation therapy to the brain can damage the pituitary gland and decrease the production of testosterone and sperm. For some types of cancers, the testicles can be protected from radiation through a procedure called testicular shielding.

- Surgery for cancers of the reproductive organs and for pelvic cancers (such as bladder, colon, prostate, and rectal cancer) can damage these organs and/or nearby nerves or lymph nodes in the pelvis, leading to infertility.

- Stem cell transplants such as bone marrow transplants and peripheral blood stem cell transplants, involve receiving high doses of chemotherapy and/or radiation. These treatments can damage sperm and sperm-forming cells.

- Other treatments: Talk with your doctor to learn whether or not other types of treatment, such as immunotherapy and targeted cancer therapy, may affect your fertility.

Fertility Preservation Options For Boys And Men

Men and boys with cancer have options to preserve their fertility. These procedures may be available at the hospital where you are receiving cancer treatment or at a fertility preservation clinic.

Talk with your doctor about the best option(s) for you based on your age, the type of cancer you have, and the specific treatment(s) you will be receiving. The success rate, financial cost, and availability of these procedures varies.

- Sperm banking (also called semen cryopreservation) is the most common and easy option for young men of reproductive age who would like to have children one day. Samples of semen are collected and checked under a microscope in the laboratory. The sperm are then frozen and stored (banked) for the future. Sperm can be frozen for an indefinite amount of time.

- Testicular shielding (also called gonadal shielding) is a procedure in which a protective cover is placed on the outside of the body to shield the testicles from scatter radiation to the pelvis when other parts of the body are being treated with radiation.

- Testicular sperm extraction (TESE) is a procedure for males who are not able to produce a semen sample. Sperm is collected through a medical procedure and frozen for future use.

- Testicular tissue freezing (also called testicular tissue cryopreservation) is still considered an experimental procedure at most hospitals. For boys who have not gone through puberty and are at high risk of infertility, this procedure may be an option.

If you choose to take steps to preserve your fertility, your doctor and a fertility specialist will work together to develop a treatment plan that includes fertility preservation procedures whenever possible.

Chapter 52

Food Safety For People With Cancer

Food Safety: It's Especially Important For You

As a cancer patient, your healthcare provider may have recommended that you take chemotherapy, radiation, or medications to help fight your disease. A side effect of these therapies is that they may weaken your immune system. Cancer also may weaken your immune system over time due to its chronic disease process.

- A properly functioning immune system works to clear infection and other foreign agents from the body. However, cancer and its treatments can weaken your immune system making you more susceptible to many types of infections. These infections include those that can be brought on by disease-causing bacteria and other pathogens that cause foodborne illness.

- Because you have cancer and are receiving cancer treatment, you are more likely to have a lengthier illness, undergo hospitalization, or even die, should you contract a foodborne illness.

- To avoid contracting a foodborne illness, you must be vigilant when handling, preparing, and consuming foods.

Make safe handling a lifelong commitment to minimize your risk of foodborne illness. Be aware that as you age, your immunity to infection naturally is weakened.

About This Chapter: Text under the heading "Food Safety: It's Especially Important For You" is excerpted from "Food Safety For People With Cancer," U.S. Food and Drug Administration (FDA), November 8, 2017; Text under the heading "After Cancer Treatment" is excerpted from "Eating Hints: Before, During, And After Cancer Treatment," National Cancer Institute (NCI), January 2011. Reviewed December 2017.

After Cancer Treatment

Many Eating Problems Go Away When Treatment Ends

Once you finish cancer treatment, many of your eating problems will get better. Some eating problems, such as weight loss and changes in taste or smell, may last longer than your course of treatment. If you had treatment for head and neck cancer or surgery to remove part of your stomach or intestines, then eating problems may always be part of your life.

Return To Healthy Eating

While healthy eating by itself cannot keep cancer from coming back, it can help you regain strength, rebuild tissue, and improve how you feel after treatment ends. Here are some ways to eat well after treatment ends:

- Prepare simple meals that you like and are easy to make.

- Cook 2 or 3 meals at a time. Freeze the extras to eat later on.

- Stock up on frozen dinners.

- Make cooking easy, such as buying cut up vegetables from a salad bar.

- Eat many different kinds of foods. No single food has all the vitamins and nutrients you need.

- Eat lots of fruits and vegetables. This includes eating raw and cooked vegetables, fruits, and fruit juices. These all have vitamins, minerals, and fiber.

- Eat whole wheat bread, oats, brown rice, or other whole grains and cereals.

- These have needed complex carbohydrates, vitamins, minerals, and fiber.

- Add beans, peas, and lentils to your diet and eat them often.

- Go easy on fat, salt, sugar, alcohol, and smoked or pickled foods.

- Choose low-fat milk products.

- Eat small portions (about 6–7 ounces each day) of lean meat and poultry without skin.

- Use low-fat cooking methods, such as broiling, steaming, grilling, and roasting.

Talk With A Dietitian

You may find it helpful to talk with a dietitian even when you are finished with cancer treatment. A dietitian can help you return to healthy eating or discuss ways to manage any lasting eating problems.

Table 52.1. Eating Problems That May Be Caused By Certain Cancer Treatments

Cancer Treatment	What Sometimes Happens: Side Effects
Surgery	• Surgery may slow digestion (how the body uses food). It can also affect eating if you have surgery of the mouth, stomach, intestines, or throat.
	• After surgery, some people have trouble getting back to normal eating. If this happens, you may need to get nutrients through a feeding tube or IV (through a needle directly into a vein). **Note:** Surgery increases your need for good nutrition. If you are weak or underweight, you may need to eat a high-protein, high-calorie diet before surgery.
Radiation Therapy	Radiation therapy damages healthy cells as well as cancer cells. When you have radiation therapy to the head, neck, chest, oresophagus, you may have eating problems such as: • Changes in your sense of taste • Dry mouth • Sore mouth • Sore throat • Tooth and jaw problems • Trouble swallowing When you have radiation therapy to the abdomen or pelvis, you may have problems with: • Cramps, bloating • Diarrhea • Nausea • Vomiting

Table 52.1. Continued

Cancer Treatment	What Sometimes Happens: Side Effects
Chemotherapy	Chemotherapy works by stopping or slowing the growth of cancer cells, which grow and divide quickly. But it can also harm healthy cells that grow and divide quickly, such as those in the lining of your mouth and intestines. Damage to healthy cells can lead to side effects. Some of these side effects can lead to eating problems, such as: • Appetite loss • Changes in your sense of taste • Constipation • Diarrhea • Nausea • Sore mouth • Sore throat • Vomiting • Weight gain • Weight loss
Biological Therapy (Immunotherapy)	Biological therapy can affect your interest in food or ability to eat. Problems can include: • Changes in your sense of taste • Diarrhea • Dry mouth • Appetite loss caused by flu-like symptoms, such as muscle aches, fatigue, and fever • Nausea • Sore mouth • Vomiting • Weight loss, severe
Hormone Therapy	Hormone therapy can affect your interest in food or ability to eat. Problems can include: • Changes in your sense of taste • Diarrhea

Part Five
When A Loved One Has Cancer

Chapter 53

When Your Parent Has Cancer

You've Just Learned That Your Parent Has Cancer

You've just learned that one of the most important people in your life has cancer. Do you feel shocked, numb, angry, or afraid? Do you feel like life is unfair? One thing is certain—you don't feel good.

Your Feelings

As you deal with your parent's cancer, you'll probably feel all kinds of things. Many other teens who have a parent with cancer have felt the same way you do now. Some of these emotions are listed below. Think about people you can talk with about your feelings.

Check off the feelings you have:

- **Scared.** It's normal to feel scared when your parent has cancer. Some of your fears may be real. Others may be based on things that won't happen. And some fears may lessen over time.

- **Guilty.** You may feel bad about having fun when your parent is sick. However, having fun doesn't mean that you care any less. In fact, it will probably help your parent to see you doing things you enjoy.

- **Angry.** Anger often covers up other feelings that are harder to show. Try not to let your anger build up.

About This Chapter: This chapter includes text excerpted from "When Your Parent Has Cancer—A Guide For Teens," National Cancer Institute (NCI), February 2012. Reviewed December 2017.

- **Neglected.** When a parent has cancer, it's common for the family's focus to change. Some people in the family may feel left out. Your parent with cancer may be using his or her energy to get better. Your well parent may be focused on helping your parent with cancer. Your parents don't mean for you to feel left out. It just happens because so much is going on.

- **Lonely.** We look at some things you can do to help situations with friends. For now, try to remember that these feelings won't last forever.

- **Embarrassed.** Many teens who feel embarrassed about having a parent with cancer say it gets easier to deal with over time.

What you're feeling is normal. There is no one "right" way to feel. And you're not alone—many other teens in your situation have felt the same way. Some have said that having a parent with cancer changes the way they look at things in life. Some even said that it made them stronger.

Dealing With Your Feelings

A lot of people are uncomfortable sharing their feelings. They ignore them and hope they'll go away. Other people choose to act cheerful when they're really not. They think that by acting upbeat they won't feel sad or angry anymore. This may help for a little while, but not over the long run. Actually, holding your feelings inside can keep you from getting the help you need.

Try these tips:

- Talk with family and friends who you feel close to. You owe it to yourself. Write down your thoughts in a journal.

- Join a support group to talk with other teens who are facing some of the same things you are. It is probably hard to imagine right now, but, if you let yourself, you can grow stronger as a person through this experience.

Many kids think that they need to protect their parents by not making them worry. They think that they have to be perfect and not cause any trouble because one of their parents is sick. If you feel this way, remember that no one can be perfect all the time. You need time to vent, to feel sad, and to be happy. Try to let your parents know how you feel—even if you have to start the conversation.

What Your Parent May Be Feeling

Knowing what your parent may be feeling could help you figure out how to help, or at least to understand where he or she is coming from. You may be surprised to learn that they are feeling a lot of the same things you are:

- **Sad or depressed.** People with cancer sometimes can't do things they used to do. They may miss these activities and their friends. Feeling sad or down can range from a mild case of the blues to depression, which a doctor can treat.

- **Afraid.** Your parent may be afraid of how cancer will change his or her life and the lives of family members. He or she may be scared about treatment. Your parent may even be scared that he or she will die.

- **Anxious.** Your parent may be worried about a lot of things. Your mom or dad may feel stressed about going to work or paying the bills. Or he or she may be concerned about looking different because of treatment. And your mom or dad is probably very concerned about how you are doing. All these worries may upset your parent.

- **Angry.** Cancer treatment and its side effects can be difficult to go through. Anger sometimes comes from feelings that are hard to show, such as fear or frustration. Chances are your parent is angry at the disease, not at you.

- **Lonely.** People with cancer often feel lonely or distant from others. They may find that their friends have a hard time dealing with their cancer and may not visit. They may be too sick to take part in activities they used to enjoy. They may feel that no one understands what they're going through.

- **Hopeful.** There are many reasons for your parent to feel hopeful. Millions of people who have had cancer are alive today. People with cancer can lead active lives, even during treatment. Your parent's chances of surviving cancer are better today than ever before.

Changes In Your Family

Changes In Your Family Routines And Responsibilities

Whatever your family situation, chances are that things have changed since your parent got sick. Does this sound like your home?

- Are you doing more chores?

- Are you spending more time with relatives or friends?

- Are you home alone more?

- Are you asked to help make dinner or do the laundry?

- Are you looking after younger brothers or sisters more?

- Do you want to just hang out with your friends when you are needed at home?

Figure 53.1. Changes In Your Family Routines And Responsibilities

Let your parents know if you feel that there is more to do than you can handle. Together, you can work it out.

Touching Base When Things Are Changing

Families say that it helps to make time to talk together, even if it's only for a short time each week. Talking can help your family stay connected. Here are some things to consider when talking with:

Brothers and sisters

- If you are the oldest child, your brothers or sisters may look to you for support. Help them as much as you can. It's okay to let them know that you're having a tough time, too.

- If you are looking to your older brother or sister for help, tell them how you are feeling. They can help, but won't have all the answers.

Your parent who is well

- Expect your parent to feel some stress, just as you do.
- Your parent may snap at you. He or she may not always do or say the right thing.
- Lend a hand when you can.

Your parent with cancer

- Your mom or dad may be sick from the treatment or just very tired. Or maybe your parent will feel okay and want your company.
- Try talking if your mom or dad feels up to it. Let your parent know how much you love them.

Keeping Family And Friends In The Loop

Is it getting to be too much to answer the phone and tell people how your mom or dad is doing? That can be a lot for anyone. Ask others to help you share news of how your parent is doing and what help your family needs. Maybe a relative or family friend can be the contact person. Some families use telephone chains. Others use e-mail, a blog, or a social media site.

Growing Stronger As A Family

Some families can grow apart for a while when a parent has cancer. But there are ways to help your family grow stronger and closer. Teens who saw their families grow closer say that it happened because people in their family:

- **Tried** to put themselves in the other person's shoes and thought about how they would feel if they were the other person.
- **Understood** that even though people reacted differently to situations, they were all hurting. Some cried a lot. Others showed little emotion. Some used humor to get by.
- **Learned** to respect and talk about differences. The more they asked about how others were feeling, the more they could help each other.

Asking Others For Help

You and your family may need support from others. It can be hard to ask. Yet most of the time people really want to help you and your family.

People who your mom, dad, or you may ask for help:

- Aunts, uncles, and grandparents

- Family friends

- Neighbors

- Teachers or coaches

- School nurses or guidance counselors

- People from your religious community

- Your friends or their parents

Things people can do to help:

- Go grocery shopping or run errands

- Make meals

- Mow the lawn

- Do chores around the house

- Keep your parent company

Other ways people can help you and your family:

- Give rides to school, practice, or appointments

- Help with homework

- Invite you over for a meal or a day trip

- Talk with and listen to you

Your Relationship With Your Parents

Your mom or dad may ask you to take on more responsibility than other kids your age. You might resent it at first. Then again, you may learn a lot from the experience and grow to appreciate the trust your parents have in you.

Taking Care Of Yourself

It's important to "stay fit"—both inside and out.

Dealing With Stress

Stress can make you forgetful, frustrated, and more likely to catch a cold or the flu. Here are some tips that have helped other teens manage stress. Check one or two things to do each week.

Take Care Of Your Mind And Body

Stay connected

- Spend some time at a friend's house.
- Stay involved with sports or clubs.

Relax and get enough sleep

- Take breaks. You'll have more energy and be in a better frame of mind.
- Get at least 8 hours of sleep each night.
- Pray or meditate.
- Make or listen to music.

Help others

- Join a walk against cancer.
- Plan a bake sale or other charity event to raise money to fight cancer.

Put your creative side to work

- Keep a journal to write down your thoughts and experiences.
- Draw, paint, or take photographs.
- Read biographies to learn what helped others make it through challenging times.

Eat and drink well

- Drink plenty of water each day.
- In the evening, switch to caffeine-free drinks that won't keep you awake.
- Grab fresh fruit, whole grain breads, and lean meats like chicken or turkey when you have a choice.
- Avoid sugary foods.

Be active

- Play a sport, or go for a walk or run.
- Learn about different stretching and breathing exercises.

Take Steps To Keep Things Simple

Staying organized can also keep your stress level under control. Here are some tips to get you started.

At home

- Make a list of things you want to do and put the most important ones at the top.

- Make a big calendar to help your family stay on top of things.

At school

- Try to get as much done in school as you can.

- Let your teachers know what's happening at home, without using it as an excuse.

- Talk to your teachers or a counselor if you are falling behind.

Get Help When You Feel Down And Out

Many teens feel low or down when their parent is sick. It's normal to feel sad or "blue" during difficult times. However, if these feelings last for two weeks or more and start to interfere with things you used to enjoy, you may be depressed. The good news is that there is hope and there is help. Often, talking with a counselor can help. Below are some signs that you may need to see a counselor.

Are you:

- Feeling helpless and hopeless? Thinking that life has no meaning?

- Losing interest in being with family or friends?

- Finding that everything or everyone seems to get on your nerves?

- Feeling really angry a lot of the time?

- Thinking of hurting yourself?

Do you find that you are:

- Losing interest in the activities you used to enjoy?

- Eating too little or a lot more than usual?

- Crying easily or many times each day?

- Using drugs or alcohol to help you forget?

- Sleeping more than you used to? Less than you used to?

- Feeling tired a lot?

If you answered "yes" to any of these questions, it's important to talk to someone you trust.

Finding Support

It may not be easy to reach out for support—but there are people who can help you.

Tips For Talking With Your Parent

Prepare before you talk

- **Step 1:** Think about what you want to say.

- **Step 2:** Think about how your parent might react. How will you respond to him or her?

Find a good time and place

- **Step 1:** Ask your mom or dad if they have a few minutes to talk.

- **Step 2:** Find a private place—maybe in your room or on the front steps. Or maybe you can talk while taking a walk, shooting hoops, or doing an activity you both enjoy.

Take things slowly

- **Step 1:** Don't expect to solve everything right away. Difficult problems often don't have simple solutions.

- **Step 2:** Work together to find a way through these challenges. Some conversations will go better than others.

Keep it up

- **Step 1:** Don't think you have to have just one big conversation. Have lots of small ones.

- **Step 2:** Make time to talk a little each day if you can, even if it's just for a few minutes.

Talking With A Counselor

It can be helpful to talk with someone outside the family—someone who doesn't take sides. A counselor is a person who will listen to you. They will help you find ways to better handle the things that bother you and gain strength in your situation.

Finding A Counselor

- Talk with your mom, dad, or someone else you trust. Let them know you would like to talk to a counselor. Ask for help making appointments and getting to visits. Sometimes the counselor will even let you bring a friend.

- Ask a nurse or social worker at the hospital if they know someone you can talk to.

- Talk with your guidance counselor at school.

Don't Be Shy About Asking For Help

You may think: "I can solve all my own problems." However, when faced with tough situations, both teens and adults need support from others!

Joining A Support Group

Another good outlet is a support group. Some groups meet in person; others meet online. Some groups go out and have fun together. In these groups you'll meet other teens going through some of the same things that you are. At first this may not sound like something you want to do. Other teens say they thought the same thing—until they went to a meeting. They were surprised that so many others felt the same way they did and had advice that really seemed to work. A doctor, nurse, or social worker can help you find a support group.

How You Can Help Your Parent

Here are some things that others have done to help their parent at home. Pick one or two things to try each week.

Help With Care

Spend time with your parent. Watch a movie together. Read the paper to your parent. Ask for help with your homework. Give hugs. Say, "I love you." Or just hang out in silence.

Lend a hand. Bring water or offer to make a snack or small meal.

Help By Being Thoughtful

Try to be upbeat, but be "real," too. Being positive can be good for you and your whole family. But don't feel like you always have to act cheerful, especially if it's not how you really feel. It's okay to share your thoughts with your parent—and let them comfort you. Be yourself.

Be patient. You are all under stress. If you find you are losing your cool, listen to music, read, or go outside to shoot hoops or go for a run.

Share a laugh. You've probably heard that laughter is good medicine. Watch a comedy on TV with your parent or tell jokes if that's your thing. Also, remember that you're not responsible for making everyone happy. You can only do so much.

Buy your parent a new scarf or hat. Your parent might enjoy a new hat or scarf if he or she has lost their hair during treatment.

Help By Staying Involved

Keep your parent in the loop. Tell your parent what you did today. Try to share what is going on in your life. Ask your parent how his or her day was.

Talk about family history. Ask your parent about the past. Look through pictures or photo albums. Talk about what you're both most proud of, your best memories, and how you both have met challenges. Write, or make drawings, about what you and your parent share with each other.

Keep a journal together. Write thoughts or poems, draw, or put photos in a notebook that the two of you share. This can help you share your feelings when it might be hard to speak them aloud.

Help with younger brothers and sisters. Play with your brothers and sisters to give your parent a break. Pull out games or read a book with your siblings. This will help you stay close and also give your parent time to rest.

After Treatment

When your parent is finally done with treatment, you may feel a whole range of emotions. Part of you is glad it is over. Another part of you may miss the freedom or new responsibilities you had while your parent was getting treatment. You may feel confused that your parent still looks sick and is weaker than you expected.

You may be afraid the cancer will come back. You may look at life differently now. All these feelings are normal. If you and your family are still feeling that life after treatment is harder than you thought it might be, you might want to talk to a counselor to get guidance through this time.

Things may not go back to exactly how they were before cancer came into your lives. Getting back to your "old life" may take a long time—or it may not happen as you expect.

What If Treatment Doesn't Help?

If treatment doesn't help your parent, you and your family will face even more challenges. Hearing that your parent might die is very difficult. You may feel many of the same emotions you felt when you first learned that your mom or dad had cancer.

When the future is so uncertain, teens say it helps to:

- **Make the most of the time you have.** Do special things as a family. At home, make time for your mom or dad. Call and visit as much as you can if your parent is in the hospital. Write notes and draw pictures. Say "I love you" often. If possible, try to have some special times together. If you have not gotten along in the past, you may want to let your parent know you love him or her.

- **Stay on track.** When people get bad news, they often feel like they're living outside of themselves—that life is moving along without them. That's why it's important to keep a schedule. Get up at the same time each day. Go to school. Meet with friends.

- **Get help when you feel alone.** Make sure you find people who can help you. In addition to your family, it may help to talk to a social worker, counselor, or people in a support group.

If Your Parent Passes Away

If your parent passes away, know that:

- **You'll always have memories.** Your parent will always be part of your life. Hold on to your memories of the good times. Don't feel guilty that you're not respecting your parents' memory when you think about something funny that your parent did or said. By laughing and smiling you are bringing back just a little of what was so special about your parent.

- **The pain will get less intense with time.** At first the pain may be so strong that you might wonder whether you will ever feel happy again. Time has a way of healing. Not being sad every day doesn't mean that you have forgotten your parent. It just means that you are starting to heal.

- **Everyone grieves in his or her own way.** Some teens grieve for their parent's death by crying. Others get quiet and spend time by themselves. Some find that they need to be around friends and talk. Others get very angry. In any case, most people find it helps to keep a regular routine. There is no right way or wrong way to grieve. It's okay to deal with loss at your own pace.

- **Your parent would want you to be happy.** Stay open to new experiences. Write about your thoughts. Make small changes that give your life new meaning.

- **Life will change.** Life won't be the same as before, but it can be rich and full again. Keep believing this.

Chapter 54

When Your Brother Or Sister Has Cancer

You've just learned that your brother or sister has cancer. You may have a lot of emotions—feeling numb, afraid, lonely, or angry. One thing is certain—you don't feel good.

For now, try to focus on these facts:

- **Many kids survive cancer.** You have good reason to be hopeful that your brother or sister will get better. Today, as many as 8 in 10 kids diagnosed with cancer survive their illness. Many go on to live normal lives. That's because scientists are discovering new and better ways to find and treat cancer.

- **You're not alone.** Right now it might seem like no one else in the world feels the way you do. In a way you're right. No one can feel exactly like you do. But it might help to know that there are other kids who have a brother or sister with cancer. Talking to others may help you sort out your feelings. Remember, you are not alone.

- **You're not to blame.** Cancer is a disease with many causes, many of which doctors don't fully understand. But your brother or sister did not get cancer because of anything you did, thought, or said.

- **You can't protect, but you can give comfort.** Sometimes you'll be strong for your brother or sister, and sometimes your brother or sister will be strong for you. It's okay to talk about how hard it is and even cry together.

- **Knowledge is power.** It can help to learn more about cancer and cancer treatments. Sometimes what you imagine is actually worse than the reality.

About This Chapter: This chapter includes text excerpted from "When Your Brother Or Sister Has Cancer—A Guide For Teens," National Cancer Institute (NCI), November 2013. Reviewed December 2017.

Your Feelings

As you deal with your sibling's cancer, you may feel lots of different emotions. Some of the emotions you may feel are listed below.

Scared

- My world is falling apart.

- I'm afraid that my brother or sister might die.

- I'm afraid that someone else in my family might catch cancer. (They can't.)

It's normal to feel scared. Some of your fears may be real. Others may be based on things that won't happen. And some fears may lessen over time.

Guilty

- I feel guilty because I'm healthy and my brother or sister is sick.

- I feel guilty when I laugh and have fun.

You might feel guilty about having fun when your sibling is sick. This shows how much you care about them. But you should know that it is both okay and important for you to do things that make you happy.

Angry

- I am mad that my brother or sister is sick.

- I am angry at God for letting this happen.

- I am angry at myself for feeling the way I do.

- I am mad because I have to do all the chores now.

Anger often covers up other feelings that are harder to show. If having cancer in your family means that you can't do what you like to do and go where you used to go, it can be hard. Even if you understand why it's happening, you don't have to like it. But, don't let anger build up inside. Try to let it out. And when you get mad, remember that it doesn't mean you're a bad person or you don't love your sibling. It just means you're mad.

Neglected

- I feel left out.

- I don't get any attention anymore.

- No one ever tells me what's going on.

- My family never talks anymore.

When your brother or sister has cancer, it's common for the family's focus to change. Your parents don't mean for you to feel left out. It just happens because so much is going on. You may want to tell your parents how you feel and what you think might help. Try to remember that you are important and loved and that you deserve to feel that way, even though you might not get as much attention from your parents right now.

Lonely

- My friends don't come over anymore.

- My friends don't seem to know what to say to me anymore.

- I miss being with my brother or sister the way we used to be.

We look at some things that may help you deal with changes in friendships, and at things others have done to stay close to their siblings. For now, try to remember that these feelings won't last forever.

Embarrassed

- I'm sometimes embarrassed to be out in public with my sibling because of how they look.

- I feel silly when I don't know how to answer people's questions.

It can help to know that other teens also feel embarrassed. So do their siblings. In time it gets easier, and you will find yourself feeling more comfortable.

Jealous

- I'm feeling upset that my brother or sister is getting all the attention.

Even if you understand why you are getting less attention, it's still not easy. Others who have a brother or sister with cancer have felt the same way. Try to share your feelings with your parents and talk about what you think might help.

What You're Feeling Is Normal

There is no one "right" way to feel. And you're not alone—many other teens in your situation have felt the same way. Some have said that having a brother or sister with cancer changes the way they look at things in life. Some even said that it made them stronger.

Dealing With Your Feelings

A lot of people are uncomfortable sharing their feelings. They ignore them and hope they'll go away. Others choose to act cheerful when they're really not. They think that by acting upbeat they won't feel sad or angry anymore. This may help for a while, but not over the long run. Actually, holding your feelings inside can keep you from getting the help that you need.

Try These Tips

- Talk with family and friends that you feel close to. You owe it to yourself.

- Write your thoughts down in a journal.

- Join a support group to meet other kids who are facing some of the same things you are. Or meet with a counselor.

It is probably hard to imagine right now, but, if you let yourself, you can grow stronger as a person through this experience.

What Your Brother Or Sister May Be Feeling

Just like everyone else, your brother or sister may be worried, scared, or confused. They may also feel tired and sick because of the treatment. Some kids feel embarrassed because treatment has changed the way they look and feel. You both may be having a lot of the same feelings.

Look At The World Through Your Brother's Or Sister's Eyes

Knowing how your brother or sister might be feeling could help you figure out how to help, or at least understand where they are coming from.

Here are a few things young people with cancer have felt:

- **Afraid.** Depending on how old your brother or sister is and how they react to tough situations, they may be more or less afraid.

- **Sad or depressed.** People with cancer sometimes can't do things they used to do. They may miss these activities and their friends. Feeling sad or down can range from a mild case of the blues to depression, which a doctor can treat.

- **Angry.** Cancer and treatment side effects can cause your brother or sister to be mad or grumpy. Anger sometimes comes from feelings that are hard to show, like being afraid, being very sad, or feeling helpless. Chances are your sibling is angry at the disease, not at you.

- **Guilty.** Your brother or sister may feel guilty that they caused changes in your family's life. But just as you did not cause this situation to happen, neither did your brother or sister.

- **Hopeful.** There are many reasons for your brother or sister to feel hopeful. Most kids survive cancer, and treatments are getting better all the time. Hope can be an important part of your brother's or sister's recovery.

All of these feelings are normal for a person living with cancer. You might want to share this list with your sibling. Ask them how they are feeling.

Changing Routines And Responsibilities In Your Family

Your family may be going through a lot of changes. You may be the oldest, youngest, or middle child in your family. You may live with one parent or two. Whatever your family situation, chances are that things have changed since your brother or sister got sick.

Does this sound like your home?

- Are you doing more chores?

- Are you spending more time with relatives or friends?

- Are you home alone more?

- Are you asked to help make dinner or do the laundry?

- Are you looking after younger brothers or sisters more?

- Do you want to just hang out with your friends when you are needed at home?

Does this sound like you?

- Do you feel like you have to be perfect and good all the time?

- Do you try to protect your parents from anything that might worry them?

- Do you feel like yelling, but hold it in because you don't want to cause trouble?

No one can be perfect all the time. You need time to feel sad or angry, as well as time to be happy. Try to let your parents and others you trust know how you're feeling—even if you have to start the conversation.

Your Relationship With Your Parents

Your parents may ask you to take on more responsibility than others your age. Your parents may be spending more time with your brother or sister. You might resent it at first. Then again, you may grow and learn a lot from the experience.

Touching Base When Things Are Changing

Families say that it helps to make time to talk together—even if it's only for a short time each week. Talking can help your family stay connected. Here are some things to consider when talking with:

Other brothers and sisters.

- If you are the oldest child, your younger brothers or sisters may look to you for support. Help them as much as you can. It's okay to let them know that you are having a tough time, too.

- If you are looking to your older brother or sister for help, tell them how you are feeling. They can help, but they may not have all the answers.

Your parents.

- Expect your parents to feel some stress, just like you may. Your parents may not always do or say the right thing.

- Try to make the most of the time you do have with your parents. Let them know how much it means to you. Maybe you can go out to dinner together, or they can come to your sports game, from time to time.

- Sometimes you may have to take the first step to start a conversation. You may feel guilty for wanting to have your needs met—but you shouldn't. You are important and loved, too.

- Keep talking with your parents, even though it may be hard.

Your brother or sister with cancer. Your brother or sister may be sick from the treatment and want to be alone. Or maybe they feel okay and want your company.

Keeping The Conversation Going

If you're used to talking openly at home, you might find that your parents aren't sharing as much anymore. Maybe they're trying to protect you from bad news or unsure about what to tell you. Some teens want to know a lot, while others only want to know a little. Tell your parents how much you want to know.

Over the next few weeks or months, you may overhear parts of your parents' conversations. If what you hear confuses or scares you, talk with your parents about what you heard.

Keeping Family And Friends In The Loop

Challenge. It's getting to be too much to answer the phone all the time and tell people how your brother or sister is doing.

Solution. Ask others to help you share news of how your brother or sister is doing. Maybe a relative or family friend can be the contact person and help let others know how your brother or sister is doing. Some families use a website or e-mail listserv to share this information.

Getting Help When You Need It

Challenge. Your family can't keep up with the house, meals, and other activities.

Solution. Friends and neighbors often want to help make meals, clean, drive, or look after you and your siblings. Make a list with your parents of what needs to get done. Keep the list by the phone. When people ask what they can do to help, pull out the list.

Growing Stronger As A Family

Some families can grow apart for a while when a child has cancer. But there are ways to help your family grow stronger and closer. Teens who saw their families grow closer say that it happened because people in their family:

- **Tried** to put themselves in the other person's shoes and thought about how they would feel if they were the other person

- **Understood** that even though people reacted differently to situations, they were all hurting. Some cried a lot. Others showed little emotion. Some used humor to get by.

- **Learned** to respect and talk about differences. The more they asked about how others were feeling, the more they could help each other.

Asking Others For Help

You and your family may need support from others. It can be hard to ask. Yet most of the time people really want to help, so don't hesitate to ask.

People that you or your parents may ask for help:

- Grandparents, aunts, and uncles

- Family friends

- Neighbors

- Teachers and coaches

- People from your religious community

- Your friends and their parents

- School nurses and guidance counselors

Ways people can help you:

- Help with homework

- Talk with you and listen to you

- Give rides to school or practice

- Invite you over or on weekend outings

Other things people can do to help around the house:

- Buy groceries or run errands

- Make meals

- Mow the lawn

- Do chores around the house

How You Can Help Your Brother Or Sister

This chapter has some things that others have done to help their brother or sister. Pick one or two things you may want to try this week. Then pick a couple more next week.

Help By Just Being There

- **Hang out together.** Watch a movie together. Read or watch television together. Decorate your brother's or sister's bedroom with pictures or drawings. Go to the activity room at the hospital and play a game or do a project together.

- **Comfort one another.** Just being in the same room as your brother or sister can be a big comfort. Do what feels best for the two of you. Give hugs or say "I love you." Laugh or cry together. Talk to one another. Or just hang out in silence.

Help By Being Thoughtful

- **Help your brother or sister stay in touch with friends.** Ask your sibling's friends to write notes, send pictures, or record messages. Help your brother or sister send messages to their friends. If your brother or sister is up for it, invite friends to hang out with them.

- **Share a laugh.** You've probably heard that laughter is good medicine. Watch a comedy or tell jokes together, if that is your thing.

- **Be patient.** Be patient with each other. Your brother or sister may be cranky or even mean. As bad as you feel, your brother or sister is probably feeling even worse. If you find you are losing your cool, go for a run, read, or listen to music.

- **Make a snack.** Make a snack for the two of you to share. Make a picnic by putting a blanket on the porch or in the bedroom.

- **Buy a new scarf or hat.** Your brother or sister might like a new hat or scarf if they have lost their hair during treatment. Get a matching hat or scarf for yourself, too.

- **Try to be upbeat, but be "real," too.** Being positive can be good for you and your whole family. But don't feel like you have to act cheerful all the time if that's not how you really feel. Try to be yourself.

Help By Staying Involved

- **Keep a journal together.** Write thoughts or poems, doodle, or put photos in a notebook. Take turns with your sibling writing in a journal. This can help you both share your thoughts when it might be hard to talk about them.

- **Go for a walk together.** If your brother or sister feels up to it, take a walk together. Or, open a window or sit on the front porch together.

Taking Care Of Yourself

It's Important To "Stay Fit"—Both Inside And Out

You may be so focused on your sick brother or sister that you don't think about your own needs, or if you do, they don't seem important. But they are!

Dealing With Stress

Stress can make you forgetful, frustrated, and more likely to catch a cold or the flu. Any way you look at it, too much stress isn't good. Here are some tips that have worked to help other teens manage stress.

Take Care Of Your Mind And Body

Stay connected

- Spend some time at a friend's house.

- Stay involved with sports or clubs.

Relax and get enough sleep

- Take breaks. You'll have more energy and be in a better frame of mind.

- Get at least 8 hours of sleep each night.

- Pray or meditate.

- Make or listen to music.

Help others

- Join a walk against cancer.

- Plan a bake sale or other charity event to collect money to fight cancer.

Avoid risky behaviors

- Stay away from smoking, drinking, and other risky behaviors.

Put your creative side to work

- Keep a journal to write down your thoughts and experiences.

- Draw, paint, or take photographs.

- Read books or articles about people who have made it through difficult experiences in life. Learn what helped them.

Eat and drink well

- Switch to caffeine-free drinks in the evening that won't keep you awake.

- Grab fresh fruit, whole grain breads, and lean meats, like chicken, or turkey when you have a choice.

- Avoid foods that have a lot of sugar.

- Drink 6–8 glasses of water a day to help prevent fatigue.

Be active

- Play a sport or go for a run.

- Take the dog for a walk.

- Learn about different stretching and breathing exercises.

Exercise has been proven to make you feel better. Running, swimming, or even walking at a fast pace can help improve your mood.

Take Steps To Keep Things Simple

Staying organized can also keep your stress level under control. Here are some tips to get you started.

At home

- Make a list of things you want to do. Put the most important ones at the top.

- Make a big calendar to help your family stay on top of things.

At school

- Let your teachers know what's happening at home, without using it as an excuse.

- Talk to your teachers or a counselor if you are falling behind. They can help you.

Get Help When You Feel Down And Out

Many teens feel low or down when their brother or sister is sick. It's normal to feel sad or "blue" during difficult times. However, if these feelings last for two weeks or more and start to interfere with things you used to enjoy, you may be depressed. The good news is that there is hope and there is help. Often, talking with a counselor can help. Below are some signs that you may need to see a counselor.

Are you:

- Feeling helpless and hopeless? Thinking that life has no meaning?

- Losing interest in being with family or friends?

- Finding that everything or everyone seems to get on your nerves?

- Feeling really angry a lot of the time?

- Thinking of hurting yourself?

Do you find that you are:

- Losing interest in the activities you used to enjoy?

- Eating too little or a lot more than usual?

- Crying easily or many times each day?

- Using drugs or alcohol to help you forget?

- Sleeping more than you used to? Less than you used to?

- Feeling tired a lot?

If you answered "Yes" to any of these questions… It's important to talk to someone you trust. Going to see a counselor doesn't mean that you are crazy. In fact, it means that you have the strength and courage to recognize that you are going through a difficult time and need help.

Finding Support

Don't let being afraid of the way you feel keep you from talking to your parents, a counselor, or kids in a support group. For many people, starting to talk is difficult. Some teens don't have good relationships with their parents. Others are too embarrassed to talk about personal things. It can also just be hard to make the time to talk, with all that is going on. But you and your parents really can help each other.

Don't Be Shy About Asking For Help

You may think: "I can solve all my own problems." However, when faced with tough situations, both teens and adults need support from others!

Tips for Talking With Your Parents

Prepare Before You Talk

Step 1: Think about what you want to say and about some solutions to the problem.

Step 2: Think about how your parents might react. How will you respond to them?

Find A Good Time And Place

Step 1: Find a private place, whether it's your room or the front steps. Or maybe you can talk while taking a walk or shooting hoops

Step 2: Ask your parents if they have a few minutes to talk.

Take Things Slowly

Step 1: Don't expect to solve everything right away. Difficult problems often don't have simple solutions.

Step 2: Work together to find a way through these challenges. Some conversations will go better than others.

Keep It Up

Step 1: Don't think you have to have just one big conversation. Have lots of small ones.

Step 2: Make time to talk a little each day if you can, even if it's just for a few minutes.

Talking With A Counselor

Sometimes talking to friends and your parents is not enough. When you are having a hard time, it can be helpful to talk to a counselor.

Why Go To A Counselor?

Remember going to a counselor means you have the courage to recognize that you're going through a tough time and need some help. Simply put: talking to a counselor can help you feel better. Counselors are specially trained to help you sort out your feelings, gain new skills to deal with what's going on, and find solutions that work for you. Teens who've talked with a counselor say it helped to talk to someone outside their circle of friends and family who didn't take sides, who they could trust. Others say they learned a lot about themselves and felt better able to face life's challenges.

Finding A Counselor

There are many ways to find a counselor. Here are some suggestions to get you started:

- Talk to your parents or someone else that you trust. Let them know you would like help to get through this difficult time. Tell them that you would like to talk to a counselor. Ask for help making appointments and getting to visits. Sometimes you can even bring a friend.

- Ask a nurse or social worker at the hospital if they can give you the name of someone you can talk to.

- Ask your guidance counselor or school nurse if you can talk to him or her.

Joining A Support Group

A good outlet for connecting with teens that are going through the same thing that you are is a support group. Some groups meet in person; others meet online. Some groups go out and do activities together. At first this may not sound like something you want to do. Other teens have thought the same thing—until they went to a meeting. They were surprised that so many other kids felt the same way they did and had advice that really seems to work. Your parents or another trusted adult can help you find a support group.

After Treatment

When your brother or sister has finally completed treatment, you and your family may feel a whole range of emotions. Part of you is glad it is over. Another part of you may miss the freedom or new responsibilities you had while your parent was busy taking care of your sick brother or sister. Your brother or sister may still look sick and be weaker than you expected. You may be afraid the cancer will come back. You may be looking to find more meaning in your life now. All these feelings are normal. Things may not go back to exactly how they were before cancer came into your lives. Getting back to your "old life" may take a long time—and it may not happen as you expect.

What If Treatment Doesn't Help?

If treatment doesn't help your brother or sister, you and your family will face even more challenges. Hearing that your sibling might die is very difficult. You may feel many of the same emotions you felt when you first learned that your brother or sister had cancer.

When the future is so uncertain, teens say that it helps to:

- **Make the most of the time you have.** Do special things as a family. At home, make time for your brother or sister. Call and visit as much as you can if they are in the hospital. Write notes and draw pictures. Say "I love you" often. If possible, try to have some special times together. If you have not gotten along in the past, you may want to let your brother or sister know you love them.

- **Stay on track.** When people get bad news, they often feel like they're living outside of themselves—that life is moving along without them. That's why it's important to keep a schedule and stay connected. Stay involved in school. Be with friends. And let yourself take breaks from it all when you need to.

- **Have hope.** Never stop believing in tomorrow, and don't be too hard on yourself. There is more good than bad in this world—even though you might not feel that way right now.

- **Get help when you feel alone.** Make sure you find people who can help you. In addition to your family, it may help to talk to a social worker, counselor, or people in a support group. It's important to let your feelings out.

If Your Brother Or Sister Passes Away

If your brother or sister passes away, know that:

- **You'll always have memories.** Your brother or sister will always be part of your life. Hold on to your memories of the good times. It's okay to think about something funny that your brother or sister did or said. By laughing and smiling you are bringing back just a little of what was so special about them.

- **The pain will lessen with time.** At first the pain may be so strong that you might wonder whether you will ever feel happy again. Time has a way of healing. Not being sad every day doesn't mean that you have forgotten. It just means that you're starting to heal.

- **Everyone grieves in his or her own way.** Some teens grieve for their brother's or sister's death by crying. Others get quiet and spend time by themselves. Some find that they need to be around friends and talk. Others get very angry. In any case, most people finds it helps to keep a regular routine. There is no right or wrong way to grieve. It's okay to deal with loss at your own pace.

- **Your sibling would want you to be happy.** Stay open to new experiences. Make small changes that give your life new meaning. Write about your thoughts and about this experience. Don't worry about what to say, just write.

- **Life will change.** Life won't be the same as before, but it can be rich and full again. Keep believing this.

Chapter 55

Caregivers And Their Role

If you are helping your family member or friend through cancer treatment, you are a caregiver. This may mean helping with daily activities such as going to the doctor or making meals. It could also mean coordinating services and care. Or it may be giving emotional and spiritual support.

The tips below are for most cancer caregivers. But there are also more details available for caregivers dealing with advanced cancer, caregiving after treatment ends, and for teens with a family member with cancer.

Dealing With Being A Caregiver

Giving care and support during this time can be a challenge. Many caregivers put their own needs and feelings aside to focus on the person with cancer. This can be hard to maintain for a long time, and it's not good for your health. The stress can have both physical and psychological effects. If you don't take care of yourself, you won't be able to take care of others. It's important for everyone that you give care to you.

Changing Roles

Whether you're younger or older, you may find yourself in a new role as a caregiver. You may have been an active part of someone's life before, but perhaps now that they are a cancer patient, the way you support them is different. It may be in a way in which you haven't had much experience, or in a way that feels more intense than before. Even though caregiving may

About This Chapter: This chapter includes text excerpted from "Coping With Cancer—Support For Caregivers Of Cancer Patients," National Cancer Institute (NCI), November 6, 2017.

feel new to you now, many caregivers say that they learn more as they go through their loved one's cancer experience. Common situations that they describe:

- Patients may only feel comfortable with a spouse or partner taking care of them.

- Caregivers with children struggle to take care of a parent too.

- Parents may have a hard time accepting help from their adult children.

- Caregivers find it hard to balance taking care of a loved one with job responsibilities.

- Adult children with cancer may not want to rely on their parents for care.

- Caregivers may have health problems themselves, making it physically and emotionally hard to take care of someone else.

Whatever your roles are now, it's very common to feel confused and stressed at this time. If you can, try to share your feelings with others or a join support group. Or you may choose to seek help from a counselor.

What Does "Giving Care" Mean?

Giving care can mean helping with daily needs. These include going to doctor visits, making meals, and picking up medicines. It can also mean helping your loved one cope with feelings. Like when he or she feels sad or angry. Sometimes having someone to talk to is what your loved one needs most.

While giving care, it's normal to put your own needs and feelings aside. But putting your needs aside for a long time is not good for your health. You need to take care of yourself, too. If you don't, you may not be able to care for others. This is why you need to take good care of you.

(Source: "Caring For The Caregiver," National Cancer Institute (NCI).)

Ask For Help

Many caregivers say that, looking back, they took too much on themselves. Or they wish they had asked for help from friends or family sooner. Take an honest look at what you can and can't do. What things do you need or want to do yourself? What tasks can you turn over or share with people? Be willing to let go of things that others can help you do. Some examples may be:

- Helping with chores, such as cooking, cleaning, shopping, or yard work

- Taking care of the kids or picking them up from school or activities

- Driving your loved one to appointments or picking up medicines
- Being the contact person to keep others updated

Accepting help from others isn't always easy. But remember that getting help for yourself can also help your loved one—you may stay healthier, your loved one may feel less guilty about all the things that you're doing, some of your helpers may offer useful skills and have extra time to give you.

Be Prepared For Some People Not To Help

When someone has a serious illness, friends and family often reach out to help. And sometimes people you don't know very well also want to give you a hand. But it's important to realize that there are others who may not be able to help you. You might wonder why someone wouldn't offer to help you or your family when you're dealing with so much. Some common reasons are:

- Some people may be coping with their own problems.
- Some may not have the time.
- They are afraid of cancer or may have already had a bad experience with cancer. They don't want to get involved and feel pain all over again.
- Some people believe it's best to keep a distance when people are struggling.
- Sometimes people don't realize how hard things really are for you. Or they don't understand that you need help unless you ask them for it directly.
- Some people feel awkward because they don't know how to show they care.

If someone isn't giving you the help you need, you may want to talk to them and explain your needs. Or you can just let it go. But if the relationship is important, you may want to tell the person how you feel. This can help prevent resentment or stress from building up. These feelings could hurt your relationship in the long run.

Taking Care Of Yourself

All family caregivers need support. But you may feel that your needs aren't important right now since you're not the cancer patient. Or that there's no time left for yourself. You may be so used to taking care of someone else that it's hard for you to change focus. But caring for your own needs, hopes, and desires can give you the strength you need to carry on.

Ways To Take Care Of Yourself

Taking time to recharge your mind, body, and spirit can help you be a better caregiver. You may want to think about the following:

Make Time For Yourself

- Find time to relax. Take at least 15–30 minutes each day to do something for yourself. For example, try to make time for a nap, exercise, yard work, a hobby, watching television, or a movie, or whatever you find relaxing. Do gentle exercises, such as stretching or yoga. Or, take deep breaths or just sit still for a minute.

- Don't neglect your personal life. Cut back on personal activities, but do not cut them out entirely. For example, look for easy ways to connect with friends.

- Keep up your routine. If you can, try to keep doing some of your regular activities. If you don't, studies show that it can increase the stress you feel. You may have to do things at a different time of day or for less time than you normally would, but try to still do them.

- Ask for help. Find larger chunks of "off duty" time by asking for help. Find things others can do or arrange for you, such as appointments or errands.

Understand Your Feelings

Giving yourself an outlet for your own thoughts and feelings is important. Think about what would help lift your spirits. Would talking with others help ease your load? Or would you rather have quiet time by yourself? Maybe you need both, depending on what's going on in your life. It's helpful for you and others to know what you need.

Join A Support Group

Support groups can meet in person, by phone, or online. They may help you gain new insights into what is happening, get ideas about how to cope, and help you know that you're not alone. In a support group, people may talk about their feelings, trade advice, and try to help others who are dealing with the same kinds of issues. Some people like to go and just listen. And others prefer not to join support groups at all. Some people aren't comfortable with this kind of sharing.

If you can't find a group in your area, try a support group online. Some caregivers say websites with support groups have helped them a lot.

Learn More About Cancer

Sometimes, understanding your cancer patient's medical situation can make you feel more confident and in control. For example, you may want to know more about his stage of cancer. It may help you to know what to expect during treatment, such as the tests and procedures that will be done, as well as the side effects that will result.

Talk To Others About What You're Going Through

Studies show that talking with other people about what you're dealing with is very important to most caregivers. It's especially helpful when you feel overwhelmed or want to say things that you can't say to your loved one with cancer. Try to find someone you can really open up to about your feelings or fears.

You may want to talk with someone outside your inner circle. Some caregivers find it helpful to talk to a counselor, such as a social worker, psychologist, or leader in their faith or spiritual community. These types of experts may be able to help you talk about things that you don't feel you can talk about with friends or family. They can also help you find ways to express your feelings and learn ways to cope that you hadn't thought of before.

Connect With Your Loved One With Cancer

Cancer may bring you and your loved one closer together than ever before. Often people become closer as they face challenges together. If you can, take time to share special moments with one another. Try to gain strength from all you are going through together, and what you have dealt with so far. This may help you move toward the future with a positive outlook and feelings of hope.

Write In A Journal

Research shows that writing or journaling can help relieve negative thoughts and feelings. And it may actually help improve your own health. You might write about your most stressful experiences. Or you may want to express your deepest thoughts and feelings. You can also write about things that make you feel good, such as a pretty day or a kind coworker or friend.

Look For The Positive

It can be hard finding positive moments when you're busy caregiving. It also can be hard to adjust to your role as a caregiver. Caregivers say that looking for the good things in life and feeling gratitude help them feel better. And know that it's okay to laugh, even when your loved one is in treatment. In fact, it's healthy. Laughter releases tension and makes you feel better. Keeping your sense of humor in trying times is a good coping skill.

Be Thankful

You may feel thankful that you can be there for your loved one. You may be glad for a chance to do something positive and give to another person in a way you never knew you could. Some caregivers feel that they've been given the chance to build or strengthen a relationship. This doesn't mean that caregiving is easy or stress free. But finding meaning in caregiving can make it easier to manage.

Caring For Your Body

You may find yourself so busy and concerned about your loved one that you don't pay attention to your own physical health. But it's very important that you take care of your health, too. Doing so will give you strength to help others. It's important to:

- Stay up to date with your medical needs. Keep up with your own checkups, screenings, and other appointments.

- Watch for signs of depression or anxiety. Stress can cause many different feelings or body changes. But if they last for more than two weeks, talk to your doctor.

- Take your medicine as prescribed. Ask your doctor to give you a large prescription to save trips to the pharmacy. Find out if your grocery store or pharmacy delivers.

- Try to eat healthy meals. Eating well will help you keep up your strength. If your loved one is in the hospital or has long doctor's appointments, bring easy—prepare food from home. For example, sandwiches, salads, or packaged foods, and canned meats fit easily into a lunch container.

- Get enough rest. Listening to soft music or doing breathing exercises may help you fall asleep. Short naps can energize you if you aren't getting enough sleep. Be sure to talk with your doctor if lack of sleep becomes an ongoing problem.

- Exercise. Walking, swimming, running, or bike riding are only a few ways to get your body moving. Any kind of exercise (including working in the garden, cleaning, mowing, or going up stairs) can help you keep your body healthy. Finding at least 15–30 minutes a day to exercise may make you feel better and help manage your stress.

New stresses and daily demands often add to any health problems caregivers already have. And if you are sick or have an injury that requires you to be careful, it's even more important that you take care of yourself.

Here are some changes caregivers often have:

- fatigue (feeling tired)

- weaker immune system (poor ability to fight off illness)

- sleep problems

- slower healing of wounds

- higher blood pressure

- changes in appetite or weight

- headaches

- anxiety, depression, or other mood changes

Long Distance Caregiving

It can be really tough to be away from a loved one who has cancer. You may feel like you're a step behind in knowing what is happening with his or her care. Yet even if you live far away, it's possible for you to give support and be a problem solver and care coordinator.

Caregivers who live more than an hour away from their loved ones most often rely on the telephone or email as their communication link. But either of these methods can be rather limiting when trying to assess someone's needs. Aside from true medical emergencies, long-distance caregivers often need to judge whether situations can be dealt with over the phone or require an in-person visit.

Finding Contacts Near Your Loved One

Develop a relationship with one or two key members of the healthcare team, such as a social worker or patient educator. It may help you feel more at ease to have direct contact with someone involved in the medical care of your loved one. Also, many long-distance caregivers say that it helps to explore both paid and volunteer support. Ways you can do this are:

- Create a list of people who live near your loved one whom you could call day or night in a crisis or just to check in.

- Look into volunteer visitors, adult day care centers, or meal delivery services in the area.

- Make a list of websites in your loved one's area to give you quick access to resources.

- Ask if the hospital keeps visitor information packets that list area agencies and contacts.

- Remember to share a list of homework, and cell phone numbers with the healthcare team. You should also give this to others who are local in case of an emergency.

Other Tips

- Ask a local family member or friend to update you daily by email. Or, consider creating a website to share news about your loved one's condition and needs. There are a number of sites available. Examples are Caring Bridge (www.caringbridge.org) and Lotsa Helping Hands (www.lotsahelpinghands.com).

- Sign up for online ways to connect with people. Programs using video and instant messaging to communicate are very common. For example, Skype and FaceTime are ways people connect from a distance.

- Airlines or bus lines may have special deals for patients or family members. The hospital social worker may also know of other resources, such as private pilots, advocacy organizations, or companies that help people with cancer and their families with transportation.

- If you are traveling to see your loved one, time your flights or drives so that you have time to rest when you return. Many long-distance caregivers say that they don't allow themselves enough time to rest after their visits.

- Consider getting a phone card from a discount store to cut down on long-distance bills. Or, review your long-distance and cell phone plans. See if you can make any changes that would reduce your bills.

Chapter 56

Advanced Cancer And Caregiving

Sometimes, as the disease progresses, changes take place in the person with cancer. These may be due to the side effects of treatment or the cancer itself. Or they may be caused by other drugs. Some caregivers have said that they wished they had known sooner about what changes to expect.

Changes may occur in:

- Looks

- Personality or mood

- Memory

- Sleep

- Appetite or nutrition needs

The person you are caring for may or may not go through any of these changes. But you should ask the doctor whether you need to be aware of them and what you can do about them if they happen.

Looking At Living Arrangements

Sometimes questions arise about whether the person with advanced cancer should live at home or be moved to a nursing or assisted living facility. When making these decisions, here are a few good questions to ask:

- What kind of help does your loved one need?

About This Chapter: This chapter includes text excerpted from "Advanced Cancer And Caregivers—Planning For The Caregiver," National Cancer Institute (NCI), December 8, 2016.

- If you're the spouse or other loved one living with them, are you capable of taking care of them?

- If they live alone, is it risky for them to keep doing so?

- What are the options for homecare?

- How often will they need help?

You'll also need to consider how your loved one feels. They may fear:

- Losing their independence

- Being seen as weak or a burden to others

- Moving to a healthcare of other type of assisted living facility

Sometimes it's easier to consider a change in living arrangements when the advice comes from a health professional. Social workers, including visiting nurses, those who work with older adults, and others may be able to help you talk to your loved one about these decisions.

Talking To Your Loved One With Advanced Cancer

Whether it's a spouse, family member, or friend, talking about serious issues is never easy. It's normal to not know what to say to someone with advanced cancer, or to worry that you'll say the wrong thing. But the most important thing is not what you say, but that you are showing your care.

It's likely that you and your loved one with cancer are both having the same thoughts and fears about the end of life. There will come a time when you will need to talk about these issues together. These might include the stage of the cancer, preparing for the future, fears of death, or wishes at the end of life. Some families talk openly about these sorts of things, while others don't. There is no right or wrong way to communicate. But studies show that families who talk things out feel better about the care they get and the decisions they make. A few things to remember are:

- **You and your loved one can still have hope for longer life or an unexpected recovery.** But it's also a good idea to talk about the fact that the future is uncertain. Avoiding important issues only makes them harder to deal with later. Talking over your concerns can bring comfort to all involved.

- **Keeping the truth from each other isn't healthy.** You may find that you both are thinking the same things. Or you may find you're thinking very different things. This makes it all the more important to get any thoughts or concerns you have out in the open.

- **Often the best way to communicate with someone is to just listen.** This is one of the main ways of showing that you're there for them. It's important to be supportive of whatever your loved one wants to say. It's their life and their cancer. They needs to process their thoughts and fears in their own time and their own way.

If you have trouble talking about painful issues, ask for professional advice. A mental health expert may be able to help you and your loved one explore topics that you don't feel able to on your own. And if the cancer patient doesn't want to go, you can always go alone. You may hear some ideas for how to bring up these topics. You can also talk about other concerns and feelings that you are dealing with right now.

Understanding Your Loved One's Wishes For Care

An advanced cancer diagnosis (ACD) brings up a number of decisions to make. These may be about what type of care or treatment to receive. Or they may be about what kind of information patients want to hear. For many families, it's important that the person with cancer be in charge of making decisions. But in some families and also in some cultures, it's common for family caregivers to make most of the decisions. And they may make them with or without the patient knowing. Or, sometimes the patient wants the caregiver to make all the decisions. Making these decisions may be hard on you for a number of reasons including:

- Your own desires for your loved one's care may make it hard to decide what is best for him.

- Your ideas about how to move forward may differ from those of other family members and friends.

- The patient may have different beliefs about care than you or other loved ones.

- The opinions of your healthcare team may differ from the patient's or yours.

If you and your loved one with advanced cancer have different opinions about next steps for care, you should share your opinions. However, in the end, it's the patient's choice. If you can't agree, you may want to ask someone else to guide the conversation between you both. You might talk to a member of your faith community, a social worker, other people dealing with cancer, or a hospice worker.

There may also come a time when you have to make decisions for your loved one because he can't anymore. It's important to get a sense of how he feels about certain issues while he can still tell you. For example, would he like you to be in charge of his medical decisions? Has he signed advance directives to let you know what kind of care he would like to receive?

Knowing what your loved one wants may mean letting go of some of your own opinions. For example, you may want to keep him alive, whatever it takes. But he may wish to stop receiving life sustaining measures at a certain point. Try to keep things in perspective by looking at how the disease has advanced. Get the facts about the care you want him to keep receiving.

If advance directives can't be found and your loved one can't speak for himself, you may feel anxious and stressed as you decide what choices to make for his care. Think about what he would want or imagine what he would say if he could talk. Try to remember if he said something in the past that would help you decide.

Know that it's common for family members to disagree on what kind of care to give your loved one. If this is the case for you, ask a member of your healthcare team to hold a family meeting and lead a discussion. They can explain the goals of the medical care being offered. For example, is it to stop the cancer? Lessen pain? Prolong life? Having this talk with everyone present may lessen the conflicts and help the family reach a decision for your loved one.

Signs That Death Is Near

Certain signs and symptoms can help a caregiver know when death is near. It's important to know that not every patient has all of these signs or symptoms. Also, even if any of them are present, it doesn't always mean that your loved one is close to death. A member of the patient's healthcare team can give you more guidance about what to expect.

- **Drowsiness and sleeping more.** As your loved one nears the end of life, he will be sleeping more and may not respond as often to you. Plan visits for times when your loved one is alert.

- **Confusion about time, place, or identity of friends and family members.** Your loved one may also seem restless, or have visions of people and places that are not present. Or she may see, hear, and talk to loved ones who have died. She also may pull at bed linens or clothing. Try to be calm and reassuring. These visions should not be treated as hallucinations. You don't need to convince her that what she sees isn't real.

- **Being more withdrawn and unresponsive.** Most patients are still able to hear after they're no longer able to speak. Don't try to arouse or shake your loved one if he doesn't respond. Speak to him directly and let him know you are there for him. He may be aware and able to hear, but unable to respond. Some experts say that giving the patient permission to "let go" can be helpful.

- **Less need for food and liquids, and loss of appetite.** Allow your loved one to choose if and when to eat or drink. Ice chips, water, or juice may be refreshing if she can swallow. Lip balm may help to keep the mouth and lips moist.

- **Loss of bladder or bowel control.** Keep your loved one clean, dry, and as comfortable as possible. Place disposable pads on the bed beneath the patient and remove them when they become soiled.

- **Dark urine or decreased amount of urine.** The healthcare or hospice team may see a need for a catheter to help the patient urinate. However this would not be necessary in the final hours of life.

- **Skin becomes cool to the touch or bluish in color.** Use blankets to warm your loved one. Avoid warming with electric blankets or heating pads, which can cause burns. Take comfort knowing that even though the skin may be cool, the patient is probably not aware of feeling cold.

- **Rattling or gurgling sounds while breathing.** These may seem loud or may seem irregular and shallow. Your loved one may also breathe fast and then slow. Turning his body to the side and placing pillows under the head and behind the back may help. Although this kind of breathing may seem scary to you, it doesn't cause discomfort to your loved one. An extra source of oxygen, ice chips, or a cool mist humidifier may help make the patient more comfortable.

- **Turning the head toward a light source.** Leave soft, indirect lights on in the room.

- **Pain becomes hard to control.** It's important to keep providing the pain medicines as the doctor has prescribed. You should contact the doctor if the current dose doesn't seem to help. With the help of the healthcare team, you can also look into other methods to help with pain such as massage and relaxation.

Part Six
If You Need More Information

Chapter 57

Online Support And Mobile Apps For Cancer Patients And Survivors

Online Support

American Cancer Society

American Cancer Society is engaged in funding and conducting research, sharing expert information, supporting patients, and spreading the word about prevention.
Website: www.cancer.org

CancerCompass

CancerCompass offers information and interaction on the web for people who have been touched by cancer.
Website: cancercompass.com/about.htm

CancerHelp Online

CancerHelp Online is a mobile friendly, cancer patient education program that combines the best patient resources from the National Cancer Institute (NCI) in English and Spanish.
Website: cancerhelp.org

CaringBridge®

A CaringBridge website provides all the information your family and friends need so they can give you all the support you need.
Website: www.caringbridge.org

About This Chapter: Resources in this chapter were compiled from several sources deemed reliable; all contact information was verified and updated in December 2017.

Cervivor

Cervivor is a community, a learning tool, an advocacy resource, and an online retreat for healing, connecting, and thriving.
Website: cervivor.org

4th Angel

4th Angel provides free, one-on-one, confidential telephone support for people with cancer and their caregivers.
Website: www.4thangel.org

Inspire

Inspire operates groups for people with cancer and their caregivers. You can also join groups for other health conditions besides cancer. Once you join a group, you can post questions and comments on discussion boards and connect with other group members.
Website: www.inspire.com

MyLifeLine Cancer Foundation

MyLifeLine Cancer Foundation provides free websites for people with cancer and caregivers to keep family and friends updated.
Website: www.mylifeline.org

Navigating Cancer

Navigating Cancer is a free website specifically for cancer patients and their supporters, offering tools and cancer resources that empower patients to take control of their health and partner more closely with their physicians, support network, and other like patients.
Website: www.navigatingcancer.com/provider

Peer Support Network

Peer Support Network provides online support for people newly diagnosed with cancer, cancer survivors, and caregivers.
Website: peersforprogress.org/npscln

Smart Patients

Smart Patients is an online community where patients and their families affected by a variety of illnesses learn from each other about treatments, challenges, and how it all fits into the context of their experience.
Website: www.smartpatients.com

Mobile Apps

CareZone
CareZone aims to simplify the process by offering a number of features that help you stay on top of your treatment.
Website: play.google.com/store/apps/details?id=com.carezone.caredroid.careapp.medications&hl=en

Pocket Cancer Care Guide
Pocket Cancer Care Guide turns your phone into a handy dictaphone so you can record answers from your doctors and nurses.
Website: itunes.apple.com/us/app/pocket-cancer-care-guide/id453059212

Create to Heal
Create to Heal focuses on how creativity and stress relief could complement your care plan. Tested over five years with hundreds of cancer patients, you can expect guided meditations, music, and art that aim to reduce stress and aid the healing process.
Website: itunes.apple.com/us/app/create-to-heal/id882453467

My Chemo Brain
My Chemo Brain, created by a cancer survivor, empowers patients by doing the remembering for them.
Website: itunes.apple.com/us/app/chemo-brain-doc-notes-free/id766256080?mt=8

PearlPoint The Cancer Side Effects Helper
PearlPoint The Cancer Side Effects Helper aims to guide patients to strength, wellness, and side-effect recovery. The app also links to PearlPoint's online archive where emotional, financial, and practical support can be found.
Website: play.google.com/store/apps/details?id=com.pearlpoint.cancersideeffects&hl=en

CaringBridge
CaringBridge encourages patients to create online health journals that could improve their treatment and can be shared with friends and family and inspire other patients around the globe.
Website: play.google.com/store/apps/details?id=com.caringbridge.app&hl=en

eCO Study
eCO Study mobile application and infrastructure are used by healthcare providers and their adult female patients with recurrent ovarian cancer who are being treated with the investigational drug combination of Olaparib-Cediranib.
Website: itunes.apple.com/us/app/eco-study/id1077666555?mt=8&ign-mpt=uo%3D8

SkinVision

SkinVision enables you to find skin cancer early and get to a doctor at the right time.
Website: www.skinvision.com

CureSearch CancerCare App

CureSearch CancerCare App helps to keep track of everything from appointments and treatments to allergies and side effects.
Website: play.google.com/store/apps/details?id=com.curesearch.caremanager&hl=en

MoovCare™

MoovCare™ is a medical software device used to detect cancer relapse or complications during the follow-up of lung cancer patients at high risk of relapse.
Website: www.sivan-innovation.com/moovcare

Chapter 58

Web-Based Resources And Support Groups

American Brain Tumor Association (ABTA)
Phone: 773-577-8750
Toll-Free: 800-886-2282
Fax: 773-577-8738
Website: www.abta.org
E-mail: info@abta.org
Activities: Supports research and offers information to brain tumor patients and their families.

American Cancer Society (ACS)
Toll-Free: 800-227-2345
Website: www.cancer.org
Activities: Provides services and programs for cancer patients and their families, supports research, and offers cancer-related information.

American Institute for Cancer Research (AICR)
Toll-Free: 800-843-8114
Fax: 202-328-7226
Website: www.aicr.org
E-mail: aicrweb@aicr.org
Activities: Provides information about cancer prevention and nutrition concerns.

About This Chapter: Resources in this chapter were compiled from several sources deemed reliable; all contact information was verified and updated in December 2017.

American Psychosocial Oncology Society (APOS)

Phone: 615-432-0090
Website: www.apos-society.org
E-mail: info@apos-society.org
Activities: Works to help people with cancer find counseling services in their own communities.

American Society of Clinical Oncology—Cancer.Net (ASCO)

Phone: 571-483-1780
Toll-Free: 888-651-3038
Fax: 571-366-9537
Website: www.cancer.net/coping/age-specific-information/cancer-teens
E-mail: contactus@cancer.net
Activities: Cancer.Net provides oncologist-approved information on cancer specific to teens.

CancerCare

Phone: 212-712-8400
Toll-Free: 800-813-4673
Fax: 212-712-8495
Website: www.cancercare.org
Activities: Provides free professional counseling, educational programs, practical help, and financial assistance to people affected by cancer.

Cancer Financial Assistance Coalition (CFAC)

Website: www.cancerfac.org
E-mail: contact@cancerfac.org
Activities: Coalition of 14 organizations provides database to help cancer patients and caregivers manage their financial challenges.

Cancer Support Community—Group Loop

Phone: 202-659-9709
Toll-Free: 888-793-9355
Website: www.grouploop.org
Activities: Provides online site for teens to find support and education while dealing with a cancer diagnosis.

CaringBridge

Phone: 651-452-7940
Fax: 651-681-7115
Website: www.caringbridge.org
Activities: Offers personal websites to help patients and family stay connected to others during illness, treatment, and recovery.

Children's Brain Tumor Foundation (CBTF)
Phone: 212-448-9494
Toll-Free: 866-228-4673
Website: www.cbtf.org
E-mail: info@cbtf.org
Activities: Works to improve treatment, quality of life, and long-term outlook for children with brain and spinal cord tumors.

CureSearch
Toll-Free: 800-458-6223
Fax: 301-718-0047
Website: www.curesearch.org
E-mail: info@curesearch.org
Activities: Supports research and provides treatment information and support resources to patients, families, and health professionals.

FORCE: Facing Our Risk of Cancer Empowered (F.O.R.C.E.)
Toll-Free: 866-288-7475
Fax: 954-827-2200
Website: www.facingourrisk.org
E-mail: info@facingourrisk.org
Activities: A resource for people affected by hereditary and ovarian cancers.

4th Angel Mentoring Program
Toll-Free: 866-520-3197
Website: www.4thangel.org
E-mail: 4thAngel@ccf.org
Activities: Pairs cancer patients or caregivers with trained mentors to provide emotional support.

Joe's House
Toll-Free: 877-563-7468
Website: www.joeshouse.org
E-mail: info@joeshouse.org
Activities: Lists thousands of places to stay across the country near hospitals and treatments centers that offer a discount for traveling patients and their loved ones.

Leukemia & Lymphoma Society (LLS)
Phone: 914-949-5213
Toll-Free: 800-955-4572
Fax: 914-949-6691
Website: www.lls.org
Activities: Supports research to find a cure for blood cancers and works to help patients and their families.

LIVESTRONG Foundation
Toll-Free: 877-236-8820
Website: www.livestrong.org
Activities: Offers support and financial assistance to cancer survivors.

Look Good Feel Better (LGFB)
Toll-Free: 800-395-LOOK (800-395-5665)
Website: lookgoodfeelbetter.org
Activities: Seeks to meet the appearance-related and social needs of teens (aged 13–17) with cancer, a program of the American Cancer Society.

Lymphoma Foundation of America (LFA)
Phone: 734-222-1100
Toll-Free: 800-385-1060
Fax: 734-222-0044
Website: www.lymphomahelp.org
E-mail: LFA@lymphomahelp.org
Activities: Offers counseling and support for lymphoma survivors.

Lynch Syndrome International (LSI)
Phone: 203-779-5034
Website: www.lynchcancers.com
E-mail: info@lynchcancers.org
Activities: Provides support for individuals afflicted with the hereditary condition Lynch syndrome.

Max Foundation
Phone: 425-778-8660
Toll-Free: 888-462-9368
Website: www.themaxfoundation.org
Activities: Helps underserved people with rare cancers and blood cancers get access to programs and services.

National Bone Marrow Transplant Link (NBMT)

Toll-Free: 800-546-5268
Website: www.nbmtlink.org
E-mail: info@nbmtlink.org
Activities: Serves stem cell transplant patients.

National Cancer Institute (NCI)

Toll-Free: 800-422-6237
Toll-Free TTY: 877-448-7848
Website: www.cancer.gov
Activities: The federal government's principal agency for cancer research.

National Children's Cancer Society (NCCS)

Phone: 314-241-1600
Toll-Free: 800-5-FAMILY (800-532-6459)
Website: www.thenccs.org
Activities: Works to improve the lives of children with cancer and provides assistance to families.

National Hospice and Palliative Care Organization (NHPCO)

Phone: 703-837-1500
Toll-Free: 800-646-6460
Fax: 703-837-1233
Website: www.nhpco.org
E-mail: nhpco_info@nhpco.org
Activities: A professional organization for those who seek to improve care at the end of life.

National Patient Travel Center

Toll-Free Fax: 800-550-1767
Website: www.patienttravel.org
E-mail: info@nationalpatienttravelcenter.org
Activities: Helps patients find medical air transportation.

Patient Advocate Foundation (PAF)

Toll-Free: 800-532-5274
Fax: 757-873-8999
Website: www.patientadvocate.org
Activities: Provides professional case management services to help patients maintain their financial stability and safeguard their access to healthcare, insurance, and employment.

Prevent Cancer Foundation

Phone: 703-836-4412
Toll-Free: 800-227-2732
Fax: 703-836-4413
Website: preventcancer.org
E-mail: pcf@preventcancer.org
Activities: Supports cancer prevention research and works to educate the public.

R.A. Bloch Cancer Foundation, Inc.

Phone: 816-854-5050
Toll-Free: 800-433-0464
Fax: 816-854-8024
Website: blochcancer.org
E-mail: hotline@blochcancer.org
Activities: Matches cancer patients with trained volunteers who have been treated for the same kind of cancer.

St. Jude Children's Research Hospital—Cure4Kids

Website: www.cure4kids.org
Activities: Educates health professionals, scientists, parents, educators, and kids on cancer and other serious illnesses.

Sisters Network® Inc.

Phone: 713-781-0255
Toll-Free: 866-781-1808
Website: www.sistersnetworkinc.org
E-mail: infonet@sistersnetworkinc.org
Activities: Works to help meet the needs of African American breast cancer survivors.

Skin Cancer Foundation

Phone: 212-725-5176
Website: www.skincancer.org
Activities: Promotes prevention, early detection, and effective treatment of skin cancer.

Starlight Children's Foundation

Phone: 310-479-1212
Website: www.starlight.org
E-mail: info@starlight.org
Activities: Builds playrooms and teen lounges in hospitals and works to improve the quality of life for children with serious medical concerns.

Stupid Cancer

Toll-Free: 877-735-4673
Website: stupidcancer.org
E-mail: contact@stupidcancer.org
Activities: Raises awareness that cancer affects young adults and works to ensure that they receive age-appropriate resources.

13thirty Cancer Connect

Phone: 585-563-6221
Website: 13thirty.org
E-mail: staff@13thirty.org
Activities: Provides support and information to teens with cancer.

ThyCa: Thyroid Cancer Survivors' Association, Inc.

Toll-Free: 877-588-7904
Fax: 630-604-6078
Website: www.thyca.org
E-mail: thyca@thyca.org
Activities: Offers support and other services to thyroid cancer survivors, family members, and others.

Young Survival Coalition (YSC)

Phone: 646-257-3000
Toll-Free: 877-972-1011
Fax: 646-257-3030
Website: www.youngsurvival.org
E-mail: info@youngsurvival.org
Activities: Provides resources, connections, and outreach to young women who are diagnosed with breast cancer.

Chapter 59

How To Find Clinical Cancer Trials

Steps To Find Clinical Cancer Trials

If you are thinking about joining a clinical trial as a treatment option, the best place to start is to talk with your doctor or another member of your healthcare team. Often, your doctor may know about a clinical trial that could be a good option for you. He or she may also be able to search for a trial for you, provide information, and answer questions to help you decide about joining a clinical trial.

Some doctors may not be aware of or recommend clinical trials that could be appropriate for you. If so, you may want to get a second opinion about your treatment options, including taking part in a clinical trial.

If you decide to look for trials on your own, the following steps can guide you in your search.

Step One: Gather Details About Your Cancer

If you decide to look for a clinical trial, you must know certain details about your cancer diagnosis. You will need to compare these details with the eligibility criteria of any trial that interests you. Eligibility criteria are the guidelines for who can and cannot take part in a certain clinical trial.

About This Chapter: Text under the heading "Steps To Find Clinical Cancer Trials" is excerpted from "Steps To Find A Clinical Trial," National Cancer Institute (NCI), June 23, 2016; Information listed under the heading "Other Resources For Finding Clinical Trials" was compiled from various sources deemed reliable. Website information was updated in December 2017.

ep Two: **Find Clinical Trials**

There are many lists of cancer clinical trials taking place in the United States. Some trials re funded by nonprofit organizations, including the U.S. government. Others are funded by for-profit groups, such as drug companies. Hospitals and academic medical centers also sponsor trials conducted by their own researchers. Because of the many types of sponsors, no single list contains every clinical trial.

Other Lists Of Trials

Other places to look for lists of cancer clinical trials include:

ClinicalTrials.gov. ClinicalTrials.gov, which is part of the U.S. National Library of Medicine (NLM), lists clinical trials for cancer and many other diseases and conditions. It contains trials that are in National Cancer Institute's (NCI) list of cancer trials as well as trials sponsored by pharmaceutical or biotech companies that may not be on NCI's list.

Cancer centers and clinics that conduct cancer clinical trials. Many cancer centers across the United States, including NCI-Designated Cancer Centers, sponsor or take part in cancer clinical trials. The websites of these centers usually have a list of the clinical trials taking place at their institutions. Some of the trials included in these lists may not be on NCI's list.

Keep in mind that the amount of information about clinical trials on these websites can vary. You may have to contact a cancer center clinical trials office to get more information about the trials that interest you.

Drug and biotechnology companies. Many companies provide lists of the clinical trials that they sponsor on their websites. Sometimes, a company's website may refer you to the website of another organization that helps the company find patients for its trials. The other organization may be paid fees for this service.

The website of the Pharmaceutical Research and Manufacturers of America (PhRMA) includes a list of its member companies, many of which sponsor cancer clinical trials. PhRMA is a trade organization that represents drug and biotechnology companies in the United States.

Clinical trial listing services. Some organizations provide lists of clinical trials as a part of their business. These organizations generally do not sponsor or take part in clinical trials. Some of them may receive fees from drug or biotechnology companies for listing their trials or helping find patients for their trials.

Keep the following points in mind about clinical trial listing services:

- The lists of trials provided by these organizations often draw from the trial lists that are available from the U.S. government (NCI and ClinicalTrials.gov).

- The websites of these organizations may not be updated regularly.

- The websites of these organizations may require you to register to search for clinical trials or to obtain trial contact information for trials that interest you.

Cancer advocacy groups. Cancer advocacy groups provide education, support, financial assistance, and advocacy to help patients and families who are dealing with cancer, its treatment, and survivorship. These organizations recognize that clinical trials are important to improving cancer care. They work to educate and empower people to find information and obtain access to appropriate treatment.

Advocacy groups work hard to know about the latest advances in cancer research. Some will have information about clinical trials that are enrolling patients.

To find trials, search the websites of advocacy groups for specific types of cancer. Many of these websites have lists of clinical trials or refer you to the websites of organizations that match patients to trials. Or, you can contact an advocacy group directly for help finding clinical trials.

Step Three: Take A Closer Look At The Trials That Interest You

- Take a closer look at the protocol summary for each trial.

- Use the questions below to narrow your list to include only those trials for which you would like to get more information.

Step Four: Contact The Team Running The Trial

There are a few ways to reach the clinical trial team.

- **Contact the trial team directly.** The protocol summary should include the phone number of a person or an office that you can contact for more information. You do not need to talk to the lead researcher (called the "protocol chair" or "principal investigator") at this time, even if his or her name is given along with the telephone number. Instead, call the number and ask to speak with the "trial coordinator." This person can answer questions from patients and their doctors. It is also the trial coordinator's job to decide whether you are likely to be eligible to join the trial. However, a final decision will probably not be made until you have met with a doctor who is part of the trial team.

- **Ask your doctor or another healthcare team member to contact the trial team for you.** The clinical trial coordinator will ask questions about your cancer diagnosis and your current general health that you may not be sure how to answer. So, you may want to ask your doctor or someone else on your healthcare team to contact the trial coordinator for you.

- **The trial team may contact you.** If you have registered to use the website of a clinical trial listing service and found a trial that interests you, the clinical trial team may contact you directly by using the phone number and email address you provide when you register.

Step Five: Ask Questions

Whether you or someone from your healthcare team speaks with the clinical trial team, this is the time to get answers to questions that will help you decide whether or not to take part in this particular clinical trial.

Talk With Your Doctor

To make a final decision, you will want to know the potential risks and benefits of all treatment options available to you. If you have any remaining questions or concerns, you should discuss them with your doctor. Ask your doctor some of the same questions that you asked the trial coordinator. You should also ask your doctor about the risks and benefits of standard treatment for your cancer. Then, you and your doctor can compare the risks and benefits of standard treatment with those of treatment in a clinical trial. You may decide that joining a trial is your best option, or you may decide not to join a trial. It's your choice.

Step Six: Make An Appointment

If you decide to join a clinical trial for which you are eligible, schedule a visit with the team running the trial.

Other Resources For Finding Clinical Trials

Governmental Organizations

National Center for Complementary and Integrative Health (NCCIH)
Website: nccih.nih.gov/research/clinicaltrials

National Institute of Arthritis and Musculoskeletal and Skin Diseases (NIAMS)
Website: www.niams.nih.gov/labs/siegel-lab-clinical-trials

National Institute of Diabetes and Digestive and Kidney Diseases (NIDDK)
Website: www.niddk.nih.gov/health-information/clinical-trials

National Institute of Environmental Health Sciences (NIEHS)
Website: www.niehs.nih.gov/research/clinical

NIH Clinical Center
Website: www.cc.nih.gov

Private Organizations

American Cancer Society
Website: www.cancer.org/treatment/treatmentsandsideeffects/clinicaltrials/app/clinical-trials-matching-service

CancerConnect
Website: news.cancerconnect.com/clinical-trials

Cancer Research UK
Website: www.cancerresearchuk.org/cancer-help/trials

CenterWatch
Website: www.centerwatch.com/clinical-trials/listings

Clinical Trials and Noteworthy Treatments for Brain Tumors
Website: www.virtualtrials.com

CureSearch: Children's Oncology Group
Website: www.curesearch.org

Current Controlled Trials (International)
Website: www.controlled-trials.com

EmergingMed
Website: www.emergingmed.com

TrialCheck
Website: www.eviticlinicaltrials.com/services

Index

Index

Page numbers that appear in *Italics* refer to tables or illustrations. Page numbers that have a small 'n' after the page number refer to citation information shown as Notes. Page numbers that appear in **Bold** refer to information contained in boxes within the chapters.

Y

Z